Privatizing Educational Choice

Privatizing Educational Choice

Consequences for Parents, Schools, and Public Policy

Clive R. Belfield
and
Henry M. Levin

Paradigm Publishers
Boulder • London

Copyright © 2005 Paradigm Publishers

Published in the United States by Paradigm Publishers, 3360 Mitchell Lane Suite E, Boulder, CO 80301 USA.

Paradigm Publishers is the trade name of Birkenkamp & Company, LLC, Dean Birkenkamp, President and Publisher.

Library of Congress Cataloging-in-Publication Data

Belfield, C. R.
   Privatizing educational choice : consequences for parents, schools, and public policy / Clive R. Belfield and Henry M. Levin.
     p. cm.
   Includes bibliographical references and index.
   ISBN 1-59451-114-4 (hard : alk. paper) — ISBN 1-59451-115-2 (pbk. : alk. paper)
    1. Privatization in education—United States.   2. School choice—United States.   3. Education and state—United States.   I. Levin, Henry M.   II. Title.
   LB2806.36.B42 2005
   379.1'11'0973—dc22

                                                           2005015678

Printed and bound in the United States of America on acid-free paper that meets the standards of the American National Standard for Permanence of Paper for Printed Library Materials.

Designed and typeset by Straight Creek Bookmakers.

09 08 07 06 05 1 2 3 4 5

Contents

List of Illustrations   vii

Acknowledgments   ix

Chapter 1—Education Privatization in Its Many Forms   1
    Introduction   1
    The Broad Framework of Educational Privatization   3
    Our Mission   15
    Note   20

Chapter 2—The Marketplace in Education   21
    Introduction   21
    Market Reforms in Education   23
    Internal Anatomy of Markets   28
    Education and the Public-Private Nexus   33
    Evidence on Vouchers and Choice   41
    Future Developments   53
    Power of Ideology   55
    Notes   57

Part I: The Family   59

Chapter 3—Families as Contractual Partners in Education   61
    Introduction   61
    Families, Schools, and Educational Attainments   62
    Developing a Metaphorical Family Contract   68
    Implementing the Contract   73
    Note   77

Chapter 4—Modeling School Choice: A Comparison of Public,
    Private–Independent, Private–Religious, and
    Home-Schooled Students   79
    Introduction   79
    The Economics of School Choice   80
    Data   83
    Estimation of School Choice   84
    Conclusion   89
    Note   90

Chapter 5—Home-Schooling   93
   Introduction   93
   The Home-Schooling Movement   94
   A Framework for Evaluating Home-Schooling   103
   The Impact of Home-Schooling on U.S. Education   112
   Notes   115

Part II: The Private Market   **117**

Chapter 6—The Effects of Competition on Educational
   Outcomes: A Review of U.S. Evidence   119
   Introduction   119
   Identifying the Evidence on Competition   120
   Competition and Academic Outcomes   124
   Competition and Educational Quality   130
   Sensitivity Analysis   136
   Policy Reform and Competition   137
   Conclusion   141
   Notes   141

Chapter 7—School Choice and the Supply of Private
   Schooling Places (with Heather Schwartz)   145
   Introduction   145
   The Importance of School Supply in Education Reform   146
   Supply Responsiveness in the Milwaukee Parental
      Choice Program   152
   Conclusion   159
   Notes   161

Chapter 8—The Potential of For-Profit Schools for
   Educational Reform   163
   Introduction   163
   Can For-Profit EMOs Be Profitable?   164
   Do EMOs Contribute to Educational Reform?   172
   What Has Been Learnt?   175

Chapter 9—Postcompulsory Entitlements: Vouchers for
   Life-Long Learning   179
   Introduction   179
   Vouchers for Postsecondary Education   180
   Evaluating Postcompulsory Entitlements   183
   Can PCEs Work?   192
   Conclusion   194
   Notes   194

References   *197*
Index   *213*
About the Authors   *225*

Illustrations

Tables

1.1 A Framework for Considering Public and Private Dimensions
of Elementary and Secondary Schooling 4
2.1 Effects of Competition between Schools or Districts 45
2.2 Summary of Catholic School Effects 47
2.3 Summary of Charter School Effects 48
2.4 Summary of Impact of Voucher Experimental Trials 49
2.5 Summary of Correlations between School Type and Civic
Education 53
3.1 Home Environment Pathways between Socioeconomic Status
and Student Achievement 70
3.2 Out-of-School Pathways between SES and Student Achievement 71
3.3 Parental Involvement with Schooling Pathways between SES and
Student Achievement 71
4.1 Household and Maternal Determinants of the Choice between
Public School, Home-School, or Religious or Nonreligious
Private School 86
4.2 Student-level Determinants of the Choice between
Public School, Home-School, or Religious or Nonreligious
Private School 87
4.3 Community-level Determinants of the Choice between
Public School, Home-School, or Religious or Nonreligious
Private School 88
5.1 Home-Schooling Estimates by State 98
5.2 Home-Schooling and District Reporting 99
5.3 Characteristics of SAT-takers by School Type 101
5.4 SAT Test-Scores by School Type 107

5.5 SAT Test-Score Gradients by Socioeconomic Status by
School Type 111
6.1 Summary of the Effects of Increases in Competition by One
Standard Deviation 125
7.1 The Growth in Private Schooling across the United States,
1993–2000 148
7.2 Parameter Estimates for Elasticity of Supply of
Private Schooling 151
7.3 Schools Participating in Milwaukee Parental Choice Program 154
7.4 Students Participating in Milwaukee Parental Choice Program 155
7.5 Concentration of Voucher Students within Participating
Schools in Milwaukee Parental Choice Program 156
7.6 Schools Where Voucher Students Comprise 80 Percent or
More of School Population 156
7.7 Age of Participating Schools in MPCP 157

Figures

2.1 Supply and Demand Framework 29
2.2 Comparative Static Analysis 30

Acknowledgments

We would like to acknowledge the great help of colleagues at Teachers College, Columbia University. In particular, Elizabeth Rigby contributed greatly to the materials in Chapter 3.

Several of these chapters have appeared in revised form in other publications: *Review of Research in Education* (Chapter 2); *UCLA Law Review* (Chapter 3); *Educational Policy Analysis Archives* (Chapter 4); *Review of Educational Research* (Chapter 6); *Education Next* (Chapter 8); and *International Journal of Entrepreneurship Education* (Chapter 9).

Clive R. Belfield
Henry M. Levin

Chapter 1

Education Privatization in Its Many Forms

Introduction

Educational privatization has emerged as a central topic of educational policy in the twenty-first century. More specifically, it has arisen in the form of new initiatives that have been proposed for funding education such as educational vouchers and tuition tax credits as well as methods of providing public support for private schooling. Most observers have at least some opinion on the subject, although accurate information on what is meant by privatization is much scarcer. A major public opinion poll found that about 80 percent of those questioned clearly favored or opposed educational vouchers, a particular approach by which government would fund private school tuition (Public Agenda, 1999). But only about one-third of the respondents could provide even a simple description of educational vouchers. This book represents an attempt to broaden knowledge and understanding of educational privatization by demonstrating its diverse forms and consequences. It is important to note that we are neither advocates nor opponents of educational privatization. We both have a strong belief that policy on the subject needs to be informed by knowledge and understanding rather than emotions and symbolism. Thus, this book is written in the spirit of an attempt at balanced analysis on a controversial subject.

In most industrialized countries of the world, including the United States, elementary and secondary education is an official responsibility of government. This commitment has been met by establishing elementary and secondary schools that are sponsored and funded by the government with compulsory

1

attendance requirements for all young persons of a certain age group, for example, ages 6–16. Although private schools and other forms of private instruction have existed prior to public schools almost everywhere, and continue to exist, even these are regulated by governments.

Recent years have witnessed a rising debate in the United States, Europe, Asia, Australia, and Latin America over whether this is the best way for a society to provide basic schooling for its young. In particular, a range of alternative approaches has been posited by those who are unhappy with the present system of public schools and who argue that a government-funded system of private schools can be more effective, efficient, and equitable. This advocacy has been accompanied by specific recommendations. For example, tuition tax credits could be provided to parents to partially or fully compensate them for private school tuition; publicly funded educational vouchers or certificates could be used to pay for private schools; and public education authorities could contract with private, for-profit entities to operate their schools.

Much of the advocacy for or opposition to these forms of privatization is ideological in nature. Free-market advocates believe that the discipline of the marketplace will provide choice and competition that are currently absent from the existing system of public schools, and that these features will provide greater parental freedom and more efficient use of resources. Skeptics believe that privatization is simply a ploy to create emerging opportunities for investment and profits for business entities by shifting $500 billion in government revenues to private enterprises as well as to establish more effective mechanisms for segregating the educational system by income, religion, and race as parental values and wealth determine school choice. As we will note in this book, the evidence is neither unequivocal nor clearly persuasive on either side, so strong belief seems to underlie these opinions rather than clear facts.

These types of debates are further confounded by the fact that education has both public and private purposes. Students and families derive private benefits from education, which provides experiences that develop skills, values, and personal attributes. These benefits are widely linked to increased productivity, earnings, health status, and many other personal outcomes that improve the welfare of the individual and family (Haveman and Wolfe, 1984). What should be noted is that the process of education in itself has both public and private components, where *private* refers to those dimensions that are purely of value to the student and his or her family and *public* refers to those that spill over to improve the larger society.

Unfortunately, current discussions on the meaning and consequences of educational privatization have been far narrower in scope than the topic demands.

Most of the discourse is simplified to a level where it is assumed that privatization refers only to whether schools sponsored by private entities are supported by government funds. In fact, educational privatization takes many forms that extend well beyond the more restrictive concerns of school funding and sponsorship. All of these need to be taken into account when considering both the merits and drawbacks of educational privatization. What follows is an attempt to broaden the context of privatization to demonstrate its many intertwined facets as a prelude for considering its consequences.

The Broad Framework of Educational Privatization

Table 1.1 provides a view of five dimensions of schooling for four types of school organizations as parsed according to public and private influences. Even a first glance at the table suggests that the public and private characteristics of schools are much less separable than the conventional wisdom and discussions on the subject suggest. Rather than there being clear distinctions of public and private for each type of schooling, a mixture prevails. Next we will discuss this phenomenon by briefly describing each type of schooling and how each broad characteristic is reflected in public and private dimensions.

At least five key dimensions of educational privatization should be considered: school sponsorship; governance; funding; production; and outcomes. Table 1.1 summarizes the public and private involvement of each of these dimensions for four types of schooling.

Home-schooling refers to the most privatized form of recognized schooling where the family takes formal responsibility for educating its offspring. Normally, this type of schooling takes place in the household under the supervision of parents or other family members, possibly with collaboration among households and with some outside assistance. An estimated 1–2 million elementary and secondary students in the United States are home-schooled, and the number is believed to be growing rapidly. As we note in Chapter 3, the educational efforts of the family, both purposive and incidental, represent the most complete form of privatization.

Private schools or independent schools refer to institutions that are sponsored by nongovernmental entities other than families. Private schools are found in all of the states. Approximately 30,000 private schools serve 4.6 million elementary and secondary students or almost 11 percent of the country's students. This percentage is down from 14 percent in 1960. About 83 percent of students in private schools are in religiously affiliated institutions. Although recent debate about

Table 1.1 A Framework for Considering Public and Private Dimensions of Elementary and Secondary Schooling

	Home-Schooling	Private Schools	Charter Schools	Public Schools
Sponsorship	Private	Private	Public and private	Public
Governance	Public and private	Public and private	Public and private	Public and private
Funding	Mostly private	Mostly private	Mostly public	Mostly public
Production	Private	Mostly private	Public and private	Mostly public
Outcomes	Mostly private	Mixed	Mixed	Mixed

privatization often addresses the issue of public funds payments to for-profit schools, only a very small proportion of private schools in the United States are for-profit, probably less than 5 percent. The dominant share comprises not-for-profit institutions with a religious or educational mission.

Charter schools are public educational institutions for which state and local laws and other requirements that govern traditional public schools have been waived. They are a relatively new institutional form, dating back only to 1992. In exchange for such autonomy, they are expected to pursue themes and goals set out in their formal application for charter status, and their performance is reviewed every few years (generally 3–5) to determine if the charter school is meeting its goals. At present charter school provisions are found in about 41 states, with more than 3,000 charter schools enrolling about 740,000 students. Each state has different rules for authorization and establishment of charter schools, and the numbers of such schools vary enormously among states. The five states with the largest number of charter schools in 2003 were California (537), Arizona (495), Florida (258), Texas (241), and Michigan (216) (http://www.uscharterschools.org/pub/uscs_docs/sp/index.htm).

Public schools refer to the dominant form of schooling in the United States and account for 47 million students in 90,000 elementary and secondary schools in 2003. Such schools are funded primarily by state and local governments with a modest amount of assistance from the federal government. These schools are typically operated by local school districts, except in Hawaii where the state operates all schools. Enrollments in public schools are generally based upon neighborhood attendance zones, although in recent years considerable numbers of such schools have been open to parental and student choice, both within and among school districts.

As table 1.1 demonstrates, the designation of public or private descriptors for each type of school is a vast oversimplification or distortion for most purposes. The degree to which all four types of schools have public or private characteristics depends upon the specific dimensions of schooling that are analyzed. We view the term *private* as relating to schooling provided for and by individuals, groups, institutions, or entities that are primarily devoted to meeting the private goals of the participants and sponsors of those institutions and that are closely associated with the prerogatives of private property. In contrast, the term *public* is viewed as relating to entities and purposes that have a broader societal impact beyond that conferred upon the direct participants and is usually associated with a government role. What we will see is that there are considerable intermingling and overlap of public and private attributes among school types rather than pure demarcation.

Sponsorship

Sponsorship refers to who establishes schools and provides schooling. Perhaps in the area of sponsorship we see the clearest division of public versus private spheres. Both home-schooling and private schools are characterized by private sponsors. Charter schools represent a mixed activity of public and private. Often schools are proposed by private groups and proposed for public charters and funding. Public schools are sponsored by government entities.

Governance of Education

Governance refers to the overall authorization for operation of schools and responsibility for schooling decisions as vested in the domains of private or public control. Even private schools and home-schooling, although privately sponsored, are jointly governed by both public and private authorities. The reason for this is that all of the states sponsor constitutions that establish schools and mandate compulsory attendance between certain ages. Throughout the eighteenth and early nineteenth centuries, there was continuing litigation on the issue of whether private schools satisfied the requirements of the compulsory attendance laws. The U.S. Supreme Court decided the issue in 1925 in *Pierce v. Society of Sisters* (1925), which determined that schooling under private auspices could meet compulsory attendance requirements by meeting the standards that the states set out for such schools. As a result of that decision, all students and their schools—including those who are in home-schooling and in private schools—are considered to be responsible to public authorities.

> No question is raised concerning the power of the State reasonably to regulate all schools, to inspect, supervise and examine them, their teachers and pupils; to require that all children of proper age attend some school, that teachers shall be of good moral character and patriotic disposition, that certain studies plainly essential to good citizenship must be taught, and that nothing be taught which is manifestly inimical for the public welfare. (*Pierce v. Society of Sisters,* 1925)

All the direct sponsorship of home-schooling and private schools is the responsibility of private entities in that they are operated by families and private school governing boards or owners, respectively, but they are subject to public authority in most of their important operations and functions. State governments and their local educational agencies have been reluctant to set out and administer these details in the case of private schools and home-schooling, giving the impression that these entities are largely "off-limits" for public control and regulation. Indeed, the states have been reluctant to fully use the powers granted to them by the U.S. Supreme Court, probably because of the political battles that would ensue over an issue that affects only a relatively small portion of the population, some of it quite powerful. But this should not distort the reality that the states have authority to do so, a point that should be kept in mind in discussions of the growth and expansion of private schools and home-schooling if such expansion were induced by publicly funded mechanisms.

Charter schools, too, are both sponsored and governed by public and private authorities, even though they are considered to be public schools. Some charter schools are sponsored directly by school districts with a governing board that is answerable to the district. Others are sponsored by groups represented by private boards that are answerable to the state and to chartering authorities. Chartering authorities are, themselves, defined by and approved by the states. Some charter schools not only have privately constituted governing boards, but contract their operations to private firms called educational management organizations (EMOs) that are paid to manage and operate the school. Although EMOs are viewed as operating under the governance of the governing boards of the schools, the fact that they have extensive de facto property rights and limited communication with such boards means that they, too, play an independent role in school governance.

There are many forms and combinations of public and private governance that characterize the many charter schools depending largely on state legislation and, particularly, the authorizing provisions. Although states can waive state and local requirements for charter schools, they are still subject to federal laws under which they are held accountable if they participate. Typically, states have provided charter schools with considerable autonomy in meeting the goals of their charter.

Finally, public schools are governed by public authorities, typically under state constitutional provisions and legislation that are implemented by a state department of education through local educational agencies. Public schools are highly limited in terms of their autonomy because they are governed by permissive legislation and can carry out only those functions that the legislature assigns to them. Much of the legislation is highly detailed on such matters as curriculum, personnel, finances, educational procedures, and the responsibilities of local governing boards; there is considerable monitoring of these functions by states and their agencies.

But even for public schools, there is an argument for suggesting that they might have mixed governance. First, public schools also contract with EMOs to run their schools, providing a buffer between direct public intervention and school operations beyond the overall contract. Second, teacher unions and other privately constituted groups often negotiate contracts in which the provisions of the agreement have a direct bearing on control and decision making at school sites. For example, it is common for such contracts to include agreements on average and maximum class sizes and on the limits of supervisory oversight of teachers as well as other details of daily operations and governance. Although states generally restrict or proscribe collective bargaining that addresses specific school policies, the resulting agreements typically infringe on the scope of governance because agreements on working conditions such as class size or supervision set limits on educational governance. Because public sector bargaining opens the door for the direct participation of private labor or professional organizations and negotiations over school policies, such organizations have a potentially strong private influence in the governing process.

Funding of Education

Funding refers to the provision of resources for schooling, not only in its financial forms but also in contributed resources. Home-schoolers have generally provided full support for their children's education through their own efforts at teaching or the provision of other instructional arrangements for their children. They have also purchased the instructional materials needed, although many states provide these at public expense. Beyond this, many home-schoolers obtain a part of their education under public circumstances by taking specific courses or obtaining other specific instructional services from the schooling authorities (Lines, 2002). This is especially common at the secondary level where particular specialized courses beyond what families can offer or sports activities sponsored by the schools are accessed by home-schoolers.

More recently, home-schoolers in some states have been able to gain resources for their children's education through publicly funded "virtual charter schools" that provide curriculum through the Internet as well as resources for instructional materials such as books and computers and limited technical assistance (Huerta and Fernandez, 2004). This development has been a source of controversy as such charter schools with few personnel and facilities and low costs have received compensation from the states that is comparable to the more costly brick-and-mortar charter schools, providing rich profit opportunities for the virtual charter providers. There are also important monitoring challenges with respect to the number of students actively using virtual charter schools and accountability for achievement comparable to that of public schools.

Private schools are also predominantly supported by private funding and resources, but not exclusively. The principal private sources of support include tuition and contributed resources, some cash and some in-kind contributions. However, in virtually all states private schools receive public services and, as nonprofit educational entities, are exempt from taxes. Sullivan (1974) has suggested that this amount is considerable (although no data have been produced in recent years). In some states school districts and other levels of government provide textbooks and transportation. Private schools are eligible for federal and state support for targeted groups of students such as those in special education or compensatory education. Often such services are provided by personnel from local school districts. Thus, although most of the funding for private schools comes from private sources, some funding is also derived from public sources depending upon the provisions of particular states and whether targeted services are provided by private schools. It should be noted that many private schools do not enroll special education students or those who require compensatory educational services such as those funded by the federal Title I legislation.

Charter schools are predominantly funded by public resources on the basis of formulas established by the state. However, such schools have been given great autonomy in raising private funds and obtaining other private resources. In most states the funding provisions are not adequate for acquiring the use of facilities that are comparable to those of public schools except in those instances where regular public schools are converted to charter schools. Thus, many charter schools search for facilities in vacant schools or space provided by sympathetic organizations such as churches and community groups in which to locate their activities. Others establish capital funds and engage in extensive fund-raising for facilities, often relying on a relatively small number of large donors. In addition, charter schools enlist boards of directors that are sympathetic with their mission to help seek operating funds from private sources. The financial results from these activities vary considerably. In some cases schools are able to obtain regular infusions of funding from major philanthropic foundations and private sponsors or patrons that account for a considerable portion of their budgets. In other cases the amounts raised are very small, particularly if the sponsorship of the school lacks the connections or the educational theme that will attract such funds.

Public schools are also predominantly funded by a combination of local tax revenues, drawn primarily from local property taxes, and state and federal revenues designated for schools. There is considerable variance, both among states and among local jurisdictions within states, in the public revenues that are provided for education, leading to litigation in recent years in many states to improve the equity or adequacy of funding by applying specific provisions of the states' constitutions. However, public schools also draw upon some private sources of funding by requiring students to pay for some extracurricular activities, uniforms, and school supplies (e.g., calculators) and by establishing local philanthropic foundations for the express purpose of raising private funds to support the schools. Although there are no reliable estimates of these amounts, they are thought to have risen in recent years; however, they still constitute a very small part of the funding for U.S. public schools. In contrast, in developing societies, both cash and in-kind private contributions represent a considerable portion of the funding requirements of public schools, typically in the range of 25–60 percent (Tsang, 2002).

Production of Educational Services

Production of education refers to the process by which students acquire knowledge and skills. Such a process is characterized by organization, procedures, curriculum content, and reporting requirements. Although we refer to only four types of schooling in table 1.1, it is important to note that the production of education and its outcomes are not limited to schools and schooling. Education is produced by the interactions of families, schools, and other influences such as neighborhoods and student peers. Of these determinants, the evidence consistently supports the role of the family as the dominant educational influence. What families do on their own makes a substantial difference in educational results, and these differences are closely reflected in the socioeconomic characteristics of families. More educated and higher-income families are able to provide their children with better home conditions, richer experiences, and greater exposure to verbal skills and knowledge, a difference that results in substantial advantages in academic proficiencies and school readiness even prior to entering school (Hart and Risley, 1995; Lee and Burkam, 2002). But, in addition, children of more advantaged parents are better prepared to accommodate successfully school routines and expectations. Because the family is the most private unit in our society, the production of education has a major private component for all children, regardless of the type of formal schooling entity. The central role of the family as an agent of privatization and how it can be harnessed to improve school results will be highlighted in Chapter 3. Acknowledging the important role of families, the following analysis limits itself to the public and private influences on the four schooling entities in table 1.1.

Home-schooling is produced under private auspices, except in those cases where students receive some of their instruction in public institutions. However, even home-schooling must meet public regulations such as attendance, content, and testing set out by public authorities, constituting a public influence on the schooling process. Nevertheless, what home-schooling families do is so hidden from public accountability that it is safe to consider the home production of education to be a private affair. Private schools also produce schooling under predominantly private means within regulations set out by government. But in the case of private schools, the government influence can be more visible. Still, in the cases of both home-schooling and private schooling, the most important components of organization, content, and process are determined privately with public influence limited in scope and by the fact that government monitoring is rare and costly or even limited or prohibited in the case of religious schools by the First Amendment of the U.S. Constitution. In *Lemon v. Kurtzman* (1971), the U.S. Supreme Court ruled that government monitoring of religious versus secular content of education in religiously affiliated schools may create excessive entanglement of the government with religion, violating the establishment clause of the First Amendment.

Charter schools have both public and private components in the production of education. Many charter schools contract with private educational management organizations to operate their schools. Although the details of the contract are negotiated and approved by governing boards of these schools, the design of the schooling process, its implementation, and school operations are relegated to the EMO. Public and private agencies adopt or work as partners with some charter schools, for example, high schools that emphasize the arts, health care, criminal justice, and other themes that require collaboration in instruction and placement of students in internships. Thus, charter schools are likely to have mixed modes of educational production between both public and private sectors.

Of the four types of schooling, public schools are characterized by the least private input into the educational process. Even so, public schools purchase or contract for significant private inputs including textbooks, equipment, consulting services, and instructional contracting with EMOs. In recent years EMOs have become particularly active in providing supplementary services such as extended-day sessions, summer school, and tutoring to students in schools that are considered to be failing according to the guidelines of the federal law No Child Left Behind. So, although the educational process of the public schools is dominated by the laws and regulations of state and local educational authorities, it also has some private components.

Educational Outcomes

Educational outcomes can be thought of as both private and public. Private outcomes benefit primarily the individuals being educated and their immediate families. Public ones benefit the larger society. Clearly what students learn in school confers private benefits upon them in terms of skills, knowledge, values, behaviors, and understanding. These, in turn, enhance their capabilities in the workplace and other settings, raising access to further educational opportunities and translating into better jobs, earnings, health, and personal satisfaction.

But beyond these private benefits, children's experiences at school provide benefits for the larger society. These public benefits are used to justify public funding of education. Under ideal conditions, schools can provide students with a common set of values and knowledge to contribute to their functioning in a democratic society. Schools can also contribute to equality of social, economic, and political opportunities among persons of different racial and social class origins, making for a fairer society. Schools are expected to play a major role in contributing to economic growth and high employment for the nation and its regions. Schooling is a contributor to cultural and scientific progress and to the defense of the nation. These represent some of the areas in which education must be perceived as a social or public good beyond any contribution that it makes to fulfilling private needs. This is also the main reason that schooling is compulsory and bound by regulations that are perceived to be instrumental in producing these important public benefits.

Home-schooling is dedicated primarily to those goals and values that the family deems important. Although government regulations surrounding schooling may be imposed to ensure social benefits, they are difficult to monitor and enforce so that home-schooling is dominated by what families believe to be in their own interest rather than that of society. For example, children are unlikely to be exposed to values and beliefs that are counter to those of their families, even though democratic discourse requires that one understand alternative perspectives in resolving differences and disputes. Thus, table 1.1 characterizes home-schooling as producing educational outcomes that are predominantly private rather than public in their focus.

Private schools represent a range of mixes between private and public outcomes in their focus, from those that are highly dedicated to social concerns to those devoted to the narrow goals of their clientele as embodied in religious practices or political indoctrination. For example, many Catholic schools emphasize social justice issues, potentially producing outcomes with public consequences and social benefits for equity and democracy. In contrast, Peshkin (1986) studied a fundamentalist Christian school that focused on preparing its students for the Kingdom of Heaven, a much more restricted concern that was limited to its adherents. Although there is a tendency to believe that private schools focus on education only for meeting the needs of their own students, these schools can also incorporate social and public goals that are believed to underlie civic education and democratic participation. Our experience suggests that private schools have a mix of such outcomes, perhaps with more emphasis on the private goals of its clientele than the public goals of society. The lack of careful research on how private schools address the public goals of education, however, leaves us with some ambiguity overall, along with the knowledge that great differences are likely among individual private schools, depending upon their sponsorship.

Designed to be public schools in that they represent the public interest, charter schools differentiate themselves to attract students with specific needs, interests, and learning styles. To some degree, we might expect charter schools to focus more fully on the public benefits of education because they are somewhat more exposed to public educational requirements than private schools. Although most state and local requirements may be waived, charter schools are still required to meet certain curriculum and testing requirements in the various states as well as meet specific personnel qualifications in their teaching staffs. Further, their personnel have public school credentials, which emphasize equity and democratic ideals. These conditions are likely to encourage charter schools to pay greater attention to the public goals of schooling than private schools.

Finally, public schools provide a mix of outcomes to meet the private needs of families, particularly through the family's choice of its residential neighborhood (a prominent feature of U.S. schooling, where neighborhoods represent attendance zones for schools). Increasingly, other forms of school choice both within and among districts also emphasize the private concerns that families have for the education of their children. However, public schools are the most exposed to the curriculum, teaching, and testing requirements of the state and other required school practices. To the degree that these requirements emphasize the public purposes of education, the public schools have a mix of educational outcomes with a higher concentration of public outcomes than the other types of schools.

The Complexity of Educational Privatization

Unlike the simple dichotomy of public versus private that has emerged in the public debates on the subject, the phenomenon of educational privatization has many forms and meanings in education and is often embedded in our system of "public education." If we compare inner-city schools with their wealthy, suburban counterparts, the differences are closely linked to differences in private wealth, not only in terms of financial support for schools but in the educational advantages of families as they affect schools. Clearly, differences between resource-poor inner-city schools and wealthier suburban schools and similar disparities in student enrollments reflect primarily the parallel disparities in the private resources of families. Families with the income to afford housing in communities with outstanding public schools are able to make private choices to live in those communities. Poor families do not have those options. In this respect, public schools in wealthier communities take on many "private" characteristics in exclusivity and selectivity according to parental wealth and in customizing education to the private goals and values of the students. And to the degree that their peers have an important influence on the learning and educational success of individual students, a valuable school resource for promoting student achievement is highly "privatized" in the process.

Further, as we showed in table 1.1, some mix of public and private features is found among all types of schools when we look carefully at the different organizational dimensions of schooling with differentiation largely by degree rather than archetype. Of course, some types of schools and forms of school organization tend to be characterized more by public features in their sponsorship, governance, funding, production, and outcomes while others are characterized more by their private characteristics. However, in some cases the tendency toward public or private is so strong that for all practical purposes it is useful to fully differentiate by calling such schools public or private. Nevertheless, we should not forget that most schooling arrangements have at least some features of both public and private.

This book's message is that the details of what is meant by public versus private must be examined, without making simple conclusions about whether government or private entities sponsor a particular school. This is the main message of the various chapters in this book. Different forms of educational privatization can produce diverse consequences, which can be affected by the way schools are financed, regulated, and supported by other features (e.g., the provision of transportation and information). In what follows next, we present a range of perspectives on educational privatization varying from the role of families to that of the marketplace.

Our Mission

It was precisely the oversimplification of the public-private dichotomy in education that was the rationale for establishing the National Center for the Study of Privatization in Education (NCSPE) at Teachers College, Columbia University, in 1999 (http://www.ncspe.org). As debates over educational vouchers, tuition tax credits, home-schooling, and for-profit, educational management organizations heated up during the 1990s, it was clear that the issues were distorted in two ways. First, they were cast in the simple terminology of public versus private when the divisions between the two were far more ambiguous. Indeed, the presentation of the two terms as polar opposites in education enabled each side to throw down a gauntlet that was highly misleading. Second, the issues were placed in an advocacy framework of public versus private in the absence of analysis of the details of what was actually being considered. Thus, organizations and spokespersons addressing such topics as educational vouchers did not attempt to provide a balanced view of their strengths or weaknesses, a situation that has not changed much. Proponents laud educational vouchers as an educational panacea (e.g., Chubb and Moe, 1990); opponents castigate them as attempts to destroy public education (e.g., Apple, 2001). These rhetorical generalizations do not consider the details of alternative proposals but simply characterize all of them as educational saviors or destroyers. This is hardly a useful forum for thoughtful consideration of future educational policy.

Established to fill in the enormous expanse of territory between these poles, the NCSPE emphasized a balanced consideration of the issues. In particular, it focused on the specific designs of privatization proposals to ascertain how the details of finance, regulation, and support services interact to determine educational consequences. Moreover, the NCSPE set out four major goals of education to consider: choice, efficiency, equity, and social cohesion. The premise was that a balanced understanding of approaches to educational privatization could not be undertaken without examining the specific details of a proposal and measuring its consequences against the four goals. At the same time, it was important to consider the emerging evidence of competition, choice, and privatization on each of the educational outcomes.

In order to address this ambitious agenda, the NCSPE held conferences and other events, undertook an extensive program of research and publication of papers on that research, as well as disseminated information on policy issues, all available on its Web site. This book provides an overall synthesis of considerations and findings on a number of aspects of educational privatization that have been little discussed in the literature. We have not intended the following chapters to be a comprehensive review of all the topics of educational privatization but a selective range on which there are current policy discussions.

Chapter 2 sets out a framework for analyzing some of the recent attempts to privatize education more fully by using the marketplace as the provider. In particular, this chapter explores educational vouchers, tuition tax credits, charter schools, and educational management organizations in the economic context of markets. Further, it introduces a set of policy tools that are used to design such market interventions in terms of the provisions for finance, regulation, and support services as well as discusses their consequences for promoting such outcomes as choice, efficiency, equity, and social cohesion. This chapter also reviews the empirical literature on the effects of competition, comparisons of achievement between public and private schools, early studies of charter school effectiveness, and results of voucher experiments.[1] This chapter concludes with a short section on why ideology dominates this subject rather than evidence.

Chapter 3 addresses the most elemental form of privatization, the direct educational impact of families on their children. In this respect, all families are immersed in "home-schooling," in that about 90 percent of children's waking hours from birth to 18 are not spent attending school but are spent under the direct influence of their families. It is not surprising that the research literature documents overwhelmingly that differences in the socioeconomic status of families far outweigh differences in schools in determining educational outcomes of the young. This chapter provides an analysis of findings on what families of different socioeconomic levels do that contributes so markedly to differences in student achievement and attainment. It reinforces the common sense notion that strong families, strong schools, and strong communities and neighborhoods, working together, are requisite for nurturing the young to a healthy and productive adulthood and educational success.

However, instead of just acknowledging what common sense and the research literature assert, Chapter 3 asks what societal contracts might be established to identify collective responsibilities of families and schools, as well as government and social institutions, if they were to undertake collaborative responsibility to support and promote productive educational behaviors and outcomes. Moreover, what institutional changes in policy would be needed to implement such agreements? We call these metaphorical contracts in the sense that they symbolize an agreement of the responsibilities that families, schools, and other social institutions might undertake to provide good educational results, especially for the children of families that are educationally and economically disadvantaged. By placing these obligations in a contractual framework, we can ask what different constituencies would be obligated to do if an effective and productive contract were drawn up. Such a contract can set guidelines for what must be done if we are serious about making all children into capable students and adults. The purpose of placing this chapter at the outset is to emphasize that privatization of educational advantage has impacts long before children arrive at school and that family influences persist while children are attending school. Indeed, any substantial improvement in educational outcomes will require resources for families and neighborhoods (Rothstein, 2004).

As we emphasize in Chapter 2, many, if not most, families have considerable choice in selecting schooling experiences for their offspring. These can consist of choices among public schools, both within school districts and among them, and through residential moves and charter schools; private schools and home-schooling are also options. Little is known about the patterns of school choice, and particularly what kinds of families choose what types of schools. Chapter 4 makes a pioneering attempt to understand the determinants of family choice of different types of schooling experiences. The presentation is unique because it considers choices of four types of schooling: public schools, private-independent schools, religious schools, and home-schooling. This is a somewhat technical analysis using two major data sets. However, the findings can be understood and discussed to build a picture of why different families choose different types of schools. We believe that this exploratory study can provide a basis for further research and provocative discussions of educational policies.

Chapter 5 addresses one of the least understood and underresearched areas of educational privatization and choice, that of home-schooling. Currently, there are wildly different estimates of the numbers of students who are home-schooled. This chapter attempts to provide a basic picture of the numbers and characteristics of children who receive home-schooling. It also applies our overall evaluation framework to home-schooling, considering issues of choice, efficiency, equity, and social cohesion. The dearth of information is a serious handicap to answering these questions, so attention is devoted to the roles of the states in addressing home-schooling and evaluating the consequences for children and for society. Although there are disagreements on the total numbers of children who are being home-schooled, there is wide accord that the numbers are rising rapidly. Chapter 5 presents a context for addressing policy challenges stemming from this expansion.

Chapter 6 goes to the heart of one of the major debates over market approaches to education. Market advocates assert that the efficiency of the educational system will increase through both choice and competition for student clientele. Through choice, it is argued that families will determine the most effective educational approaches and schools that will meet their child's needs. Through competition, schools will have incentives to excel in order to attract sufficient numbers of students to maximize profits or promote their missions in the case of nonprofit providers. In recent years a large number of econometric studies have addressed the relation between competition among schools and educational achievement of students as well as other educational outcomes.

Chapter 6 attempts a rigorous summarization of these studies to ascertain the effects of competition among schools and school districts. A total of 41 empirical studies are reviewed and analyzed systematically. The findings of these studies show a pattern that provides mild support for the competitive hypothesis. That is, there is a consistent finding, with a few exceptions, of greater educational achievement the higher the degree of competition. However, the measurable competitive effects are modest enough in magnitude that they may be offset by other consequences of competition such as the costs of establishing and monitoring more educational suppliers.

Clearly, choice and competition in an educational marketplace depends on the number and variety of schools wishing to participate. Chapter 7 examines the determinants of school supply, generally, and applies the discussion to the Milwaukee Parental Choice Program, a publicly funded voucher program that has been in operation since 1990 and included almost 15,000 students in 2005. An important determinant of the supply of schools entering the marketplace is the size of the voucher. In the case of Milwaukee, it is fairly sizable at almost $6,000 per student. Although this is considerably lower than the average expenditure per pupil in the Milwaukee Public Schools, it does not entail the cost of transportation and other services borne by the Milwaukee Public Schools or the costs of educating moderate and severely handicapped students, an expensive function relegated to the public schools. The relatively high voucher use and the inclusion of religiously sponsored schools have stimulated a substantial supply of private schools that accept voucher students in Milwaukee. In 2003 some 106 schools were participating, with great diversity in sponsorship. Chapter 7 (with Heather Schwartz) analyzes the pattern of school sponsorship and the degree to which such private schools are enrolled in predominantly by voucher students. The reason that this is an important issue is that vouchers are limited to low-income families in Milwaukee, so a school that enrolls only these students will have a high concentration of low-income students. Because the literature on the educational effectiveness of schools suggests that having a mix of higher-achieving and more advantaged peers can have positive impacts on student achievement and that concentrating students from poorer areas reduces achievement, the composition of students enrolled at voucher schools is an important consideration in policy. Indeed, the hope is that these students will be absorbed by schools that have diverse student bodies, given that they are no longer restricted to relatively segregated public schools.

One of the major movements in the past decade has been the role of educational management organizations—for-profit companies that contract to operate and manage conventional public schools and charter schools. Enthusiasts of this trend have suggested that such institutions would raise the efficiency of schools in their use of resources, improve and reform educational practices, obtain better student results, and still provide adequate profits. In addition, the competition for students among themselves and with traditional public schools would provide incentives for conventional public schools to improve in order to retain clientele. The first decade of EMOs has not borne out these expectations, with little impact on educational practices and financial losses that have been far in excess of profits. Chapter 8 represents an analytical attempt to understand why the results have been at variance with predictions and, particularly, the assumptions about school organization and operations that led to the strategies pursued by this first wave of EMOs.

Although the attempt to use marketplace mechanisms to address elementary and secondary schools has predominated among proposals to expand privatization in education, this discussion has been less prominent in postsecondary education, with the notable exception of Milton Friedman's plan for financing higher education with income-contingent loans (Friedman, 1962). Under an income-contingent loan plan, most subsidies to colleges and universities would be eliminated, and students would finance their education by taking loans that would be repaid according to the additional income generated by the educational investment. It is paradoxical that voucher-type proposals have not been prominent in higher education given the apparent success of the GI Bill over 60 years in financing the education of more than 18 million returning military veterans with voucher-like payments. Chapter 9 presents a framework for consideration and analysis of postcompulsory entitlements or vouchers for funding higher education and lifelong learning. The implications of this system of finance are compared along grounds of choice, efficiency, and equity as well as comprehensiveness and flexibility.

It is hoped that these chapters illustrate both the strengths and challenges associated with the move toward greater privatization in education. In addition, we demonstrate that the provisions of finance, regulation, and support services for any privatization alternative can provide dramatically different consequences and that these cannot be understood in the absence of such details. Finally, we show that at least four important criteria must be considered in evaluating the consequences of privatization approaches: freedom of choice, productive efficiency, equity, and social cohesion. These criteria should also be used in evaluating traditional approaches to schooling and other alternatives.

Note

1. At the time that this book went to press, a number of new studies were released. For example, see National Center for Education Statistics, *America's Charter Schools: Results from the NAEP 2003 Pilot Study* (Washington, D.C.: NCES, 2005).

Chapter 2

The Marketplace in Education

Introduction

For at least a century and a half, universal schooling has been viewed as a primary obligation of government. In the United States, state and local governments, with federal support in recent years, have accommodated this responsibility by making substantial legal commitments and providing funding and facilities to discharge that obligation. Although private schools existed prior to the historical establishment of public schools, today they account for only about 11 percent of enrollments at the elementary and secondary levels (NCES, 2003a, table 3; for a discussion of trends in public school districts, see Kenny and Schmidt, 1994). Thus, the public provision of elementary and secondary schooling has long been accepted as a government function and responsibility.

Starting in the 1970s and increasing in intensity in recent years, both the public funding and provision of schooling have been questioned (Friedman, 1993; Lott, 1987). Proposals have been raised to shift school governance and at least some of the funding of education to the private marketplace. Historically, even public schools had a strong component of privatization in the sense that local communities were able to mold their schools to reflect their political, educational, and religious values (Katz, 1971). Resources available to schools depended heavily on local property wealth so that schools in richer communities were better endowed than those in poorer communities (Murray et al., 1998). Parents with adequate means could move to neighborhoods that had better schools or ones that more closely matched their child-rearing and educational values or could send their children to private schools.

Although significant differences may still exist among public schools, these differences have been reduced considerably by court and legislative decisions that have more nearly equalized school funding; reduced racial inequalities; provided more rights and opportunities for the handicapped, the poor, and females; and proscribed religious practices. This trend was particularly pronounced in the latter half of the twentieth century as court and legislative decisions forced school policies and practices to become more alike, at least procedurally, so that differences among schools were reduced considerably (Husted and Kenny, 2002).

Starting in the 1970s cities began to create districtwide schools based upon academic or vocational themes that might attract students from among different neighborhoods. These magnet schools were designed primarily to encourage racial integration by drawing students away from segregated neighborhoods (Wells and Crain, 2005). But the notion of providing school choice was also a response to the pressures from families whose neighborhood schools no longer reflected the differences permitted in an earlier time.

By the 1980s these movements had expanded to incorporate broader intradistrict and interdistrict options. Especially notable were the establishment of charter schools in which most state and local regulations were waived in exchange for a school commitment to particular educational goals and results. That movement has expanded from its establishment in 1992 to as many as 2,556 charter schools by 2002 (according to the Center for Educational Reform, an advocacy center for charter schools and school choice; see http://www.edreform.com). Even more profound—and politically contentious—were the emergence of proposals to shift schools from government sponsorship to the private marketplace with government funding via educational vouchers or tuition tax credits (Carnoy, 1997; Levin, 1998; Belfield and Levin, 2003; for a general overview, see NCES, 2003b).

Under these funding approaches, a private market of schools would replace all or most public schools. Parents would be provided with a voucher, a certificate for tuition that could be redeemed with the state, or tax credits, reductions in tax burdens for all or a portion of tuition. In some cases, parents would be able to supplement these public funds with their own finances to obtain more costly schooling for their children. The motivations behind these approaches were to provide greater freedom of choice of schools as a right and more alternatives for families as a response to the increasing uniformity of schools; to use market competition to make schools more effective with given resources; and to improve options for students in public schools that are economically and racially segregated. These solutions were also consistent with the general movement toward less reliance on government and greater reliance on markets and other forms of decentralization. In exciting a flurry of plans and proposals, educational markets have also been associated with considerable political controversy and strong ideological positions, both from advocates and opponents.[1]

In this chapter we address the educational marketplace by describing the principal reform proposals and the assumptions about market behaviors that motivate them. We show that all educational arrangements, including market approaches, face a conflicting set of goals, and they require tradeoffs—that is, sacrifice of some goals in order to obtain others. The movement to an educational marketplace must confront this dilemma, particularly the conflicts that may arise between the private and public purposes of education. We review the tools that can be used to orient educational market approaches toward specific goals and their consequences. Finally, we provide a brief review of the available evidence on the impacts of educational markets.[2] Although there are many ways to introduce markets into the education system, we pay particular attention to educational voucher programs because these programs typically would introduce multiple features of a market simultaneously.

Market Reforms in Education

Voucher Programs

The most prominent market reform in education is that of educational vouchers. The concept is found as early as the eighteenth century in a plan proposed by Thomas Paine (West, 1967). However, the present discussions on vouchers date back to an important essay published by Milton Friedman (1962) that asked what the government role should be in education. Friedman concluded that "a stable and democratic society is impossible without a minimum degree of literacy and knowledge on the part of most citizens and without widespread acceptance of some common set of values" (p. 86). Because education contributes substantially to these goals, Friedman agrees that some minimal public subsidy is justified. But he argues that public funding for schooling is not an argument for government schools. Rather, the operation of a private marketplace of schools will provide greater benefits in efficiency and technical progress by promoting choice and competition. To combine public funding with private provision, Friedman proposed that "governments could require a minimum level of schooling financed by giving parents vouchers redeemable for a specified maximum sum per child per year if spent on 'approved' educational services" (Friedman, 1962: 89). All educational voucher plans utilize this basic concept, although each may contain different provisions with respect to the size of the voucher, the opportunities for parents to add to the voucher, and other details.

An attempt was made to establish an educational voucher demonstration in the early 1970s by the U.S. Office of Economic Opportunity (Center for the Study of Public Policy, 1970; Weiler, 1974). No state was willing to use public funds for private schools even with federal assistance, so the demonstration was modified to an exercise in public school choice by creating minischools within existing public schools in a California school district and by allowing parents to choose among minischools within the district. The public discussions of vouchers also led to attempts by partisans to establish statewide voucher plans during the 1970s and 1980s (e.g., Coons and Sugarman, 1978). Historically, smaller districts in Maine and Vermont had used a voucher-like mechanism to pay tuition to private schools and other public school districts to educate their children in lieu of establishing schools in the home district (Hammons, 2001b). By 2003, publicly funded voucher programs had been implemented in several U.S. cities and proposed in several others (e.g., Washington, D.C.). But the total number of participants is very small as a proportion of public school enrollments. (There is also a network of privately funded voucher programs, providing scholarship grants to more than 100,000 students; see Howell and Peterson, 2002, table 2.1.)

Milwaukee Parental Choice Program

A formal voucher program for K–12 schooling did not exist in the United States until the state of Wisconsin established one for Milwaukee in 1990. The Milwaukee Parental Choice Program was limited to low-income families and to no more than 1 percent of students from the Milwaukee Public Schools (later, the limit was raised to 1.5 percent and subsequently removed). The amount of the voucher rose from $2,446 in 1990 to $4,894 in 1998 and $5,882 in 2003–04, amounts predicated upon the amount of state aid to local school districts. Until 1995 the Milwaukee voucher was limited to attendance in nonreligious schools and only about a dozen schools and about 830 students participated by the fifth year. In 1998 religious schools were declared eligible by state law for the voucher, an action that was upheld subsequently by Wisconsin courts and the U.S. Supreme Court. This broadening of school eligibility promoted a large expansion: by 2003–04, 107 schools were enrolling almost 12,778 voucher students and two-thirds of voucher recipients were enrolled in religious schools.

Evaluations of the impact of the Milwaukee voucher plan on academic achievement cover only the period from 1990–95 (Witte, 1999). The evaluations of the earlier period were controversial and contradictory, complicated by a problematic data set (missing data, considerable attrition, instability among comparison groups). The initial evaluation for the state of Wisconsin showed no difference in achievement between voucher and nonvoucher students (Witte, 1999). A reanalysis by Greene, Peterson, and Du (1998) using a somewhat different approach found achievement advantages for longer-term, voucher students in both mathematics and reading. A third evaluation that made considerable adjustments for the data problems showed no difference in achievement for reading and a slight advantage for the voucher students in mathematics (Rouse, 1998).

Because the earlier period was characterized by relatively few schools and students, a more valid evaluation of the impact of the Choice Program would ideally build on the present situation. Unfortunately, after 1995, schools receiving vouchers were not required to report test results (or even pertinent information on the characteristics of enrollees), so no such analysis could be done.

Cleveland Scholarship and Tutoring Program

The second of the existing voucher plans was established by the state of Ohio for the city of Cleveland beginning in 1995. Known as the Cleveland Scholarship and Tutoring Program, it has particular prominence because it was the focus of a U.S. Supreme Court decision that resulted in the legal approval (at the federal level) of inclusion of religious schools in a voucher plan (*Zelman v. Simmons-Harris*, 2002). Low-income families were given preference for vouchers in Cleveland, with those below 200 percent of the poverty level (about $36,000 for a family of four) provided with 90 percent of tuition or $2,250, whichever is lower. Families above 200 percent of the poverty level were provided with 75 percent of tuition or $1,875, whichever is lower. About one-quarter of the students came from the latter group.

The vast majority of students in the program chose religious schools; this was not surprising because such schools represent three-quarters or more of existing private enrollments more generally and are the only ones available at the tuition levels of the Cleveland voucher. There were no differences in achievement in any subject between voucher and nonvoucher students over the period of evaluation, kindergarten to fourth grade (Metcalf et al., 2003).

Florida Opportunity Scholarship Program

The Florida voucher program, established in 1999, has two components. Schools that receive an F for two years out of four on the Florida educational assessment system must allow their students to select another public school or to receive a voucher to go to a private school. The voucher has a value of up to about $4,500. Some 542 students were using the voucher in 2002–03.

Florida also sponsors the McKay Scholarships for students with disabilities, a voucher approach. Parents who decide that their children with disabilities are not progressing in public schools can apply what is spent in the public schools toward private schools. In 2002–03 almost 9,000 out of 375,000 students with disabilities were taking advantage of this finance mechanism. The amount that could be allocated to the voucher was a maximum of more than $21,000, depending on the services that were being provided in the public school for that child. Parents could add on to the voucher amount to pay for a more expensive placement. No evaluations of the impact of vouchers on student performance have been done other than a general analysis that argues that schools that might have met the failure criteria improved because of their fear of the voucher (Greene, 2001). But, other incentives were also in place, making it very difficult to disentangle the impact of the voucher threat from the stigma of failure or from the effects of special state assistance for schools at the precipice of failure (Kupermintz, 2001; Camilli and Bulkley, 2001).

Colorado Opportunity Contract Pilot Program

In the spring of 2003 the state of Colorado passed a voucher plan to take effect in the autumn of 2004. It would provide vouchers to students from low-income families with low academic performance if they are in districts where eight or more schools in 2001–02 had low or unsatisfactory performance (or are in a district that participates in the program voluntarily). The amount of the voucher would depend on the grade level and district expenditure: it would amount to the lesser of the actual cost of educating the child in the private schools or 37.5 percent of district expenditure for kindergarten; 75 percent of district expenditure for grades 1–8; and 85 percent of district expenditure for grades 9–12. The plan would start with a maximum of 1 percent of student enrollments in eligible districts and rise to no more than 6 percent by 2007 (see Lenti, 2003). In December 2003 the Colorado plan was struck down, being judged to violate the Colorado Constitution by depriving local school boards of control over instruction in their districts. Legal challenges are likely to continue, however.

Tuition Tax Credits

An alternative way of encouraging a private educational marketplace is a tuition tax credit (TTC) (James and Levin, 1983; Belfield and Levin, 2003). A

TTC provides a reduction in tax burden equal to a portion of tuition paid to a private school. For example, a TTC on income tax could reduce the tax liability of the taxpayer by some sum, for example, up to $1,000 a year. Since 1997, six states have enacted tuition tax credits for education, and thirteen states have tax deduction programs (for schooling expenditures). A tax credit is different from a tax deduction. Some states allow a portion of tuition to be deducted from income in computing a tax, but this only reduces the tax burden by the tax rate on the allowable deduction rather than providing a reduction in the tax burden of that amount. Some states also permit businesses to contribute up to a specific maximum amount to cover the tuition of students in private schools. A TTC serves as a subsidy to households with children in private schools, reducing the effective tuition cost to them, thus increasing the demand for private enrollment. Poorer households can take less advantage of a tax credit because they have less tax liability, although it is possible to design a plan that refunds the credit if tax liability is not adequate to offset it.

Charter Schools

Charter schools are public schools that are able to waive compliance with state and local regulations in exchange for adhering successfully to a specific mission, their charter. In 2002–03 there were 2,556 charter schools serving 685,000 students in 36 states and Washington, D.C., according to the Center for Educational Reform (http://www.edreform.com_upload/ncsw-numbers.pdf). These schools simulate some of the dynamics of a market by increasing the supply of alternatives to parents and by competing with existing public schools. In addition, many of them contract with for-profit, educational management organizations to operate their schools (Miron and Nelson, 2002: 170–193). Typically, they also have their own boards of trustees and considerable autonomy relative to public schools in their states. Although they are not components of a private marketplace, they contain features of choice and competition, which some analysts believe are good predictors of behavior in such a marketplace (see Kane and Lauricella, 2001; Sugarman, 2002).

Because the intention of charter school legislation is to encourage flexible educational provision in response to local needs, charter schools themselves are heterogeneous (on virtual/cyber charter school laws, see Huerta and Gonzalez, 2004). As well as exemption from regulations in hiring unionized teachers, charter schools can choose a nontraditional pedagogy and or curriculum; they can also select the mode of delivery (classroom-based or through distance learning) and school facilities. Given this heterogeneity, the evidence on charter schools' performance (at least as reflected in test score comparisons) is mixed (on charter schools in California, see Zimmer and Buddin, 2003). For advocates, the charter school movement represents a freedom from government intrusion—not only in how the education is provided but also in how it should be assessed.

Educational Management Organizations

In the past decade, for-profit businesses have risen to manage schools. Businesses have long sold products and services and managed some operations of schools such as transportation, cafeterias, maintenance, and construction as well as school textbooks, supplies, and equipment such as furnishings and computers (even including curricular packages and assessment systems). But the rise of educational management organizations (EMOs) has represented a marketplace in itself where such entities compete to manage entire schools under contract to school districts or to charter school boards. In general, EMOs and their schools are in competition because they typically are premised upon school choice by clientele and promise to outperform comparable schools administered by the school district. In fact, school districts often contract with EMOs to operate schools that have done poorly under district administration (for insights into the challenges of establishing and maintaining a profitable educational management organization, see Chapter 8). Thus, EMOs provide two major dimensions of a market, choice and competition, features that we discuss in the next section.

Internal Anatomy of Markets

What is a market and what is assumed about its behavior?[3] Markets are places (literally or figuratively) where buyers and sellers come together to establish purchase of goods and services at an agreed-upon price. The purely competitive market is considered the ideal. In such a market there are a very large number of buyers and sellers so that no one buyer or seller can influence the price. There is perfect information on the alternatives open to market participants. There is freedom of entry into the market by either buyers or sellers, meaning that there are no obstacles to either producing or purchasing the good or service. Buyers wish to maximize total satisfaction or utility subject to the limitation of their resource capacity or income. Sellers wish to maximize profits.

Given these assumptions, a supply curve can show the amount of a particular good or service that will be supplied at each and every price at any point in time. Each supply curve refers to a given quality of the good or service. Multiple supply curves can denote different qualities offered. The supply curve will be upward sloping or increasing with price because the industry must divert resources from other uses at an increasing cost to increase output, especially over the short run. The demand curve will be downward sloping or inversely related to price because as prices rise they reduce the amount of other goods and services that might be purchased and encourage the purchase of relatively cheaper substitute goods and services. Under these conditions, there is an intersection of the supply and demand curve and an equilibrium price for clearing the market. All suppliers and consumers pay the market price. See figures 2.1 and 2.2 for the basic schema of supply and demand.

Although suppliers may want a price that is higher than the market price, competition for clientele will push down the price to that point where firms simply cover all of their costs plus a minimal profit, enough to stay in business. Firms have a choice of which goods or services to produce, so they can decide to enter or even leave the industry if they cannot succeed at the equilibrium price. Firms that are less efficient and cannot produce their output at the market price will fail and will leave the marketplace. Consumers may wish to get a

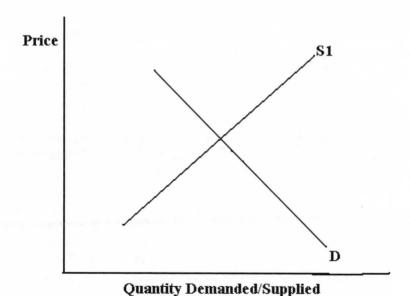

Figure 2.1 Supply and Demand Framework

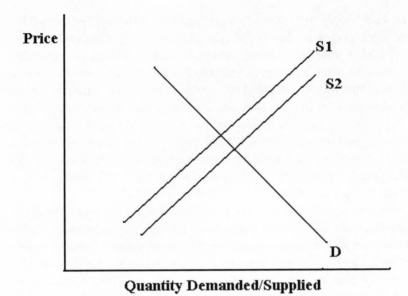

Figure 2.2 Comparative Static Analysis

price below the market equilibrium, but they will be unable to purchase goods at below-market prices in the long run because firms will not be able to sustain themselves at a price level below the cost of production. The key dynamics of the market are choice and competition. Households have a choice of suppliers, so firms must compete for their business by providing goods or services at the lowest price.

This is not to say that prices will be invariant over time. Prices may change as a function of overall supply and demand conditions such as the production technologies or changes in household preferences and income. But the competitive market equilibrium will ensure that the new price is consistent with efficient production. Figure 2.2 shows what happens when there is a technology breakthrough that lowers the cost of production: the supply curve shifts to the right (to S2), which establishes a new and lower equilibrium price. Presumably, competition provides incentives to improve productivity so as to gain larger profits at the market equilibrium. However, such competitive advantages may be short-lived because other competitors may be able to emulate the conditions that lead to gains. Therefore, market prices will fall, as figure 2.2 shows, ensuring only a competitive market return.

It is this model that provides claims for those who seek to shift the production of schooling from governments to the private marketplace. They believe that by providing choice and competition, the quality of schooling will rise when costs are constant or the costs will fall for a given quality. In addition, advocates may wish to provide greater choice in types of schooling, providing a range of submarkets for families because of differences in educational preferences (values, religion, philosophy) rather than requiring each school to provide a uniform type of education (Chubb and Moe, 1990). By replacing a local school monopoly with market competition, efficiency can be brought to the consumer in two ways.[4] First, there will be incentives to compete by providing schooling services at the lowest possible costs. Second, households will be better matched to the types of schooling that meet their needs because of the variety of schools that will emerge and the incentives of schools to be responsive to the needs of their clientele.

Market advocates would argue that the market approach leads to choice and competition overall, increasing productive behavior on the part of parents and students as well as schools. Parents and students have incentives to choose schools wisely. They also have incentives to keep schools attentive with the implicit option of switching to other schools if they are dissatisfied. Schools have incentives to be responsive to student needs to both attract and retain students and to get to the maximum size consistent with good education (it should be noted that most private schools are considerably smaller than their public school counterparts; see Andrews et al., 2002). At the same time they have incentives to innovate over the long run to gain market advantages, a dynamic that can make the industry technologically and organizationally progressive as other competitors imitate those improvements to increase their own effectiveness. These incentives arise primarily from choice and competition promoted by the marketplace.

Finally, even in markets where there is considerable competition, government regulation is necessary. Governments should set basic standards to capture the public interest in schooling, a matter which is addressed in the following section. At issue is how extensive this regulatory framework should be, not whether it should exist.

Imperfect Competition

Few markets are perfectly competitive. In many cases there are few suppliers of a particular product or service, and even these firms may choose to collude rather than compete. Further, a key resource used by firms may be controlled by a single entity such as another firm or a union. Consumers may not have good information, and the nature of the good or service may make accurate information difficult to acquire. Certainly, all of these factors are a reality in education. Particularly in rural areas there may be too few potential students to establish competitive schools that can operate efficiently. For example, in Chile about one-quarter of the municipalities were too small to have even a single competitor to the community's school (McEwan and Carnoy, 2000). Teachers' unions may constrain the ability of schools to adjust employment, benefits, and salaries to market realities or to change the organization of educational services. And parents may have difficulties obtaining and evaluating school quality with schools providing information that is designed primarily for marketing and promotional goals rather than for useful comparisons. Although each of these may reduce the efficiency of the marketplace, the issue is whether introducing greater choice and competition improves educational processes and outcomes, not whether the improvement is optimal.

As long as some choice and competition are available, it is believed that the outcomes will be better than when there are no choices at all. This does not mean that only competition can be used to obtain efficiency in the use of educational resources to gain maximal performance. In his classic book *Exit, Voice, and Loyalty,* Albert Hirschman suggests that both exit (market choice) and voice (informing the provider of how to improve) are important to efficiency and that the easy option of abandoning a supplier may undermine the incentive to guide and pressure them directly to improve services. In the case of education, such school involvement may also be key to student and family engagement, which contributes to learning. McMillan (2004) has found some evidence of this in reviewing the impact of choice on parental participation and student achievement.

To make appropriate choices families need to have good information. In part, this is the motivation for more prescriptive standards and testing in schools—so that families will have information about school quality and will be able to compare schools and hold them accountable. However, there has been considerable debate over whether school quality can be easily codified and quantified (or even manipulated), leading to the possibility that parents will be making choices based on false information (for discussion, see Kane and Staiger, 2002). In addition, although the intentions of most families are aligned toward their children's well-being, some families may make poor or inappropriate choices.

Market Failure and Externalities

Probably the greatest challenge to the view of market efficiency in education is created by the presence of externalities. Externalities refer to effects that "spill over" to the larger society from the individual transactions of the marketplace. That is, by virtue of producing and selling goods and services, firms may have an impact that extends beyond the internal production and sale of products to consumers. At the same time, the choice of such services and their consumption by consumers may also have effects beyond the purchasers. Externalities can be divided into those that represent social costs and those that represent social benefits. An example of the former is the spewing of pollution by firms in their quest to be narrowly efficient in the production of goods or services. An example of the latter is the reduction in risk of contracting communicable diseases for all society as more and more individuals receive inoculations that reduce the incidence of such diseases. That is, the probability of contagion is reduced, even for those who do not receive inoculations, by the acts of those who do get vaccine protection.

Schooling is considered to be a primary source of external social benefits because the results of an education benefit not only the individual, but the society of which the child is a part. That is, even those who are not in school are expected to benefit from a more highly educated society. It has long been held that one of the central purposes of schools is to improve the cohesion and stability of society through the provision of a common experience that prepares the young for adult roles and responsibilities (Gutmann, 1987). Schools are expected not only to educate students as individuals but also to contribute to the overall effectiveness of society through creating competent adult citizens. Even Friedman (1962: 86), a prime advocate of replacing government schools with those of the marketplace, has acknowledged this external benefit of schools by asserting that a democracy requires a minimal level of literacy and knowledge and a common set of values to function effectively. This supposition underlies Friedman's argument for public funding of education. He asserts that this externality (or "neighborhood" effect) can be addressed by setting "minimum standards" for schools in a marketplace without further government intervention. Friedman does not attempt to suggest what these minimum standards might be or how they might be satisfied, providing a blank canvas on which other designers have sketched their own interpretations. That there is broad agreement that schools must meet more than the narrower requirements of individual students and their families is evident. The larger question is how to reconcile the private choices of families with the public requirements of education for democratic knowledge and values.

Education and the Public-Private Nexus

When families choose the type of education that they want for their offspring, the decision revolves primarily upon their values as well as their perception of their children's needs. That education yields private benefits to children and their families is obvious. More and better education is closely associated with higher income and status and greater access to worldly knowledge, both technical and cultural. Because parents want their children to succeed, they will prefer schools that meet high standards. Beyond that, parents usually have political, religious, and philosophical values that they believe are important and should be transmitted to their children. Accordingly, they will seek schools that reflect these values or, at least, do not undermine them. The range of household choices for schooling will be largely predicated on the diversity of backgrounds and educational beliefs of the heterogeneous populations that are found in the United States (Hochschild and Scovronick, 2003). Increasingly, this diversity is reflected in other nations as immigration and religious radicalism increase throughout much of the world.

If the market responds only to these diverse demands, it will not seek a homogeneous set of school offerings with substantially common experiences for all students. Instead, it will tend to divide into market segments or niches that appeal to a particular group of households, segments based upon religion, child philosophy, instructional approaches, and so on. James (1987, 1993) has found that diversity in the population is an important statistical predictor of the extent of private schooling internationally. Coons and Sugarman (1978) and Chubb and Moe (1990) argue that this is the most appropriate way to serve competing needs rather than expecting a single institution to serve all needs. Under a market approach, schools will seek market niches through product differentiation. That is, they will compete by matching their appeal to particular educational preferences of parents rather than trying to produce a standardized educational product. The problem is that serving well a wide variety of different values and preferences is likely to undermine the social goals of providing a unifying educational influence around societal institutions and values.

In general, the social purpose of schools is to prepare the young for democratic participation in the political, social, and economic institutions that unite society into nations, regions, and communities. Successful citizen participation in a free and democratic society requires a common language, values and knowledge for economic and political understanding and participation, as well as an acquaintance with a common set of social goals. In addition, democratic societies are concerned with the provision of fairness in access to life's rewards so that effort and talent, rather than private privilege, are the determinants. These goals argue for a common educational experience rather than one that is differentiated according to family political, religious, and philosophical preferences. That is, the very externalities of education that justify public support argue in favor of a common educational experience rather than one premised upon private choice.

How are these conflicting goals to be reconciled? That conflict is at the heart of all educational systems. On the one hand, the right to influence the way in which one's child is reared means that parents should have the options of choosing the school that matches most closely their child-rearing preferences. On the other hand, the right of a society to maintain an effective and stable democracy and a fair society requires that children have a common educational experience. The existing educational system in the United States, in which 90 percent of students are in government-sponsored schools, has faced this historic challenge. But even more so, a market system that bases its appeal on differentiation and choice must adopt a mechanism to ensure common experiences across schools to prepare students for their civic rights and responsibilities.

Clearly, there is no perfect system as much as a search for a "best system" in providing a balance among these and competing aims (Tyack, 1974). In this context, we can denote four major criteria for addressing an effective educational system: a) freedom of choice; b) productive efficiency; c) equity; and d) social cohesion.

1. Freedom of Choice—This criterion emphasizes the private benefits of education and the liberty to ensure that schools are chosen that are consistent with the child-rearing practices of families. Voucher advocates typically place great weight on this criterion relative to voucher detractors.
2. Productive Efficiency—This criterion refers to the maximization of educational results for any given resource constraint. Educational voucher advocates assume that market competition for students among schools will create strong incentives, not only to meet student needs but to improve educational productivity. Voucher detractors believe that the assumptions that make competition effective will not be present in the educational marketplace.
3. Equity—This criterion refers to the quest for fairness in access to educational opportunities, resources, and outcomes by gender, social class, race, language origins, disability, and geographical location of students. Voucher advocates argue that the ability to choose schools will open up possibilities for students who are locked into inferior neighborhood schools and that the competitive marketplace will have great incentives to meet the needs of all students more fully than existing schools. Challengers argue that vouchers will create greater inequities because parents with education and income are better informed and have greater resources such as

access to transportation. In addition, they believe that the choices themselves will further segregate the poor and disenfranchised as those with power and status will select schools with students like themselves and schools will also select students by such criteria.

4. Social Cohesion—This criterion refers to the provision of a common educational experience that will orient all students to grow to adulthood as full participants in the social, political, and economic institutions of our society. This is usually interpreted as necessitating common elements of schooling with regard to curriculum, social values, goals, language, and political institutions. Voucher advocates believe that this will take place in schools without making special provisions or that it will require only minimal regulations.

Vouchers by Design

There is not a single voucher plan, but many different ones, each emphasizing a somewhat different mix of priorities among the four criteria. Although some refer to "the voucher plan," differences among voucher plans can have profoundly different results. Within limits, educational voucher arrangements are highly malleable. Plans can be constructed with particular features to address each of the four criteria by using three design instruments: (1) finance; (2) regulation; and (3) support services.[5]

1. Finance—Finance refers to the overall magnitude of the educational voucher—how it is allocated and whether schools can add tuition charges to the government voucher for families willing and able to purchase a more costly education. A larger voucher will promote more options in the marketplace with greater freedom of choice and competition. If the educational voucher is differentiated by educational need such as larger vouchers for those with disabilities and from poverty backgrounds, some issues of equity will be addressed. Schools will have greater incentives to attract such students and provide the resources and programs to address their needs. If families can add on to vouchers from their private resources as Friedman proposed, however, those with higher incomes will be able to send their children to more expensive and restrictive schools with potential increases in inequities relative to the present system.

2. Regulation—Regulation refers to the requirements set out by government for eligibility of schools to participate in the voucher system as well as any other rules that must be adhered to by schools and families in using educational vouchers. Presumably, only schools that meet certain standards will be eligible to redeem vouchers. Some voucher plans have

emphasized a common curriculum and uniform testing as a condition of school participation to ensure that students are meeting goals of social cohesion and that schools can be compared for their productive efficiency along common measures of student achievement. Admissions requirements have also been a matter of scrutiny where schools with more applicants than available places would be required to choose a portion of students by lottery to ensure fairness in selection procedures. Eligibility for vouchers may be restricted to certain populations in the name of equity. For example, public and private voucher programs in Milwaukee and Cleveland have been limited to children from poorer families in order to give them choices outside their neighborhoods. Florida's legislation has limited vouchers to children in failing public schools.

3. Support Services—Support services refer to those types of publicly provided services designed to increase the effectiveness of the market in providing freedom of choice, productive efficiency, and equity. Competitive markets assume that consumers will have access to a wide variety of choices as well as useful information for selecting among them. In the United States, the availability of public transportation is very limited, necessitating a system of school transportation from children's neighborhoods to schools of choice. In the absence of school transportation, school choices and competition for students will be limited, reducing both the competitive efficiency of schools and creating inequities for those who cannot afford private transportation.

Information must be widely available for families to make informed choices about the schools that they select for their children. Accurate information on school programs and effectiveness as well as other important aspects of school philosophy and practice would need to be collected and disseminated to parents to assist in making decisions (Schneider et al., 2000). It could be argued that the schools will provide their own information through promotional materials and informational sessions to parents. However, there is little assurance that the information will be accurate and balanced, and it may be especially difficult to process for less-educated parents.[6] Technical assistance might also be provided by government agencies through information and training to new schools to advance the productivity of the entire sector.

Different Voucher Plans

Different voucher plans have incorporated specific designs that utilize these three policy instruments to achieve particular goals. Depending on the specifics, a given voucher plan may differ from another plan in its impact on choice, efficiency, equity, and social cohesion. In essence, each plan uses the design tools to construct a plan that either implicitly or explicitly places greater weight on some goals rather than on others.[7]

1. Designs for Freedom of Choice—A voucher plan that maximized choice would allow for a very broad definition of education that would encompass most types of schools and schooling; would provide either a large voucher to all or a smaller voucher with parents permitted to add to it out of private resources; would minimize regulation of curriculum, admissions, and other dimensions of school operations; and would provide a good system of comparative information on schools as well as an adequate system of transportation. Such a design would ensure a large number of alternatives on the supply side that parents could choose from. This type of plan is especially attractive to Libertarians who prefer to see the least government interference in the marketplace, especially if the voucher is modest and parents are able to add to it. Libertarians may believe that the support services of information and transportation are unwarranted because the cost of government intervention exceeds its value, and they may favor add-ons rather than a large basic voucher from public funding.[8]

2. Designs for Productive Efficiency—Productive efficiency is maximized when schools produce a given level and type of education for the least cost. That is, they are operating at the lowest point on their average cost curve. This is somewhat difficult to assess because, under a system of freedom of choice, schools may be producing very different types of education. It is the matching of these educational offerings to the preferences of families in a competitive environment that is viewed as the heart of efficiency. Accordingly, designs that focus on efficiency would have a voucher that is high enough (including parental add-ons) to attract many competitors into the marketplace. Regulations would be minimal because they would tend to inhibit competition. However, some would argue that academic achievement is so central to the productivity of all schools that testing of student achievement should be required and reported. Support services such as information and transportation would raise efficiency through increased competition, but the cost of those services would have to be taken into account relative to the efficiency gains.

3. Designs for Equity—Equity in education refers to equality in access, resources, and educational outcomes for groups that have traditionally faced differences on these dimensions. From a finance perspective, an equitable design

would seek compensatory vouchers where more funding was available for students with greater educational needs such as those in educationally at-risk and disabled categories. In addition, families could not add on to the voucher so that income differences would be neutralized. The most fundamental regulation on equity is the question of who is eligible to receive and use a voucher. Thus far, all of the voucher plans in the United States have been limited to students from low-income families or those enrolled in failing schools. Thus, the voucher has been accessible to students who are the worst off educationally, providing greater equity in choice for them as it has been provided traditionally through residential location and private schools for those who are more affluent. Equity-oriented regulations would also embrace a provision of nondiscrimination in admissions. Schools would be required to choose some portion of their students by lottery if there were more applicants than openings. Provisions encouraging or requiring that schools not limit themselves to a narrow social or ethnic population are likely, given the evidence that peers have an important impact on educational outcomes (Zimmer and Toma, 2000). Transportation and information would be required support services to provide access to those who are less advantaged and to provide an informed basis for choosing schools.

4. Designs for Social Cohesion—Social cohesion connotes a common educational experience, one that prepares all students for civic responsibilities and participation (see the discussions in Wolfe, 2003). The voucher would have to be large enough to provide a common educational experience beyond specialized and elective subjects and activities. The voucher would have to be structured so that all students could gain access to schools where they would be exposed to peers from a variety of backgrounds. This means that parental add-ons to the voucher would probably be proscribed because they would tend to place students from different income strata into different schools. Regulations would focus on establishing common elements in curriculum and certain school activities including the possibility of all students engaging in community service. Support services might focus on the provision of technical assistance in helping schools develop a common educational core as well as the information and transportation to enable families to find and gain access to schools with heterogeneous students.

Incompatibilities and Trade-offs

Moe (1995) has suggested that molding particular objectives into voucher plans is a matter of design. To some degree he is correct, but such a perspective does not acknowledge the tensions and conflicts among criteria and goals in themselves that suggest that gains in fulfilling one criterion may reduce the ability to fulfill others. This means that intrinsically there must be trade-offs. Some goals cannot be attained without sacrificing others.

A plan such as Friedman's focuses on freedom of choice and productive efficiency through heightened competition, arguably at the expense of equity and social cohesion. Friedman proposes a modest, flat voucher at public expense. Parents could add to the voucher out of private resources, and schools could set their own tuition. Regulation would be minimal, and there would be no provision for transportation and information. This would promote a very large number of alternatives at different levels of tuition, *for those who could afford them,* with few restrictions on schools that enter the marketplace, promoting a large supply of alternatives. Clearly, social cohesion and equity goals would not be paramount.

Conversely, plans that emphasize social cohesion and equity tend to reduce freedom of choice and productive efficiency by establishing a variety of regulations and support services. For example, the Jencks plan (Center for the Study of Public Policy, 1970) would regulate admissions and curriculum and require standardized testing and reporting of results (see also the proposal by Godwin and Kemerer, 2002). It would also provide larger vouchers for the poor—compensatory vouchers—and a system of transportation and information. In addition, vouchers could not be augmented from private resources. The regulations and a fixed-government voucher with no private augmentation would reduce freedom of choice relative to the Friedman plan. The high costs of providing information and transportation and monitoring the regulations for eligible schools would add considerably to the costs of the voucher system and reduce productive efficiency (Levin and Driver, 1997). But the larger vouchers for the poor, regulations on admissions, and information and transportation services would increase equity. The common curriculum and testing requirements would be expected to improve social cohesion.

Although some design provisions would improve outcomes among more than one criterion, almost all would also reduce outcomes on other criteria. Provision of information and transportation will improve choice options for all participants, but especially for those from families with the least access to these resources, the poor. But such provision would also raise the costs of the overall educational system, probably reducing productive efficiency unless gains from competition due to better information and access offset the costs of the transportation and information. The establishment of regulations with continuous monitoring and enforcement could be used to increase equity and social cohesion but would sacrifice freedom of choice and productive efficiency.

There is no optimal system that provides maximal results among all four criteria. Ultimately, the choice of design features will depend on specific preferences and values as transmitted through democratic institutions. Those who place a high value on freedom of choice will probably be willing to sacrifice some equity and social cohesion provisions by eschewing regulations and support services and allowing parental add-ons to vouchers. Conversely, those who place a high value on social cohesion will be willing to sacrifice some freedom of choice through establishing a common curriculum core and other standardized features of schools. Ultimately, much of the debate over the specifics of educational voucher plans revolves around the political power and preferences of the stakeholders.

It is an understatement to say that advocates of vouchers may agree on the general case for vouchers but may disagree profoundly on the specifics. There are even strong differences among persons who are often placed in the same general political category. Thus, many liberals want to see greater freedom of choice for students in the inner city through educational vouchers, even though liberals are usually viewed as antagonistic to marketplace solutions for government services. At the same time, cultural conservatives are deeply committed to a common curriculum and knowledge framework that should be required of all students and the schools where they are enrolled, a very substantial commitment to regulation (Bennett, 1987; Hirsch, 1987). Political conservatives with libertarian views reject regulatory requirements entirely in favor of market accountability, that is, letting consumers decide what they want.

Evidence on Vouchers and Choice

Educational vouchers and tuition tax credits apply to a very small proportion of school populations in the United States. Even among these situations, there have been relatively few evaluations, and virtually none that address consequences for all four of the criteria that we have set out. Nevertheless, it is possible to provide the contours of findings for each area.

Freedom of Choice

Advocates of the marketplace emphasize that parents will have greater freedom of choice than they would under a government system. In an open market, families will have the right to choose schools for their children that are premised on their values, educational philosophies, religious teachings, and political outlooks. Where there are varied preferences and/or abilities across students, this freedom of choice becomes especially important: it is too expensive and complicated for a government provider to collect and process all the information needed to allocate students to their most-preferred school. For libertarians, allowing families to make their own choices should—almost by definition—improve educational outcomes.

The evidence on choice favors the view that vouchers will increase choice considerably in terms of the numbers and diversity of options and that those who take advantage of choice will express higher satisfaction with their schools than comparable groups. Doubters of the expansion of choice often start out with the existing numbers of openings at private schools in a particular region, showing that the available openings are miniscule in comparison with the potential number of vouchers. Certainly, in the short run this is likely to be true, with little expansion of openings in response to voucher demands. Existing schools have capacity limitations that can be relieved only through longer-run expansion. In addition, there is a time lag between the stimulus to establish new schools and the ability to plan, construct, and staff them. However, in response to the new private-market demand, the long-run supply of school places will increase (as evidenced in Milwaukee between 1998 and 2002). But there is another reason that the number of school choices should expand under a market system relative to government sponsorship of schools. Private schools (and charter schools, too) tend to be about half the size of public schools in the United States (NCES, 2003c). This means that for any given population there are likely to be twice as many schools under a market regime.

The U.S. evidence strongly supports the conclusion that parents value freedom of choice (Peterson and Hassel, 1998). Many families report higher satisfaction from participation in voucher programs (Howell and Peterson, 2002) and from being able to choose charter schools over regular public schools (Zimmer and Buddin, 2003). Indeed, the fact that parents in large numbers choose different types of schools when given options is prima facie evidence of the benefits of choice, and guaranteeing freedom of choice is an important way to raise satisfaction levels within the education system (Teske and Schneider, 2001).

There are several caveats to bear in mind, however, when depending on increased choice to improve substantially the quality of education. The first is that some families may not have the resources or the capacity to make choices that are in their children's best interests; there may be a role for education professionals to guide, monitor, or regulate these choices. Also, in sparsely populated areas the limited population size may preclude the establishment of alternatives.

For example, in Chile where educational vouchers have been available for more than two decades, about one-quarter of municipalities, mostly in rural areas, do not have a single alternative to the municipal school (McEwan, 2003). A second caveat is that some families may choose schools that will lead to de facto segregation of groups; individual families may feel better off, but society as a whole may be worse off. A third caveat is that there may be only limited options to increase the range of choices. In the United States, many families already have as much choice as they feel they need—fully three-quarters of families appear satisfied with their choice of school (Henig and Sugarman, 1999). In addition, a sampling of low-income families offered a voucher of $1,400 toward attendance at private schools showed that only between 29 percent and 70 percent used the voucher for at least three years (Howell and Peterson, 2002: 44). A fourth is that private schools might deny some students access. A religious private school is likely to bar enrollment, for example, to students with atheist beliefs (or beliefs in alternative faiths). (Around 75 percent of all U.S. private schools currently in operation are religiously affiliated.) The final caveat is that private schools may be subject to increased regulations if they accept vouchers; these regulations may discourage new students (as found by Muraskin and Stullich, 1998: 49).

So parents may be "free to choose" in principle, but not in practice. Each of these factors suggests that the gains from enhanced freedom of choice in a market—although positive overall—may not be profound and may be particularly limited for some groups.

Productive Efficiency

Some economists have questioned whether the resources spent on public schools have been invested efficiently. For example, from 1973 to 1996 Hanushek (1998) charts falling NAEP science scores and stable NAEP math scores in U.S. schools, even as real current expenditure per pupil increased by around 45 percent (although this debate is controversial, compare Hanushek [1994] and Grissmer et al. [1998]). Many commentators attribute this alleged decline in performance to inefficiencies in government provision of education and a lack of competition. They contend that an educational system with a greater reliance on the marketplace through choice and competition would be more efficient.

Competitive Pressures

Economists believe that marketplace competition forces providers of a service to be more efficient. Competition exists when multiple, separate providers—

facing the same legal rules and regulations—are available to meet the demands of consumers. Where there is more competition between providers (schools/districts), then consumers (parents/children) will face lower prices for services and/or higher-quality services; providers must accept lower "profits," such that only efficient firms will remain in business. More competition should mean higher-quality schooling and enhanced educational outcomes in the education market.

The impact of competition can be assessed in terms of test scores and other outcomes from the education system. Belfield and Levin (2002) reviewed more than forty published studies from 1972 to 2002 that explicitly test for a link between competition and educational outcomes in U.S. schooling. These studies used large-scale, cross-sectional data sets, employing more than 400 individual tests for the impact of competition. Competition is measured either between schools within districts, between districts, or between the public and the private sectors. The impact is measured as the effect on educational outcomes when the extent of competition is increased by one standard deviation.

The full results are reported in Chapter 6. Table 2.1 gives a very brief summary. In general, test scores rise with the extent of competition. However, the effects are substantively modest. If competition presses schools to offer more effective schooling, students may respond by enrolling longer or by applying to college in greater numbers. No effect of competition on dropout rates is evident, but increased competition from private schools is associated with higher public school graduation rates. The effects of competition on spending are harder to predict. From the evidence, there is no clear link between educational expenditures and competition. Fundamentally, competition in the marketplace should raise educational efficiency. Indirectly, the evidence suggests that competition raises test scores modestly but does not raise expenditures.

Overall, this evidence supports the argument in favor of introducing more marketplace competition into education. Increasing competition—either intradistrict, interdistrict, or from private schools—may raise effectiveness and efficiency of public schools, as well as address other educational objectives. It is important to note that the substantive effect is modest and does not support the contention that market competition will produce radical improvements in educational results. Also, the magnitude of the reform is important. Case studies of Cleveland and San Antonio show very few pressures to improve when the competitive stimuli are limited to small-scale reforms (Hess et al., 2001).

However, this evidence only establishes the benefits of competition, and does not consider any necessary reorganization costs to foster, regulate, and monitor competition, or to promote competition broadly across the education system.

Table 2.1 Effects of Competition between Schools or Districts

Outcome Variable	Competition Measure	Effect of Increasing Competition
Academic outcomes	Herfindahl Index	Positive
	Private school enrollments or other proxies for competition	(Positive)
Attainment, graduation rates, drop-out rates	Number of districts or schools	No effect
	Private school enrollments	Positive
Spending	Number of districts in state	Negative
	Private school enrollments	Ambiguous
Efficiency	Herfindahl Index	(Positive)
	Private school enrollments	Positive

For example, Levin and Driver (1997) estimated the additional costs of a state-wide voucher system for recordkeeping and monitoring of students, transportation, adjudication, and information services and concluded that these added costs would be substantial, perhaps as much as one-fourth of existing per-pupil expenditures. Bear in mind that the centralized administration of an extremely decentralized activity (funding and regulating household and school choice) entails a huge increase in transactions and their costs. For example, in the case of California, the state would have to shift its attention from monitoring more than 1,000 school districts to concerning itself with the establishment of individual accounts for almost 7 million individual students and a doubling of existing numbers of schools to 25,000 or more.

More Efficient School Managers and Owners

The second argument that the marketplace may deliver higher-quality education rests on the belief that private owners and managers of schools will be more efficient than government ownership and management. Government-run education systems are often heavily criticized (Bok, 2000). Public schools may have excessive rules or rules applied to all schools regardless of circumstance, and they may be run "democratically," making them fraught with conflicts and compromises to appease the demands of special interest groups that have little connection to students' educational needs (Chubb and Moe, 1990). Costs may be inflated, because politicians feel that spending on public services is electorally popular and because of corruption, fraud, and waste (which taxpayers cannot escape from as easily as shareholders can divest themselves of stock in a wasteful company). In contrast, private owners have incentives—profits, typically—to closely monitor their companies to make sure that they are meeting their objectives. With more market freedom, private schools could be taken over by more efficient providers, or a for-profit company could franchise its schooling technology, for example. Whichever development takes place in the open educational marketplace, the profit motive or educational mission will induce owners and managers to raise educational quality and efficiency to attract an optimal number of students.

The evidence on the relative effectiveness in producing academic achievement of private schools over public schools has been reviewed by McEwan (2000). The evidence for Catholic schools is summarized in table 2.2 (the results for nonreligious schools are similar). Overall, it shows only small differences between private and public school types (when student intake differences are accounted for), indicating that there are not large differences in results across management and ownership structures (see also Figlio and Stone, 1999). For achievement, there appear to be modest effects on mathematics among poor, minority students in grades 2–5 (but not in grades 6–8 or among nonblack students) who attend Catholic schools; and no consistent effects on reading. For educational attainment (i.e., years of schooling), Catholic schools increase the probability of high school completion and of college attendance (particularly for minorities in urban areas).[9]

Other studies have compared the school effectiveness of specific types of choice arrangements such as charter schools or magnet schools (Gamoran, 1996). A recent comprehensive review by Miron and Nelson (2002) compares charter schools with traditional public schools. Summarized in table 2.3, the evidence indicates that, although results vary from state to state, charter schools appear on average to be no more (but also no less) effective than traditional public schools. Evidence on charter schools is continuing to accumulate.[10]

Another potential school type that might be expected to take advantage of an educational marketplace is for-profit schooling. As of summer 2003, the largest for-profit provider of education in the United States was Edison Schools, which educates approximately 80,000 students across 150 schools. However, many of the private, for-profit companies have faced difficulties in achieving profitability and in competing with nonprofit religious schools. In general, the for-profit companies have not been able to innovate more efficiently than public

Table 2.2 Summary of Catholic School Effects

Academic Outcome	Number of Positive and Significant Estimates/ Total Number of Studies	Average Effect (all studies)
K-8 math:		
Full sample	1 / 4	0.02
Minority	2 / 7	0.05
White	1 / 7	0.04
K-8 reading:		
Full sample	1 / 3	0.03
Minority	0 / 7	0.00
White	2 / 7	0.10
Secondary math:		
Full sample	2 / 5	−0.05
Minority	1 / 6	0.00
White	3 / 4	0.10
Secondary reading:		
Full sample	1 / 4	−0.05
Minority	0 / 2	0.00
White	1 / 2	0.00
High school graduation:		
Full sample	4 / 5	0.07
Minority	5 / 6	0.14
White	5 / 6	0.06
College attendance:		
Full sample	3 / 4	0.06
Minority	5 / 6	0.15
White	5 / 6	0.06

Source: McEwan (2000, table 5).

schools and have had difficulties in establishing brand equity (Levin, 2001b). Overall, private, for-profit schools have not established themselves as clearly superior to public schools, and the evidence on improved managerial competence is ambiguous.

Educational Effectiveness from Voucher Programs

Evidence from existing voucher programs and randomized field trials is relevant to the question of whether a marketplace is more efficient than a state-run system. (Most of these evaluations focus on test scores, although it may be more appropriate to consider the effect on student attainment.) Evaluations of the small-scale voucher programs in the United States show largely neutral

Table 2.3 Summary of Charter School Effects

Academic Outcome	Grade Level	State	Results for Charter Schools Relative to Comparison Group
Math	2-11	AZ	+ve (very weak)
Reading			+ve (weak)
Reading	3, 4 and 7	CO	+ve (2/3rds outperformed comparison schools)
Writing	3, 4 and 7	CO	+ve
Math	3, 4 and 7	CO	No difference
Reading/Math	4, 6, 8 and 10	CT	+ve
Reading/Math		DC	-ve (less likely to have improved; more "below basic")
Reading/Math	3, 5 +	GA	No difference
Reading/Math	4, 5, 7, 8, and 11	MI	-ve
Reading/Math	5, 6, 8, 9 and 11	PA	-ve (lower scores in cross-section) +ve (faster gains)
Reading/Math	3-8	TX	-ve, all schools +ve, at-risk schools

Source: Miron and Nelson (2002, table 3).

effects. For the Milwaukee Parental Choice Program, the results vary from no effect to an effect on mathematics, but not reading, to an effect on both mathematics and reading (compare Witte, 1999; Rouse, 1998; Greene Peterson, and Du, 1998). For the Cleveland Scholarship and Tutoring Program, there are no significant differences between scholarship and public school students on any set of educational outcomes, although those students who accept vouchers but then return to public schools report the lowest test scores (Metcalf et al., 2003). The Florida Opportunity Scholarship Program involves so few students that it is not possible to identify an educational impact as yet.

Experimental evidence also shows weak educational effects from participation in a voucher program. Using an experimental design, Howell and Peterson (2002) randomly assigned educational vouchers among a group of voucher applicants from low-income families, forming a group of voucher recipients and a similar control group. The voucher amount of about $1,400 a year was applied mainly to tuition at low-cost Catholic schools for up to three years in three cities (New York; Washington, D.C.; and Dayton, Ohio). The full results are reported in Howell and Peterson (2002) for recipients who used their vouchers at a private school; the test score impacts are summarized in table 2.4. Overall, after three years no achievement advantages were found for those who used

Table 2.4 Summary of Impact of Voucher Experimental Trials

City	Impact of Switching to a Private School on Test-Score Performance			
	Year I (NPR)	Year II (NPR)	Year III (NPR)	Year III (N)
Full sample				
New York City	1.1	0.6	1.4	1250
Dayton	2.2	4.2	..	
Washington, D.C.	-0.3	7.5**	-2.1	687
African Americans				
Three-city average	3.9	6.3**	6.6**	1175
All other groups				
Three-city average	-1.0	-1.4	-3.5	760

Notes: NPR is National Percentile Ranking.
** Statistical significance at $p<0.05$.
Source: Howell and Peterson (2002, table 6-1).

educational vouchers. Although the authors report positive gains for one specific group, African Americans, after three years of voucher enrollment, these results were challenged on methodological grounds and nonrobustness when statistical corrections were made.[11]

Considering all the evidence on the efficiency and effectiveness of markets in education, the following conclusion appears to be robust. Markets do improve educational quality over what would be provided in a fully public system, but the size of this improvement is probably modest and appears to be found for some groups and not for others. To the degree that students are stratified into schools with more nearly homogeneous student populations, the peer effects of diversity on achievement may be reduced for some groups of students as well. The educational marketplace has advantages in matching students to the types of schools that their families prefer relative to traditional assignment by attendance area. This advantage is less evident where intradistrict or interdistrict or extensive charter school choice exists. The additional costs of the infrastructure required to monitor and administer a voucher system are substantial and may outweigh the modest achievement advantages.

Equity

The concern that school systems—whether provided by markets or the state—be fair and equitable is an important one. Equity can be assessed in terms of inputs—do all students get an appropriate amount of funding and resources, commensurate with their needs? Equity can also be assessed in terms of outcomes—do all students finish their schooling with sufficient skills and a fair opportunity to progress in life?

Those who challenge education markets argue that they will produce greater social inequities, as children of parents with higher incomes may benefit most. First, families already paying for private schooling may receive a government subsidy for tuition fees, which previously they were willing to pay for independently. This windfall is intrinsic to universal voucher programs, for example, and is also likely with the introduction of a tax credit or deduction. Second, wealthier families will have more resources to purchase educational services in a private market, allowing them to purchase more education if add-ons are permitted, resulting in greater inequities in inputs.[12] Third, children of highly educated parents may gain extra benefits when choices are expanded. As Schneider et al. (2000) have shown, these parents are probably better informed about what is available to their children in the market and will be better placed to take advantage of new school services. The likely result is that children from wealthy families will use the marketplace to greater advantage. Fourth, social stratification will increase. However, there is little direct evidence that this source of advantage is significantly greater in practice than the inequities of a public school system with local financing where families with adequate income can choose school neighborhoods.

Moreover, markets can be regulated so as to avoid inequities and, in fact, help low-income families or students in failing schools. Many voucher programs—particularly the small-scale programs—have an income threshold applied to them: only families below a certain income level are eligible for a voucher. Similarly, tuition tax credits can be allocated on a merit-based or income-based criterion. The general idea is to enable low-income and minority families to enter the market with more "purchasing power" given to them from government subsidies. Furthermore, markets may make the education system more equitable through open enrollment (Godwin and Kemerer, 2002). Advocates argue that the ability to choose schools will open up possibilities for students who are locked into inferior neighborhood schools, and that the competitive marketplace will produce greater incentives to meet the needs of all students more fully than existing government schools.

More general concerns about broadening the scope of the market and the implications for educational equity should also be noted. First, private schools may refuse to admit some types of students, denying them an appropriate education. (It is difficult to find direct evidence that private schools do this overtly; see Lacireno-Paquet et al., 2002.) Second, families may seek schools that enroll students from their backgrounds with the direct or subtle exclusion of other types of students. Simply creating a curriculum and marketing appeal that is friendly to some types of ethnic and social groups can discourage others from applying. There is a reasonable amount of evidence that—when families are given school choice—they prefer schools with students of the same racial and socioeconomic background as their own (Witte, 1999; Martinez et al., 1996; Schneider et al., 2000; Fairlie and Resch, 2002; Weiher and Tedin, 2002). In addition, many families want their children to be with students of as high as possible ability and social class backgrounds. If families sort their children according to ability, high-achieving students will help each other and gain further advantages over other students.[13] Persistent and significant educational inequities may result. Recent literature has emphasized the impact that different peer groups have on the education of fellow students, and the peer consequences of choice would appear to be negative (Levin, 1998; Zimmer and Toma, 2000). Given the largely neutral impact of vouchers on participants' test scores, these sorting effects may be critical in a full evaluation of the educational marketplace.

Social Cohesion

Schools should promote the social good; this is the main reason they are publicly funded. What constitutes the "social good" will vary across societies. In a democracy, the purpose of schooling is usually interpreted as necessitating common elements of schooling with regard to curriculum, values, goals, language, and political orientation. After compulsory schooling, citizens should possess the skills and knowledge necessary for civic and economic participation in society. By introducing markets and choice into the education system, therefore, there is a risk that these common elements will be undermined.[14]

There are two routes through which an education system can generate social cohesion and order. One is by the design of the system itself: social goods are created when collective action is undertaken (i.e., when all students are offered the same system of education). This is the idea of "common schooling": social goods are created through communal activities. Clearly, reliance on the market would undermine this common schooling; when families can opt out of public schools or when they can provide extra funds for their children's education, they will not be part of this communal activity (see Levinson and Levinson, 2003). When richer families can buy more elitist and exclusive education for their children, social cohesion may be adversely affected. However, it is difficult to find empirical research that substantiates the importance of common schooling in promoting social order.

The second route to producing social goods is through the instruction that students receive within school. When students are taught socialization skills and the importance of civic virtues, social cohesion may be enhanced. Some schools may include courses such as civics or political science or religious education as part of the curriculum; others may encourage charitable acts by the students or offer instruction on (for example) environmental issues.[15] At issue is whether private schools can inculcate more of these capacities than public schools; whether families would—if schooling choices were more open—demand more of this type of education; and whether schooling does influence social cohesion.

Opponents of the marketplace are concerned that individual families are more likely to stress private advantages to themselves than broader benefits to society. Indeed, the pressure for greater freedom of choice derives from the preferences of families. Precisely how to measure the student behavior that connotes these social benefits is not settled. For example, some would measure student knowledge of political and economic institutions and modes of participation in civic life. Others would measure attitudes toward civic participation. Yet others might measure the orientation toward contributing to society.

When measuring some of these dimensions, research evidence for the United States suggests that private schools offer more "civic education" than public schools do.

Table 2.5 summarizes the empirical evidence from two cross-sectional analyses of civic education in the United States, controlling for other factors including family background. Students in assigned public schools are compared with those in four other types of schools: magnet public, private Catholic, private-religious but non-Catholic; and private-independent. Although not fully consistent, the results broadly indicate that private schools produce more community service, civic skills, civic confidence, political knowledge, and political tolerance than are available in public schools. The explanatory power of the school type on actual levels of civic-mindedness, however, is very low. Nevertheless, there is certainly no direct evidence that, were families to choose a private school from the marketplace of providers, social cohesion would fall.[16] However, this analysis is based on existing samples of private schools, not the types that would arise under a voucher plan. Analysis of the expansion of the supply of private schools accepting vouchers in Milwaukee indicates 30 percent are secular, with the rest religiously affiliated: about half of the religious students are Catholic and half are from other faiths. But there was a reasonable expansion of new schools: Just under half of the participating schools were founded after the program was introduced, suggesting the need for caution in extrapolating from existing provisions (see Belfield et al., 2003).

Table 2.5 Summary of Correlations between School Type
and Civic Education

	Relative to Assigned Public School Results in 1996/1999			
Facet of civic education	Magnet Public	Catholic	Religious, non-Catholic	Private Secular
Community service	../..	+ve/+ve	+ve/..	+ve/..
Civic skills	../..	+ve/+ve	../..	../..
Civic confidence	../..	../+ve	../+ve	+ve/+ve
Political knowledge	../..	../+ve	../..	+ve/..
Political tolerance	+ve/..	../+ve	../-ve	../+ve

Notes: Results are from probit and ordered probit estimations (details available from author). +ve or –ve indicates that there was a statistically significant difference (p<0.10) from the assigned public school category; '..' indicates no statistically significant difference. Sources: Estimates for 1999 are taken from Belfield (2003). Estimates for 1996 are taken from Campbell (2001, table 12-7).

Future Developments

What are the prospects for market approaches to education, and where are the needs for research? The market approach to education is proceeding apace in elementary and secondary education. Much of the momentum is derived from the political tides that have swept in privatization more generally in recent decades. Other reasons are the quest for many different forms of school choice and the search for radical alternatives to counter the failure of inner-city schools. Federal legislation under No Child Left Behind (NCLB) is also an important force for privatization as an extension of school choice; three main provisions serve to increase choice. Under Unsafe Schools Choice Options, students can transfer from a school identified as "persistently dangerous" or one where they were victims of a crime. Under Public School Choice, a school that fails to meet academic Adequate Yearly Progress (AYP) targets must offer students transfer alternatives to other schools. Finally, under Supplemental Educational Services, schools failing to meet AYP targets for three years must offer low-income students additional tutoring or remediation outside the regular school day. Each of these provisions will open up the educational market, both from the parents' perspective—many students may be affected—and from the providers' perspective—where private companies may offer tutoring or remediation services or charter schools may grow. Such provisions may also be politically attractive, in that choice is triggered only when the current set of educational options is deemed inadequate. As states are responsible for identifying unsafe schools and setting AYP targets, there is latitude in how much market provision is encouraged. However, given the difficulty of meeting NCLB standards over time, especially for highly mobile students who do not attend a particular school long enough to benefit from enriched services, it is possible that more and more schools will be declared "failures." This will provide political ammunition to push for educational market approaches and further privatization as a promising alternative to that "failure."

The evidential base is far from complete. About the only conclusions that we can draw at this time are that (1) market approaches increase choice considerably; (2) competition and choice are associated with small improvements in academic achievement but nothing approximating the revolutionary changes argued by advocates; (3) some evidence indicates that universal market approaches will lead to greater inequalities, but restricted ones limited to the poor may have the opposite impacts; and (4) the effects of educational markets on social cohesion are unknown and depend heavily on how social cohesion is defined and measured and what types of schools will emerge in a market expansion.

Why Is So Little Known?

Although we have been able to set out a policy and evaluation framework for educational vouchers with some confidence, the evidence needed to fill in that framework is much less comprehensive. There are a number of reasons for this:

1. Lack of Market Experience—Educational vouchers and tuition tax credits as well as charter schools and for-profit educational management organizations are a relatively recent phenomenon. They embrace only a tiny fraction of schools and students in the United States. This has meant that the empirical universe from which one can derive evidence is extremely limited. Thus, much of the evidence is derived from other forms of educational competition, international settings such as Chile, and public/ private school comparisons rather than from extensive market competition. Even the applications of educational markets are relatively small in scale and are difficult to generalize to more extensive applications.
2. Chicken versus Egg Dilemma—In the absence of more solid and persuasive evidence of superiority and the complications of trade-offs among goals, it is difficult to initiate more extensive market demonstrations. That is, to encourage dramatic departures from the traditional organization of schools, it is necessary to show that the alternatives are demonstrably

superior. But in the absence of larger-scale applications of educational markets, it is not possible to derive that evidence.

3. Too Many Variants—Clearly, the outcomes of an educational marketplace depend crucially on the specifics. There are many different combinations of arrangements for finance, regulation, and support services, each with potentially different consequences for the four criteria that have been delineated. Therefore, generalization is limited from the few implementations that exist today in the United States or in other countries. In reality, evidence must be limited to a particular application of educational vouchers or other forms of the educational marketplace, and the existing variants are too limited from which to draw extensive generalizations.

4. Extensive and Expensive Evaluations—It is one thing to do research on modest interventions in education. It is quite another to evaluate a systemwide change. Holding other things constant statistically or experimentally becomes less feasible as the scope of the intervention expands, and market approaches to education represent extensive interventions. Thus, costly evaluations of educational vouchers that have adopted experimental designs have found that even after three years of assessment, a timeline that many think is too short, serious challenges to validity arise (e.g., see Peterson and Howell, 2004; Krueger and Zhu, 2004a, 2004b). Further, even these evaluations typically address only matters of student achievement and parental satisfaction, ignoring the other important dimensions. The significant advantages in using randomized field trials to produce very precise answers and accurately identify impacts may come at the cost of relevance to broader policy questions and issues of program implementation. Although much more can be done in ascertaining the probable impact of market reforms in education on different educational outcomes, the multiplicity of educational goals and the thinness of the evidence suggest that a priori views and ideological stances will probably dominate in terms of educational policy on this topic.

Power of Ideology

We have suggested that the evidence on the impacts of the various forms of educational privatization and competition are equivocal. No one can be sure what the educational consequences are of a major shift into the educational marketplace, although the outlines of some of the results are suggested by the features of the particular design that is proposed. While we might surmise the probable effects of particular plans, we cannot predict with great confidence what their effects will be. Designs for changing the framework in which social institutions operate only set new environments to influence behavior. That is, they create new options and incentives. It is the actual behavior of such microunits as schools, governments, and families in response to those changes that will determine the educational consequences. We might expect to find both anticipated and unanticipated results. For example, it is assumed by many that increased choice will produce greater achievement by matching students to schools that better meet their needs. But more choice means greater mobility and attrition of students among schools, a phenomenon that has been shown to have an overall negative influence on student learning, even for those students remaining in the school (Hanushek et al., 2004).

If the empirical research does not permit us to say with great confidence what the results of greater educational privatization will yield, how can the advocates and detractors be so passionate in their defense or attack of such policies? We believe that it is the ideological appeal of privatization that determines one's stance to a far greater extent than evidence about the consequences (Levin and Belfield, 2005). Those who adhere to a libertarian philosophy endorse educational markets because they believe that freedom of choice is the highest priority and should be the main criterion in designing a system of educational finance and school operations as Friedman (1962) has emphasized. They also argue that efficiency and equity will follow from choice and market competition where schools will have incentives to meet consumer needs at the lowest cost and attract sufficient clientele to meet goals of profit maximization.

In contrast, those who believe that education is part of the implicit social contract required for an effective democracy place emphasis on a school system that is free, publicly funded, and guided by democratic decisions rather than marketplace ones (Apple, 2001). They emphasize to a much greater extent the centrality of democratic decisions and government schools in addressing social cohesion and equity as opposed to the goals of efficiency and choice that they attribute to market advocates. Of course, these extremes do not characterize the views of all people. Most of the public represents some combination of the two ideologies with a tendency that may be more in one direction than the other. For this reason the advocates and opponents of market privatization typically use the "evidence" that supports their positions to persuade the larger audience of the validity of a polar position.

The advocacy is compounded further by the opposing interests of narrower constituencies. Teachers' unions oppose the marketplace because of their educational beliefs and their view that such a move threatens their power to achieve their goals through collective bargaining. That is, they believe that the marketplace would undermine the union's power and teachers' interests. In contrast, business constituencies are tantalized by the potential profits in gaining access to the $400 billion elementary and secondary education sector. Although these constituencies may believe in the power of capitalism and markets to transform education, they have not lost sight of the investment opportunities that a marketplace would open to them. Given the strength of these respective interests, we conclude that it is unlikely that the evidence will decide the issue.

Notes

1. As examples on both sides of the debate, compare Smith (2003), Viteritti (1999), Coulson (1999), Henig (1994), and Cookson (1992). For analysis that relates these positions to political constituencies, see Ryan and Heise (2001).

2. There is now a considerable amount of evidence on education markets, from researchers in political science, law, education, sociology, and economics (e.g., Godwin and Kemerer, 2002; Wolfe, 2003; Hoxby, 2003b). It is therefore possible to provide only an overview of the issues (for an earlier, book-length review, see Gill et al., 2001).

3. The brief exposition that follows is designed to provide the uninformed reader with only the most rudimentary picture of a market and price determination. It is not a substitute for a more thorough presentation. Detailed expositions at an introductory level can be found in Pindyck and Rubinfeld (2000).

4. It is important to note that a large number of households exercise choice among schools and school districts in their choice of neighborhood. For some detail on existing school choice, see Henig and Sugarman (1999). For the theory on why choice of community may lead to efficient production of schooling and other public goods in local communities, see the classic article by Tiebout (1956).

5. More detail is provided in the appendix to Levin (2002a, 170–171), which presents "Questions for Analyzing Design Dimensions of Vouchers."

6. The dearth of knowledge and understanding by parents is heavily underlined in Public Agenda (1999). Schneider, Teske, and Marschall (2000) also found class and racial differences in parents' knowledge about schools. For a detailed investigation of public attitudes, see Moe (2001).

7. See Levin (1999); for greater elaboration, see Levin (2002a). Also see Godwin and Kemerer (2002).

8. For example, E. G. West, an important supporter of private markets in education, has argued that public benefits or externalities of education are largely mythical or are not worth the burden of tax support because of the deadweight loss of public welfare created by that level of taxation. His views imply that the provision of payment for education should be privately arranged rather than being a matter for the government. See West (1967; 1991).

9. There have been a number of attempts to identify alternative outcomes for schooling besides test scores and to compare these outcomes across school types. Comparisons between private-religious and public schools show that the former reduce teen involvement in sexual activity, arrests, and the use of hard drugs, but there is no difference in alcohol, tobacco, or soft drug usage (Figlio and Ludwig, 2001).

10. Recent microlevel analysis from four states indicates that charter school students may perform better (WI), broadly equivalent (TX), or worse (CA, NC) than students in other school settings (Bifulco and Ladd, 2004; Witte, 2003; Hanushek et al., 2003; Buddin and Zimmer, 2003). These microlevel analyses also find considerable variation in academic achievement across types of charter schools.

11. These findings have been challenged by a reanalysis that concludes that these gains may not be robust to more consistent racial classification and alternative sampling schemes (see Krueger and Zhu, 2004a, 2004b; in rebuttal, see Peterson and Howell, 2004). Notwithstanding, on either set of assumptions, there is very little evidence that voucher programs make a large difference to educational outcomes for participating students.

12. Much of the present system of funding public education permits greater funding for schools in wealthier areas through the property tax. However, by basing this type of decision on individual families rather than communities, it can be shown that the inequalities are likely to increase.

13. There is more international evidence on sorting according to ability levels. In New Zealand, there is evidence of ethnic partitioning after decentralization: The proportion of minority students increased in lower-performing schools and fell in higher-performing schools (Fiske and Ladd, 2003). Similar evidence has been found in studies of schools in Scotland and the Netherlands (Williams, 1996; Karsten, 1994). In the United Kingdom, families—when given new school choice options—selected schools with students from a similar socioeconomic status as their own (Gorard and Fitz, 2000). However, the overall effect on socioeconomic partitioning was slight.

14. Often, the assumption that a government system does generate social cohesion is taken for granted. Given the substantial involvement of local, state, and federal governments in education over the past century, there has been little specific evidence adduced as to how social cohesion is being promoted and what indicators can be used to ensure that it continues.

15. A related approach is to compare the educational processes (e.g., pedagogies, cultures, classroom interactions, and textbooks) of private versus public schools (see Peshkin, 1986; Brint et al., 2001).

16. From data from the 1996 Youth Civic Involvement survey, Smith (2003: 114) reports higher levels of tolerance, civic capital efficacy, and participation in private schools, although when these correlations are adjusted for student and community characteristics only private-independent schools show an advantage. Further, this conclusion depends heavily on which schools might predominate in market expansion. Evangelical schools, which are the most rapidly growing segment at present, show less political tolerance among their students than Catholic or public schools (Godwin et al., 2001).

Part I

The Family

Chapter 3

Families as Contractual Partners in Education

Introduction

Conventionally, analysis of education privatization focuses either on enrollment in private schools or on mechanisms that would subsidize private education such as vouchers or tuition tax credits (Levin, 2001c). However, at its core, privatization in education begins with family effort, in essence the purest form of privatization. Consistently, studies of educational achievement or educational attainments find that it is differences in family circumstances that have the largest influence on educational outcomes, more so than the impacts of differences among schools. For this reason, education is already heavily "privatized."

More than 90 percent of the waking hours of a child from birth to the age of 18 is spent outside of school in an environment that is heavily conditioned, both directly and indirectly, by families (Sosniak, 2001). Yet, the thrust of formal educational policy is devoted overwhelmingly to school improvement, ostensibly to raise student achievement and improve educational equity. Of course, many schools also attempt to incorporate a variety of forms of parental involvement, but such involvement is limited largely to the margins of the educational process rather than being viewed as a dominant determinant of that process (for a comprehensive review, see Epstein, 2001; Jordan, et al., 2002). The most elemental form of educational privatization is found in the high level of control that families have over the activities that directly and indirectly determine educational outcomes. Although families may also expand their control over education through school choice mechanisms, there is little evidence at this time of a powerful effect on educational outcomes from such expansion (see Chapter 2).

This imbalance between the influence of the family and the influence of the school requires a fundamental reconsideration of how education systems should be oriented. The approach considered here is to view families as contractual partners in education, i.e., having contractual obligations in behalf of their children. To a large degree this notion of a "contract" is metaphorical since a democratic society permits families to rear their children in diverse ways with wide latitude among practices. But, one can still view the family as an educator and raise the question of what type of contractual obligations between the family and the school would maximize the child's educational success (for an earlier investigation, see Leichter, 1975). It is not assumed that all families will have the full capacity to satisfy the contract, so attention must be devoted to what types of institutions would be required to help families meet any contractual obligations. Of course, this is not the first attempt to focus on the family to improve educational achievement of their offspring. The attempt here is to do more than to propose specific programs. It is to identify in a comprehensive manner the knowledge base that links family behaviors to educational outcomes and to codify that into a metaphorical contract that might be implemented by families in conjunction with a variety of social institutions.

This chapter is divided into a number of sections. The next section documents the fact that the production of educated citizens is dependent upon both family and school influences. In spite of this knowledge, the public policy focus has been much heavier on making schools more effective than on making families more effective. The following section provides a brief review of "effective" family behaviors that contribute to educational attainment, suggesting that equal effort must be given to the latter as the former. Consequently, just as there are contractual obligations for schools, it is possible to establish a metaphorical contract of obligations for families, one that is based on evidence about effective educational practices of parenting. Finally, a conceptual framework is set out which considers how to provide families with the capacity to meet their (metaphorical) contractual obligations.

Families, Schools, and Educational Attainments

Prior to the 1960s, it was assumed that differences in school resources and other characteristics were the dominant causes of differences in such educational outcomes as achievement scores and years of schooling attained. It should be noted that in those years, fiscal support of schools was extraordinarily disparate among states, school districts, and schools (for the classic critique in educational finance, see Coons, et al., 1970). The Coleman Report, a study requested by Congress under the 1964 Civil Rights Act and published in 1966, represented a massive effort to determine the impacts of both families and schools on educational achievement (Coleman et al., 1966). It concluded that differences in family background characteristics were overwhelmingly more important than school characteristics in explaining differences in student achievement. Although the Coleman study was criticized, in part for using a statistical technique that overstated the impact of families on achievement (Bowles and Levin, 1968), its overall finding has been replicated in virtually all of the studies done over ensuing decades (for an excellent treatment which distinguishes between the absolute and relative impacts of schools, see Rothstein, 2004, pp.13–14).

If there is any controversy, it is only over the methods for measuring the relative home and school influences. For example, at one extreme Hoxby (2001) evaluated the statistical determinants of achievement among a sample of more than 16,000 students who were in twelfth grade in 1992. Hoxby found that family variables accounted for more than 93 percent of the variance in mathematics scores with less than 3 percent being explained by school input variables and the remaining 4 percent associated with neighborhood variables. Depending upon which subject is tested, family variables account for 34 to 105 times as much variation as the school input variables. In a parallel analysis for 33-year-olds in attempting to explain their educational attainments in terms of years of schooling, Hoxby (2001, pp. 98–99) finds similar results, an overwhelming influence of family background. (One criticism of this method is it uses measures of family characteristics for each individual student, but only cruder school averages for the school inputs. Therefore, the measures of school inputs are insensitive to the variance in student experiences reflected by differences among specific teachers and among classroom groups to which individual students were exposed. Using a method that accounts for some of these within-school differences, Wenglinsky (2002) finds that teaching variables might have a weight equivalent to socioeconomic (SES) variables.)

Although some argue that the family is the key to educational improvement (Steinberg, 1996) and others argue that it is the school (Edmonds, 2002; Mortimore, 1998), the conflict between the two positions lacks merit. Both families and schools are important in educational development (see Grissmer et al., 1994). From an economist's perspective, they are joint inputs into the production function for education, and they are partially interdependent rather than separable in effects. That is, school inputs and family inputs may interact in such ways that students from some backgrounds may benefit more from specific resources and school policies than do other students. For example, reductions in class size seem to have a larger impact on minority students and those from lower socioeconomic status (SES) backgrounds than Anglo students or those from middle class backgrounds (Krueger, 1999; Molnar et al., 1999). This pattern of differential effects by race and social class has also been found in other studies (Grissmer et al., 2000). Or consider that when students enter schools with stronger preparation and higher expectations, teachers are able to provide more demanding challenges than when students are less prepared.

Preoccupation with Schools

While the importance of families in determining educational outcomes is highly recognized in the literature, it is less emphasized in educational policy. The main focus of educational policy has been on institutional reforms within schools in teaching practices and curriculum or changes in the organization of the educational system (for itemized school reforms, see Block et al., 1995; Schauble and Glaser, 1996). As noted above, much of recent reform has been toward privatization and more choice, including magnet schools, open enrollment among schools within districts and states, and charter schools, as well as the provision of publicly funded, educational vouchers.

Almost all of these efforts at policy reform recognize that families are important in determining educational results of offspring. Indeed, advocates argue that school choice will energize parents to improve family practices in the education of their students, while also creating incentives for schools to improve their performance in order to maintain and attract clientele (Hoxby, 2001). School reform projects also make at least some attempt to expand parental involvement in the education of students, particularly in the school but also at home. However, most of the focus of in-school reforms is on changes in pedagogy, curriculum, and governance; much of the pressure has been from families applied to schools. More convincingly, the foremost expert on the educational role of families has concluded: "No topic about school improvement has created more rhetoric than 'parent involvement,'" rhetoric that exceeds substantially the magnitude of effective interventions (Epstein, 2001, p. 3). The substance of parental involvement has been marginal relative to the possibilities represented by families for improving the education of their children directly. School policy for improving educational outcomes has been far more obsessed with pressuring schools to change than inducing change in families.

A recent strand of school policy reform is the preoccupation with raising standards and closing the gaps among social groups (motivated by the concern about mediocre performance on achievement tests and unequal outcomes by race and socioeconomic status). The "standards movement," which is found in almost all of the states, emphasizes improving achievement test results as a condition of graduation and promotion as well as reducing test score inequalities between minority and Anglo students (Heubert and Hauser, 1998). The "standards movement" that is prevalent in the U.S. is obsessed with the school as the instrument of change by setting curriculum content standards and tests that measure progress on those standards. Often the rationale given is that of raising economic productivity and reducing economic inequality in an internationally competitive economy. But, a school-based approach without more focus on families may have disappointing results for the reason that test score gains from educational reforms that are limited to schools have been modest and such gains show only a limited relation to productivity or earnings (Levin, 2001b). For example, dramatic reductions in class size from about 25 to 15 students per class in the famous Tennessee Class Size experiment resulted in an increase in student achievement of about 0.25 standard deviations (Finn and Achilles, 1999). Minority students improved by about 0.30 standard deviations and white students by about .20 standard deviations (Krueger, 1999, n10). Only about one-tenth of the black-white achievement gap was reduced by this very costly reform (see Hedges and Nowell, 1998; Rothstein, 2004). Among reforms that have been shown to succeed in improving educational achievement, the impacts are relatively small, and little of the achievement gap has been closed. (Even these "successful results" overstate the case because they do not account for highly mobile students: they evaluate achievement gains for students who have been in the school reform continuously over one year or more yet the most disadvantaged students are highly mobile, moving frequently among schools, see Levin, 2002.)

Beyond an emphasis on standards, market advocates have pushed for greater competition among schools for students in order to provide an incentive to raise school effectiveness. But, as outlined in detail in Chapter 6 below, this reform is highly unlikely to generate impacts remotely close to the impacts that family behaviors would produce.

In summary, strategies to improve education rely primarily on schools, with some involvement from families. However, such limited tendrils reaching to families are likely to have only marginal effects on educational outcomes because so much educational success is based upon family actions, circumstances and behaviors that are not extensions of schooling or that even take place in the preschool period. Both families and schools are central to obtaining strong educational results, and the imbalance of educational policy in the direction of schools is detrimental to improving the quality and distribution of educational outcomes.

Seeking a Balance between Families and Schools

One measure of the present imbalance created by policy emphasis on schools rather than families is to compare the formal strictures placed on schools with those placed on families in behalf of producing educational results. The schools that our children attend are subject to a sheaf of laws, rules, regulations, directives, guidelines, and policies that are far too extensive for enumeration. Although providing less than 10 percent of the funding for elementary and secondary schools, the federal government sets numerous and complicated rules and procedures that affect the operations of all schools. Federal laws and regulatory provisions have especially proliferated for such functions as education for handicapped students, gender equity, economically disadvantaged students, bilingual students, racial stratification, and vocational education. The "No Child Left Behind Act" which became law in January 2002 constitutes over 1,000 pages in itself, just a single law. Implementing the law requires additional regulations.

Federal courts have also been active in setting standards for the operation of schools under the federal constitution. State laws are even more multitudinous than the federal ones and administered by activist state departments of education setting their own regulations and policies and monitoring school districts. Federal and state laws are further augmented by the actions of local school boards. And, state courts have become deeply involved in interpreting state laws and constitutions.

It is probably not even possible to fully document all of the laws, regulations, and policies that frame the operations of schools. One can view these as representing an overlapping set of contracts which might be viewed as "binding agreements among the parties." Of course, these contracts are so complex that only a small portion of them are effectively operable at any one time since the overwhelming numbers and complexities of the provisions make them impossible to fully monitor. School personnel are familiar with those provisions that are presently salient or that are monitored, but others are ignored or are found to cover such limited circumstances that they are only identified rarely and when specific circumstances arise. Monitoring of contracts is costly, so it is not surprising that only a small portion of the provisions are monitored. But, part of this leviathan of requirements can be thought of as a set of formal contracts that are enforceable by governments that have sanctions. Government agencies can withhold funds and official recognition of schools, can close and reshape institutions, or can change personnel. In addition, there are less formal agreements that might be more temporal in nature, agreements with students and their families that constitute an informal contract on school activities or expectations (Bishop, 1996). Such informal contracts are subject to change with changes in clientele and can be enforced by sanctions available to families through political channels or through the choice to leave (Hirschman, 1970).

The enforceable contracts which schools are party to have two features. First, public schools, other than those embedded in educational voucher arrangements or public choice, are largely answerable to federal, state, and local authorities rather than to parents or students. Moreover, there is little or no bargaining over contractual provisions because the schools are agencies of state government and are expected to fulfill those responsibilities mandated by federal and state authorities. The contracts are imposed, not negotiated. Second, the contracts are procedural rather than outcome-based. That is, the schools are required to follow procedures set out by Congress, courts, legislatures, and administrative branches rather than to produce specific educational outcomes. Only recently have there been sanctions for schools that are "failing" to produce specific educational results, sanctions either in terms of reconstitution of schools by external authorities or by allowing students in failing schools to seek other alternatives such as under the Florida Opportunity Scholarship Program.

But, if families have a powerful influence on the educational results for their children both separately and in concert with schools, one might expect to find formal obligations set out for them as well. In fact, the formal requirement for family participation in education as embodied in law is so trivial that it is in stark contrast to the overwhelming accretion of formal demands and procedures set on schools. Basically, there is a single requirement: a child must meet compulsory attendance requirements, that is he or she must be in attendance at a recognized school during regular school hours or must meet other participation requirements as set out for home schooling. Of course, families are not the property of the state, whereas schools are agencies of the state. But, if better educational results, and particularly, more nearly equal outcomes in education are to be achieved, it is obvious that schools cannot do it alone. (In reassessing the balance between schools and families, other writers see the school as inappropriately displacing the family rather than supplementing it, e.g., Universal Pre-School Programs or Breakfast Programs are held to weaken or undermine relationships within the family, see Roback Morse, 2002.) Rather, changes in family behavior will be necessary as well, particularly among those families in the lowest deciles of socioeconomic status whose children are most challenged in terms of educational outcomes.

Developing a Metaphorical Family Contract

Given the interdependence between the family and the school, the key issue is how to exploit this interdependence, i.e., in the terms used here, how to develop the metaphorical family contract. Presumably there is a knowledge base on what schools need to do to educate children effectively, and this is translated into financial support, resources, and procedures, much of it embodied in laws, rules, and regulations. This knowledge base is always expanding on the basis of experience and research, although it is hardly unequivocal. Debates over the choice of practices and over how they should be implemented are common in education, in part because of differences in values on what is good educational policy and practice. Chubb and Moe (1990) suggest that schools based upon democratic decisions must necessarily adopt a hodge-podge of goals and practices that are largely unworkable because they must necessarily be a compromise among many different and conflicting views. But, in fact, decisions are made and practices are adopted that are viewed as effective strategies for achieving given goals.

Paradoxically, the knowledge base on what family practices have educational consequences is less equivocal than the knowledge base for schools, but it has been less employed to impact on educational policy. (On the failure to find definitive evidence on school reform, see Hanushek, 2004.) It is therefore possible to provide an overview of what makes families effective in terms of the education of their students. Although such indicators of socioeconomic status as parental education, income, occupation, race, language, and family structure (number of parents and siblings) have been used to explain achievement, these are only markers or indicators of social class, not the family practices that account for such differences. In this case the question is: if a family contract was developed that set out the responsibilities of families to maximize their contribution to the education of their students, what would such a contract contain?

This is called a metaphorical contract because there are not ready mechanisms to enforce such a contract, and much of the contract may require resources that go beyond the capacity of some families, particularly those with low socioeconomic status (SES), to fulfill such responsibilities. However, it is useful to translate the indicators of family SES which account for such substantial portions statistically of educational success into actual behaviors which are affected by family SES. If high-SES families are following successful educational practices in the home and in relation to the school, it is important to know what those practices are. Conceptually, these activities can be placed into a metaphorical contract of good practices for all families, and then it is possible to seek ways of helping families meet the conditions of the contract. Enforcement and monitoring are problematic, but the likelihood of success for their children might be an important motivation for families.

It should be noted that this is a distinctively different approach than one finds in the literature on school-induced, parent participation or more out-of-school experiences. This school-based literature is important in improving the educational success of children at the margin by trying to get low-SES families more involved in the schooling of their students and providing additional opportunities with school-based special programs (Rothstein, 1996). These programs are useful, and reflect a genuine effort to improve educational outcomes. But, such approaches tend to be scatter-shot rather than systematic. They are not embedded in a more comprehensive picture of what is needed. Moreover, such approaches often require additional funding, rather than emphasizing the reallocation of activities toward a specific goal. In contrast, a metaphorical contract would attempt to encapsulate comprehensively the various practices that parents would need to pursue to assure a high chance of educational success for their students. As we will suggest in the final section, an overall solution to incorporating families more fully into the education of their children will require some social investments, but that is not necessarily the case for executing every aspect of the contract.

What follows is not an exhaustive catalog of parental behaviors that are linked to educational success, but a representative set that might be used to construct an initial metaphorical contract. Normally, any attempt to review the impacts of families on the educational achievement of their children is limited to measures of SES. Therefore the question is refined to: what do SES measures represent in terms of actual family practices that positively affect student achievement?

High SES Families and the Education of Children

Strong ties between SES and student educational outcomes have been affirmed in numerous studies: SES appears as an important predictor of children's cognitive development, school readiness, school achievement and school completion, as well as other measures of child and adolescent well-being (Duncan and Brooks-Gunn, 1997; Stipek and Ryan, 1997). Three specific pathways have been identified, through which the influence of SES is clearest. These pathways are summarized in tables 3.1–3.3, where the impact of being in a low SES family is described.

First, the home environment of higher SES families is more conducive to educational advancement (table 3.1). The strongest effects are through the parent-child interactions, such as the creation of "school-like" homes, stronger language and literacy relations, and less conflict within the home. In addition, higher SES families have better health and nutrition and follow a more structured daily routine at home. In terms of the local environment, higher SES families reside in more socially organized neighborhoods, and they are less likely to move residence such that their children must change school. This pathway is the most important, and yet the one most neglected in current policies and school practices.

Second, higher SES families use out-of-school time (including summertime) in a more educative way: they are more likely to use preschooling and daycare centers for their children, and they spend more time on reading (table 3.2). These differences are evident in the widening of educational performance over

Table 3.1 Home Environment Pathways between Socioeconomic Status and Student Achievement

Home Environment Variables	Impact on Children of Being in a Low-SES Family
Learning environment	Lower likelihood of a "school-like" home[1]
Language and literacy	Weaker language interaction with parents (less talking; fewer object labels; shorter, noncontingent conservations; more controlling speech)[2] Weaker literacy engagement (value placed on literacy; press for achievement; availability and instrumental use of reading materials; reading with children; and opportunities for verbal interaction)[3]
Parent-child interactions	Conflicting interactions with parents; more controlling, restrictive and disapproving parents[4]
Daily routine	Less likely to follow a daily routine[5]
Health and nutrition	Lower health; less health care (e.g., immunization delay; more conditions limiting school activity)[6]
Parents' mental health	Have parents with greater risk of depression[7]
Choice of neighborhood	Residence in more socially disorganized neighborhoods, with fewer child development resources and greater exposure to violence[8] Higher school mobility from residence mobility[9]

Sources:
[1]Epstein (2001); Bradley (1995); [2]Lareau (2000); [3]Hess and Holloway (1984); [4]Liaw and Brooks-Gunn (1995); [5]Rebello Britto, Fuligni, and Brooks-Gunn (2002); Newacheck, Stoddard, and McManus (1993); [6]Brooks-Gunn and Duncan (1997); [7]Adler et al. (1993); [8]Leventhal and Brooks-Gunn (2000); Sampson et al. (1997); [9]General Accounting Office (1994)

Table 3.2 Out-of-School Pathways between SES and Student Achievement

Out-of-School Time Variables	Impact on Children of Being in a Low-SES Family
Child care	Lower quality child care[1] Choice of child care based on cost, location rather than quality[2] Care by relatives rather than center care or nannies[3]
Pre-school	Less likely to attend pre-school[4]
After-school and summer time	Spend more time in informal play, outside play, or television watching[5] Spend less time on sports and reading[6]

Sources:
[1]Gallinsky et al. (1994); [2]Peyton et al. (2001); [3]Ehrle et al. (2001); [4] General Accounting Office (1994); [5]Lareau (2000); Posner and Vandell (1999); [6]McHale et al. (2001)

Table 3.3 Parental Involvement with Schooling Pathways between SES and Student Achievement

Parental Involvement with Schooling	Impact on Children of Being in a Low-SES Family
Choice of school	Less likely to have chosen a private school[1] Less likely to have had home location chosen in conjunction with schooling decision[1] Less likely to have taken advantage of public choice programs[2]
Communication with school and requests made	Less involved in school-based practices[3]
School involvement	Less involved in evaluation of school provision (less monitoring of child's schooling; intervention in children's program; less critical of teachers; less supplementary materials to reinforce classroom experience)[4]
Homework help	Less homework help in terms of valuing, monitoring, assisting, not interfering and doing[5]

Sources:
[1]Woodhouse (1999); Hoxby (2001); [2]Witte (2000); [3]Epstein (1996); [4]Lareau (1989); [5]Scott-Jones (2002)

the summer period: lower SES students have been found to fall further behind during the summer months (Alexander et al., 2001).

Third, high SES parents are more involved in their children's schooling (table 3.3). They are more likely to have exercised a direct preference for a particular type of school, and more likely to be involved in school-based activities. As well, higher SES parents are more likely to monitor the performance of their children's schooling more intensively and more effectively. Finally, higher SES parents are more likely to assist their children in their homework. It is this pathway that has received the most attention in terms of policy reform (and has been promoted by school choice advocates); and yet it is a relatively weak pathway to educational advancement.

Collectively, these three pathways suggest a substantial educational advantage for children of higher SES parents. We also note that these pathways refer to specific *educational* advantages that parents pass to their children, and we have not addressed more general economic, social, and behavioral advantages that may accrue. Therefore, these pathways allow us to identify specific practices and behaviors that parents can employ to improve educational outcomes that can then be introduced into the metaphorical contract. In fact, it is possible to be more precise, identifying actual tasks that parents may engage in. For example, in relation to effective parental involvement with homework, Hoover-Dempsey et al. (2001) identify how high SES parents: interact with the student's school or teacher about homework; provide general oversight of the homework process; respond to the student's homework performance; engage in homework processes and tasks with the student; and engage in metastrategies to create a fit between the task and student skill levels. Each of these tasks may enhance educational performance. Nonetheless, the information in tables 3.1–3.3 is intended to be illustrative of what might be included in a parent-school contract. Of course, some of these behaviors are only possible with higher family income. However, others require a substitution of a more effective set of behaviors for ones that are less effective.

Some schools have established contracts with parents. But, these are very brief and tend to focus on highly specific and functional contractual terms (e.g., the time the student should arrive at school, the number of hours the student should spend in school, student comportment, and parent volunteer requirements).[1] They are certainly highly incomplete specifications of behaviors that parents might exhibit to maximize the educational performance of their children. Parental contracts can be enforced if the school has the power to select its students as in many public schools of choice, charter schools, and independent schools. However, we are unaware of any enforceable contracts that reflect the activities listed in tables 3.1–3.3.

Implementing the Contract

Of course just to take what is known about the potential of the family for contributing to educational success and encapsulating that into a contract does not change very much. The real challenge is to alter family and school practices by implementing the provisions of the contract. This seems daunting because of the inability of the state to monitor and enforce family behavior, particularly given the subtleties of behavior on child development. Yet, the license provided by a metaphorical contract permits us to conceptualize the purposes that such a contract might serve, even in the absence of strict enforcement.

Incentives

Potential motivation for attempting to comport with the terms of the contract is certainly in the domain of self-interest for families. That is, families have a deep interest in the success of their children in both school and in life and so if they can be convinced that feasible actions that they might take will improve their children's chances, they will be motivated to undertake them within the their abilities and resources. This incentive is clearly a very powerful one. But, there are constraints upon families in fulfilling such contracts, a matter that is addressed below. At the same time, schools with pressures to improve student achievement—particularly among minorities and low-income students—also have incentives to mobilize family resources in behalf of better school performance. So does the larger society that will benefit from better civic behavior, economic performance, and political decisions of those whose education has improved (Haveman and Wolfe, 1984).

The information on good practices to improve the educational prospects of children is not common or widespread in a form that spells out specific actions that families can take. It is costly to obtain such information. Moreover, families are "socialized" by their experiences and circumstances to behave in certain ways and not in others. These differences are particularly poignant in Shirley Brice Heath's (1983) work on *Ways With Words* in which she compares parental language interactions with children among families of different SES and racial backgrounds (see also Taylor, 1999). They are also found in the important work of Melvyn Kohn (1969), where families are shown to prepare their children for occupational success by transmitting the values and behaviors of their own occupations. Thus, a working class adult will often emphasize conformity, obedience, following rules, and reluctance to challenge authority or seek alternatives. Children of professional parents are taught to challenge authority, negotiate, and consider options. Each is preparing offspring for success as the parent understands its requirements from their own occupational experiences, but the consequence is transmission of class status from generation-to-generation. This might be termed a "knowledge constraint," but it may also entail a "capacity constraint." These differences in child language and orientation also result in different expectations and treatments of children in school, an example of the interaction between parental and school effects (Carnoy and Levin, 1985).

By "capacity constraint" we mean that some families, even if informed of practices that will improve educational outcomes for their children, may not have the capacity to act on that knowledge. Clearly, transmitted language styles are not just determined by knowledge acquisition by parents about which approaches are more effective at socializing children for school experiences. Language is deeply embedded in culture and personality and does not simply shift through parents being informed that another style will be more advantageous for children's success (Bourdieu and Passeron, 1977; Bernstein, 1971). In other cases families do not have the income to provide expanded opportunities for their children such as enriched childcare, effective preschools, health care, nutrition, and housing. Nevertheless, there is scope for parents to be made more aware of effective practices in these domains, for such knowledge is a necessary condition for change.

Implementation Strategies

A metaphorical contract for parents could be divided into three parts, each dedicated to a different type of strategy (Kagan and Weissbourd, 1994): (1) information; (2) assistance; and (3) externally provided activities.

1. Information—A metaphorical contract for parents to enhance the education of their children would be a repository of information, much of it presently unfamiliar to families on what types of activities are effective. Simply knowing what is exemplary serves an important function as parents make decisions about their offspring. Many of the activities are feasible for almost any family such as setting aside reading time for children, rewarding good school performance, discussing school experiences, reviewing a child's schoolwork, meeting with teachers for progress reports, taking children to the library on a regular basis, guiding television viewing, and so on. We believe that there are many activities that parents would be willing to undertake both at home and in conjunction with schools if

they knew that these were activities that would have a positive effect on their child's education.

2. Assisted Activities—The metaphorical contract would contain other responsibilities that parents cannot do alone because of a lack of resources or other capacity constraints. For example, students may need help on homework that parents are unable to provide. In this case, school or community-provided homework assistance or tutoring will be necessary, even though it will be up to parents to monitor their children's needs and to make appropriate arrangements. Other areas that may require assistance are training in parenting skills; orienting children towards college and learning the academic requirements; visiting colleges; and using community services such as those provided by public agencies and nonprofit providers as well as religious organizations. All of these represent an intermediate range of activities where parents can take responsibility if they have assistance.

3. External Support—These are activities in which parents may require substantial assistance to be able to fulfill the contract. At one extreme are such basic necessities for human and educational development as decent housing in safe neighborhoods, health care, employment opportunities, and adequate income to provide amenities (for concrete evidence on the effects of housing on student achievement, see Ludwig et al., 2001; for the impact of increased family income for low-income families on achievement, see Dearing et al., 2001). In addition, they may include quality preschooling, summer schools, tutoring centers, and after-school programs and the provision of summer jobs for students and test preparation courses including those for college entrance examinations. External support may entail longer school years and school days for children to accommodate educational enrichment. Both assisted and externally supported activities will likely entail a variety of providers including schools, other governmental organizations, philanthropic groups, community organizations, and faith-based organizations.

Next Steps

The next steps in moving in these directions would be to do a fully comprehensive survey of the knowledge base that relates family activities to educational success of offspring. The approach here has been to provide a (large) sampling of that knowledge base, but clearly effective behaviors will evolve and develop as social and economic forces impinge. Then, this comprehensive and contemporary knowledge base would need to be transformed into a metaphorical contract that would set out categories and specific types of activities that families would commit themselves to on behalf of their children. The contract would also be accompanied by the "rewards" in terms of predicted educational progress associated with these types of activities.

Activities would need to be divided according to those whose performance would require one of the three intervention strategies: information, assistance, and external provision. Each of the three strategic areas would require design and implementation of programs that would be effective in assisting parents to honor substantial parts of the contract. Social policy would weigh efforts to provide support for families to fulfill their obligations relative to similar support for schools to fulfill theirs. School activities and parent involvement programs could also be refined to support parent partnership contracts. Increasingly, economists are suggesting that reforms to support family's educational activities will provide a considerably larger improvement in the education of at-risk populations than direct investments in schools.

Clearly, this exploration of metaphorical contracts for families has raised as many questions as suggestive directions to pursue. In addition to further details on the knowledge base and how it might suggest different implementation strategies, there are at least two larger issues for using the contract. As the metaphorical contract and its different parts are constructed, it is not clear who are the potential parties to the agreement beyond families. Obviously, schools become a potential partner when the child reaches school age, but probably not during the preschool years. Schools have incentives to provide assistance to families in exchange for better student performance on which schools are judged. The larger impact of educational attainments on labor force productivity, citizenship, and social participation means that society and its governmental and nongovernmental organizations also have a stake in the contract (the citizenship and social participation rationales are found in Gutmann, 1987). But, how these particular groups will participate in the contract and how this will be coordinated remains to be developed.

Second, there is the question of whether there are any grounds for enforcement of any part of the contract. Enforcement requires both monitoring and sanctions. Monitoring of family behavior—particularly the more subtle components—is not likely to be appropriate or feasible; and sanctions for most family behaviors are unlikely to be available. Thus, inevitably there must be greater reliance upon incentives, not only the rewards of better child performance, but incentives for such results as good grades, student achievement, attendance, and school completion. It is these types of questions that need to be more fully addressed in order to make significant progress on metaphorical contracts for family education partnerships.

Note

1. The parent/guardian "Achievement Agreement" at Bronx Preparatory Charter School lists eight commitments, of which only one refers to a parental role outside the school. This commitment expects the parents to: allow the child to contact the teachers about attendance and homework; read at night; attend parent/teacher conferences; make themselves available to staff; read all papers sent home; schedule student absence during the afternoons; and purchasing necessary materials. Similarly, the pledge by parents at North Star Academy Charter School of Newark has ten items, of which only one refers to the type of activities identified in tables 3.1–3.3: "we will check our child's homework each night and provide quiet time and space for the work to be completed." A third example, Hyde School, makes no reference to family behaviors beyond attendance at a school retreat. At the Accelerated School, Los Angeles, the agreement expects the parent to provide home-academic support (e.g., ensuring the child is ready to learn), provide school support, and participate in at least 3 hours of school-based activity. Other countries have developed policies on home-school agreements. In England, the School Standards and Framework Act of 1998 expects each school to adopt an agreement relating to: the standard of education; the ethos of the school; regular and punctual attendance; discipline and behavior; homework; and the information schools and parents should give to each other. Again, the actual content of the agreement is loosely specified. Similarly, school handbooks specify rules that apply within the school.

Chapter 4

Modeling School Choice

A Comparison of Public, Private–Independent, Private–Religious, and Home-Schooled Students

Introduction

Part of the agenda for privatization is that families should have a greater choice of schooling options. In particular, families are encouraged to view school choice as "active," rather than passive in the sense of accepting the provision being offered in the neighborhood public school. In part, this active role for parents in making school choices is empowering (as set out in Chapter 3 as the third pathway by which parents influence education). But it has also been fostered by a sense of disaffection with public schooling—both its effectiveness and efficiency—that has been emphatically catalogued by academic economists (e.g., Hanushek, 1998; Hoxby, 2003b; Friedman, 1993). The general population is somewhat more ambivalent (Moe, 2001), and indeed the proportions of students in private schools have remained stable over recent decades (Kenny and Schmidt, 1994). But, private schooling—either religious or sectarian—is not the only outlet for those dissatisfied with public schooling: home-schooling is now a viable option. This option adds further to the sense that parents must make an active decision about the appropriate school for their children.

The recent growth and development of home-schooling has been described in detail by numerous authors (Lines, 2000; Welner and Welner, 1999; Hammons, 2001a; Somerville, 2001; Stevens, 2001; Bauman, 2002); our investigation is in Chapter 5. The preceding literature emphasizes the legal and civic aspects of home-schooling, but there has been little quantitative assessment or economic treatment. This is surprising: home-schooling represents an extreme form of education privatization, affecting the expenditure patterns, time allocation, and labor force participation of the families involved. Furthermore, home-schooling extends school choice to four alternatives.

This chapter reports on the determinants of school choice by U.S. families, contrasting each schooling option across family characteristics. Such school choices are easily expressed using economic calculus. For example, home-schooling may be more effective than public schools for some children, and possibly less costly (if there are either high transport costs or additional expenditures mandated by schools, e.g., uniforms, learning materials). Similarly, private schools may be less effective for some children than home-schooling schools (if the former are "elitist," and appear hostile to outsiders), and possibly more costly (with high direct tuition fees). More generally, home-schooling may meet the needs of families with particular educational preferences that are not catered to by available institutions (typically for morality-based schooling, James, 1987). In this case the appropriate comparison is between home-schooling and religious schools. Thus, the question to be answered is: what are the family characteristics which motivate families to choose between the four types of schooling?

This chapter is structured as follows. The first section sets out the economic model for deciding which school type to choose. The second section describes the datasets available to test for family characteristics that might influence the school choice decision. The third section reports the findings on the determinants of the school choice decision. The last section refers back to the relevance of school choice within the current system of U.S. schooling and the growing policy reforms which seek to expand choice.

The Economics of School Choice

Prior research on school choice in the United States has mainly focused on binary options: students decide to exit public schools for the single alternative, typically held to be Catholic schooling (but see Figlio and Stone, 1999). However, this stylization elides religious and nonreligious schooling, even though these are unlikely to be close substitutes. It is also out-of-date, given: changes in the teaching staff and student composition in religious schools (on the evolution of Catholic schooling, see Sander, 2001; Grogger and Neal, 2000); the growth of other types of private school; and greater choice in the public sector (e.g., charter schooling). Instead, school enrollment is best articulated as a four-way choice: public schooling, private–religious schooling, private–independent schooling, and home-schooling.

A straightforward way to infer school choice motivation is to compare tabulations of characteristics by school type. (Another method for inference is to look at what schools are chosen by families whose choice set is expanded, e.g. through voucher programs; this literature has been summarized by Teske and Schneider, 2001.) For home-schooling, aggregate comparisons show families that are: more likely to be white and non-Hispanic; have income levels comparable to the national average (but with a more leptokurtic distribution); and have parents who were more highly educated than the average for the United States. It is not necessarily the case that families who decide to home-school possess highly idiosyncratic attributes (see Bauman, 2002). However, a full approach requires investigation of what motivates the choice of a particular school type, testing these factors statistically, and controlling for other family characteristics.

In deciding between the schooling options, households can be assumed to maximize utility, as set out by Neal (1997). As well as other commodities, household utility depends on the educational outcomes from schooling and unobserved consumption goods from schooling (e.g., religiosity, dutifulness to parents). Neal's (1997) choice model may be generalized to include the $j=4$ different types of schooling where p is public schooling, d is private–independent schooling, r is private–religious schooling, and h is home-schooling. Educational outcomes Y are therefore determined across each of the choices as:

$$(1) \quad Y_{ip} = X_i\beta_p + v_i$$
$$(2) \quad Y_{id} = X_i\beta_d + \varepsilon_{id} + \gamma_d + v_i$$
$$(3) \quad Y_{ir} = X_i\beta_r + \varepsilon_{ir} + \gamma_r + v_i$$
$$(4) \quad Y_{ih} = X_i\beta_h + \varepsilon_{ih} + \gamma_h + v_i$$

In (1)–(4), X denotes a vector of input and control variables. The ε_{ij} parameters identify the match between household i and the selected school type; it is assumed that $E(\varepsilon_{ij}|X_i)=0$. The γ_j parameters represent the mean outcome effect for school type j relative to public schooling. The v_i term is a household effect (error term) and again by assumption $E(v_i|X_i)=0$. Such modeling is necessary to estimate the treatment effects across school types, as well as exogenous instruments that may serve to identify the school choice match (see Evans and Schwab, 1995). However, this inquiry is restricted, first, to specifying the variables to be included in X, and then, second, to giving some indication of the match between household types and school types (ε_{ij}).

The estimation procedure therefore follows a multinomial logit model, where school choice is a function of the characteristics of the household, the child, the mother/father, and the local community:

(5) Pr(Choice j=1...4) = f(Household, child, mother/father, community)

The aim is to identify the statistical and substantive characteristics that motivate the choice of one school type over another. Variables capturing the child's characteristics may indicate which children (in terms of ability, gender, and maturity) favor particular school types. Parental variables may capture not only intergenerational transfers of educational attributes, but also parental capacity for home-schooling. Also of interest are the household and community characteristics that influence the school choice decision, as well as their relative importance across each school type. The household variables capture the resources available within the home for educational purposes, as well as social differences across students (see Lareau, 2000). The community variables are likely to capture the local public resources available for schooling, and the importance of neighborhood in schooling decisions (these are useful for general equilibrium modeling). Unfortunately, no school quality variables are available for analysis.

Using cross-sectional district-level data across ten states (and panel data for one state, Kentucky), Houston and Toma (2003) model the choice to home-school relative to public school. They find evidence that home-schooling proportions are greater where the public school drop-out rate is higher and where public school expenditures are lower. The strongest impact was found for the standard deviation of incomes: greater heterogeneity in incomes (and presumably preferences for education) is associated with higher proportions of home-schooling. Public schooling was also more likely in more densely populated areas. (However, Houston and Toma [2003] report a number of contrary results: district-level average male income and female education levels were positively related to public schooling enrollment; no measure of religious preferences is found to be significant.) In an extension, Houston and Toma (2003) model private school choice to home-school choice for the same datasets: home schooling is preferred where more families are married and where male income levels are lower (whereas private schooling preferences are strongly correlated with the proportions of Catholics in the district).

The approach here is to use micro-data, because many of the school choice determinants will be idiosyncratic to families within areas, rather than between areas. School choice advocates maintain that families need to be given more options so that they can exit unsatisfactory schools. However, this argument depends on what factors influence exit propensities: if such propensities are a function of fixed attributes such as gender or family background, then the effects of school choice expansion may be muted. (For an argument that parents rate schools in the same way as experts and that parents choose schools mainly based on academic quality, see Bast and Walberg [2004]; for empirical analysis that suggests a less rational and more personal approach to school choices by families, see Buckley and Schneider [2003].) Also, if the four school types serve very different families, then families may not regard them as substitutes for each other. This estimation therefore yields information on several policy-useful questions. For example, how important are household compositions (such as two-parent families) compared to the education level of the parents? Also, do families with special learning needs seek home-schooling as an alternative to public schools, rather than private schools? What school types do students of religions other than Catholicism choose? Using two similar datasets, it is possible to estimate equation (5) to answer such questions, as well as triangulate the results.

Data

Two recent datasets are available to estimate equation (5). These are the National Household Expenditure Survey (NHES99) and micro-data from SAT test-participants in 2001 (ETS01).

NHES99 is a random-digit dialing telephone survey, with a nationally representative sample of all civilian, noninstitutionalized U.S. persons. Screening interviews were administered to 57,278 households (74 percent response rate), and then parental interviews were conducted, where children were found to be in the household (88 percent response rate postscreening). The relevant sample of parent respondents is 17,640. To compensate for bias (arising from lack of telephone, nonresponse, or ethnicity), weights are applied to the data. Whereas public and private school distinctions are relatively straightforward, the identification of home-schooling is less clear. Here, home-schooling is identified using the NCES (2001) definition, which is derived from questions: "Is child being schooled at home?"; "Is child getting all of his/her instruction at home?" and "How many hours each week does child usually go to school for instruction?"; and "What are the main reasons you decided to school child at home?" So, home-schooling is identified where the child is being schooled at home; where any public schooling did not exceed 25 hours per week; and where the child is not being schooled at home for temporary reasons of health. This definition yields 270 (1.5 percent) students who are home-schooled (unweighted number). The rest of the sample is: 1,530 (8.7 percent) students who attend religious school; 560 (3.2 percent) who attend a private–independent school; and 15,280 (86.6 percent) who attend public schools.

ETS01 is the population of individuals who took the SAT college-entry examination in 2001. Before taking the SAT, each individual is required to complete a background questionnaire which requests information about the household, the individual, and the family. This information is similar to, but not exactly the same as, the information collected in NHES99. One advantage of the ETS01 data, for instance, is that individuals report their religion. For the characteristics of the community, county-level data are merged into the core dataset through the individual's school location. The county-level variable is the proportion of children aged 5 to 17 who are defined as "poor" in the Census, taken from the U.S. Census Small Area Income and Poverty Estimates 1998, State and County 1998. Importantly, each test participant declares their type of schooling; and in 2001 the questionnaire included the option "homeschooling." Based on the self-reported school types, the sample includes: 4,653 (0.01 percent) students who are home-schooled; 109,135 (11.3 percent) students who attend religious school; 32,469 (3.4 percent) who attend a private–independent school; and 822,967 (84.9 percent) who attend public schools.

Both datasets are recent, large-scale, and include an array of similar variables; they are also sufficiently up-to-date to include a home-schooling indicator.[1] The important difference is that the ETS01 data refer essentially to only one cohort of students, aged between 14 and 18 in 2001, who are attempting to gain entry to college. Given the relative novelty of home-schooling, those who appear in ETS01 are the "first-movers" into home-schooling. Moreover, school choice and desire to gain entry to college may be endogenously determined. Notwithstanding, the ETS01 test participants are all of similar ability, ages, and motivations; this may serve as a control for unobservable characteristics motivating the school choice decision. Thus, the school choice decision can be interpreted more specifically using the ETS01 data: given a student who wishes to go to college, what factors motivate the choice of school type?

Estimation of School Choice

The multinomial logit results for equation (5) using NHES99 and ETS01 datasets are summarized in tables 4.1–4.3. (The full set of estimations and the marginal effects are reported in Belfield, 2004.)

The results for both the NHES99 and ETS01 are plausible and suggestive (and these results correspond broadly with those of Figlio and Stone, 1999). Table 4.1 shows the influences of household characteristics and mother's characteristics on school choice. The datasets allow for measures of wealth, either the log of family income, or dummy variables for home-ownership, a high-income family, or the expectation of financial aid at college. The results across the two surveys are consistent: family financial resources are strongly positively correlated with private schooling as opposed to public schooling, and home schooling is adopted inversely with family resource levels. Interestingly, these financial effects are the same magnitude for both independent and religious private schooling.

The NHES99 includes further details about the household: larger numbers of adults in the household are negatively associated with religious schooling, being (weakly) associated with a shift toward public schooling. However, more children/siblings in the household are associated essentially with a switch away from private–independent and toward home-schooling.

Maternal characteristics are identified by education levels, and by whether the mother is employed or not (NHES99 only). Again, the two surveys give consistent results. Relative to mothers who had not obtained a high school equivalency, the effect of more education is to switch enrollment away from public schools but toward each of the other three options. The NHES99 results show higher maternal education is a strong influence on home-schooling, and this finding is to some extent supported by the ETS01 estimation. Again, however, these educational influences are strongest in causing a switch toward private religious schooling. Similarly, if the mother is employed, the child is much more likely to be in public school, with the other three options being equally affected positively.

Table 4.2 shows how student characteristics influence the school choice. Unsurprisingly, these play a strong role in influencing school choices. However, the results are discrepant in some cases. So, the NHES99 shows male children are less likely to attend private–religious school, whereas the ETS01 estimation indicates the opposite. For ethnicity, the results are more in accord: both African American and Latino students are more likely to attend public school, and least likely to attend private–religious school; Asian students are spread more evenly across the options, although they too are least likely to attend private–religious school. Similarly, private–religious schools are least likely to enroll non-U.S. (immigrant) citizens. The age variables in the NHES99 survey show that private schools—particularly religious ones—primarily serve younger students; home-schooling appears to be prevalent across all ages. Of special interest in the debate about choice is the disability of the child: opponents of choice have argued that private schools will subtly dissuade children with additional learning needs from enrollment (see the discussion in Howell and Peterson, 2002). For the private independent schools, there is no evidence of such dissuasion: students with disabilities or special learning needs are more likely to be in these schools. Again, home-schooling appears as a neutral option, whereas (according to NHES99, but not ETS01) private–religious schools

Table 4.1 Household and Maternal Determinants of the Choice between Public School, Home-School, or Religious or Nonreligious Private School

	Public School		Home-School		Private Religious School		Private Independent School	
	NHES 99	ETS 01	NHES 99	ETS 01	NHES 99	ETS 01	NHES 99	ETS 01
Household characteristics								
Owns home	−		:				:	
Ln (Family income)	−	−	:	−	+	+	+	+
No financial aid eligibility	:	−	:	:	−	+	:	+
Adults[a]: 2 (both parents)	:		:		:		:	
Adults[a]: 2 (one parent)	:		:		:		:	
Adults[a]: 3 or more	:		:		−		:	
Siblings for child	:		+		:		−	
Mother's characteristics								
Educ.[b]: High school	:	−	+	:	:	+	:	:
Educ.[b]: Some college	−	−	+	+	:	+	:	+
Educ.[b]: (Higher) Degree	−	−	+	+	+	+	:	+
Mother: Employed	+		−		:			

Notes: NHES 99: Parent Sample, National Household Education Survey. Log likelihood=7339, Wald Chi^2(75)=1072; N=17,640. ETS01: Educational Testing Service. Log likelihood=45063, Wald Chi^2(51)=9636, N=969,223. [a]Default adults: 1 parent only. [b]Default education level: less than high school.

Legend: Shaded boxes are statistically significant; +, positive and statistically significant, $p<0.05$; −, negative and statistically significant, $p<0.05$; .. not statistically significant, $p>0.05$; blank cells indicate test was not performed.

Table 4.2 Student-level Determinants of the Choice between Public School, Home-School, or Religious or Nonreligious Private School

Student Characteristics	Public School		Home-School		Private Religious School		Private Independent School	
	NHES 99	ETS 01	NHES 99	ETS 01	NHES 99	ETS 01	NHES 99	ETS 01
Male	..	–	..	..	..	+	..	+
Ethnicity[a]: African American	+	+	..	–	–	–	–	–
Ethnicity[a]: Asian	..	+	..	–	–	–	..	+
Ethnicity[a]: Hispanic	+	+	..	–	–	–	–	–
Born outside United States	..	+	..	–	–	–	..	–
Age[b]: 10 to 12 years	..	..	..	..		..		
Age[b]: 13 to 18 years	+	..	..	..	–	..	–	
Special learning needs	+	–		–	–			
Religion: Catholic		–				+		+
Religion: Other faiths				+		+		–

Notes: See Table 4.1. [a]Default ethnicity: white. [b]Default age: 5–9 years.

Legend: Shaded boxes are statistically significant; +, positive and statistically significant, $p>0.05$; –, negative and statistically significant, $p>0.05$; .., not statistically significant; blank cells indicate test was not performed.

Table 4.3 Community-level Determinants of the Choice between Public School, Home-School, or Religious or Nonreligious Private School

Community Characteristics	Public School		Home-School		Private Religious School		Private Independent School	
	NHES 99	ETS 01	NHES 99	ETS 01	NHES 99	ETS 01	NHES 99	ETS 01
ZIP poverty line[a]: >10%	..		..		+		..	
ZIP Hisp-Black[b]: 0–15%	+	−	..		−		−	
ZIP Hisp-Black[b]: 16–40%	..	−	..		−		..	
County poverty rate				..		..		
Region[c]: Northeast	−	−	−	−	+	+	+	+
Region[c]: South	−	+	..	..	+	−	+	+
Region[c]: Midwest	−	−	..	..	+	+	−	+
Area[d]: Urban	−		..		+		+	+
Area[d]: Suburban	−		..		..		..	

Notes: See Table 4.1. [a]Default ZIP poverty line: >19%. [b]Default ZIP Hisp-Black: >40%. [c]Default region: west. [d]Default area: rural.

Legend: Shaded boxes are statistically significant; +, positive and statistically significant, p>0.05; −, negative and statistically significant, p>0.05; .., not statistically significant; blank cells indicate test was not performed.

do enroll fewer disabled students. Finally, the ETS01 data includes information on religious status. This variable has a strong effect: students who profess any religion are more likely to be in private–religious schooling, but less likely to be in private–independent schooling. The results for home-schooling are mixed: those following the Catholic faith are less likely to be home-schooled, but other religions do dispose the family toward this choice. Notably, religion is the most important influence: the marginal coefficients for religion as a determinant of school choice is between 2 and 10 times that of any other factors. This is the family characteristic that is most associated with school choice. (Cohen-Zada and Justman [2003] also find that the largest impact on private school enrollments would come from changes in the share of Catholics in the community [and from population density].)

Finally, table 4.3 shows the effects of community characteristics. Here there are fewer clear influences on school choice. Higher rates of poverty are more likely to encourage private schooling (presumably amongst those who are not below the poverty line themselves). Plausibly, home-schooling is less common in the North East, and urban areas; these are areas where private schooling options are more common.

Before concluding, it is worthwhile noting some of the possible caveats to these findings. The first is the difficulty of measuring home-schooling, and finding out precisely what type of educational choice it represents. Some parents may temporarily home-school, e.g., for a single academic year; others may home-school part-time, e.g., enrolling only half-days at public school. For the NHES99 data, there is a reasonably agreed definition for home-schooling, but the ETS01 data includes self-reports of school type. The second caveat is that the sample of home-schoolers is too small; certainly, more efficient estimates would be obtained with larger samples (both absolute and relative to the high proportions enrolled in the other school types). Nevertheless, the ETS01 data includes over 5,000 home-schoolers in its sample. Finally, a third possible caveat is that the multinomial logit estimation may be improperly conceived. However, testing for the "irrelevance of independent assumptions"—by pooling religious and independent students—does not materially influence the coefficients (on the other two school types).

Conclusion

Here, a simple model of choice is used to explore the determinants of school choice, represented through the four options now available to parents. The aim has been modest: to see what factors are important when school choice is being decided on. In this respect the results are not surprising. However, the evidence has a more purposeful application given the growth of education reforms that are based on school choice and privatization.

First, the results show how different factors motivate different switches. Family characteristics appear more important here than student characteristics. So, families are more disposed toward home-schooling and away from private–independent schooling when there are more children in the house; but they are more disposed away from home-schooling and toward public schooling when the mother works. Income variables and community poverty rates tend to sway parents toward private schooling, but not toward home-schooling. Thus programs such as education tax credits may work to raise enrollments in private schools, not home-schooling; and demographic shifts in family structure (e.g., to fewer offspring and fewer two-parent families) may further discourage demand for home-schooling.

Second, religious belief appears as the most substantively powerful influence in choosing private schooling: in magnitude, the influence of religious persuasion far outweighs that of family resources or maternal education levels. Giving families greater choices may therefore mean an increase in the importance of religiosity in the U.S. school system, either because religious education is what parents demand or because these are the types of schools that come forward in the market. This finding supports the research on education vouchers, particularly in Cleveland where religious schools compose almost the entirety of the expanded school choice options. It suggests that charter schools, which preserve the separation of Church and State, may have relatively limited appeal.

Finally, the evidence can elucidate which type of schooling is most divergent from the public school norm, i.e., which school type has the strongest "independent" characteristics. Based on tables 4.1–4.3, it appears that the families who use private–religious schools have especial characteristics, strongly attracting them to this choice. Therefore, it is the religious schools—and not the home-schoolers—that appear the "most different" from public schools, at least along the vector of characteristics for which there are data. At issue is whether this difference will be moderated or exacerbated by the heightened demand for religious school which may come from voucher programs.

Note

1. Design effects for both surveys may also indicate some bias in the coefficients, particularly for home-schoolers who may be hard to classify. However, both surveys are applied to the general population, such that no school type is over-sampled. For the NHES99, it is important to recog-

nize that home-schoolers may be more reluctant to complete government surveys; but the SAT01 is not a government survey and is standardized nationally. Although the ETS01 dataset has 6,033 observations (large enough for sub-sample analyses), it is difficult to know how representative these individuals are of the larger home-school population. Establishing representativeness is a particular challenge if home-schooling is more likely to be a substitute for the lower grades of education. The SAT numbers may reflect the proportions of home-schoolers of high school age, but understate the count of home-schoolers who are more heavily clustered in the pre-teen years.

Chapter 5

Home-Schooling

Introduction

Home-schooling is perhaps the most radical reform of the U.S. education system in decades. It is the ultimate in privatization: the education of children who home-school is typically privately funded, privately provided, and (almost fully) privately regulated. Essentially, home-schooling gives primacy to private interests in education over a broader public interest. Recent estimates indicate that approximately 1 million students are being home-schooled, out of a student population of 55 million; a dramatic growth in numbers over the 1990s. This figure—albeit imprecise—is considerably higher than the combined numbers of students in charter schools and voucher programs, reforms that have attracted considerably more academic attention (as reviewed in Chapters 1 and 2). At the same time, home-schooling seems to be garnering broad-based support: whereas in 1985, only 16 percent of families thought home-schooling a good thing, by 2001 this figure had risen to 41 percent (Rose and Gallup, 2001: 46; see also Hammons, 2001a).

This development and increasing acceptance of home-schooling prompt many fundamental questions in relation to the organization of the U.S. school system. As an alternative to public schooling, home-schooling may satisfy families with particular educational preferences (typically religious) or those who are disaffected by publicly funded choices (see Stevens, 2001). Its growth may cast doubt on the efficiency of a schoolhouse operation, in that home provision is regarded as more effective (interview with Milton Friedman by Kane, 2002). Moreover, there are concerns about the public goods produced by home-schooling and the welfare of the children involved. Finally, home-schooling may have a strong economic impact on family expenditure patterns, time allocations, labor force participation, housing prices (near good schools), and preferences for public services.

In this light, this chapter offers a review of home-schooling and its potential implications for education policy reform. We begin by describing the characteristics of home-schoolers, drawing on information from recent surveys, reviews, and state data. We then review the factors motivating the choice of home-schooling relative to other schooling options. Next, we evaluate home-schooling using criteria set out in Chapters 1 and 2 of freedom of choice, efficiency, equity, and social cohesion. We conclude with a discussion of the policy instruments used to influence home-schooling and the implications for an education system with a sizeable home-schooling sector. To advance discussion of home-schooling across these aspects, we introduce new evidence from the highly selective cohort of home-schoolers who took the SAT in 2001.

The Home-Schooling Movement

Home-Schooling and Home-Based Educational Practices

Home-schooling is a diverse practice (Petrie, 2001: 479; Stevens, 2001). It is not a discrete and determinate form of education provision, particularly when contrasted with enrollment at a public school, which has a formal governance structure and offers a definite pedagogy and standard curriculum, taught by teachers as part of a regular instructional program fitted into the academic calendar. Indeed, home-schooling is sometimes lauded for not being "four-walls education," with some families explicitly motivated by a desire to unschool their children (Stevens, 2001; on special education, see Ensign, 2000). Other families may follow the formal approach of a school (e.g., with timetables or lesson plans). In general, the instructional mode of home-schooling appears to be characterized by its heterogeneity.

Two useful distinctions are worth noting. One is between complete home-schooling and home-based education. The former occurs where there is no interaction between the student and a school (although the student may draw on resources in the community). Home-based education occurs where the student draws on the resources of the school as desired (e.g., for specialist courses, sports, or extracurricular activities) or participates in a distance-learning program delivered by a school (e.g., an umbrella school). The latter approach is reasonably common: data indicate that 20 percent of home-school families sent their children to school for part of the day (NCES, 2001). The second useful distinction is the duration of home-schooling: although difficult to estimate, many home-schoolers do attend schools for a large period of their childhood (perhaps spending only two years home-schooling; see Lines, 2002; Isenberg's (2002) data show similar durations, with home-schoolers enrolling in public schools by later grades; see also Rudner, 1999). Others may be home-schooled throughout childhood. Thus, the duration of home-schooling is likely to be bimodal, with averages masking the distinction between short-term home-schoolers and those who are fully home-schooled.

Home-schooling is also a diverse practice in terms of regulations and laws (for a legal history, see Buss, 2000; Somerville, 2001). Although legal across all states, as reviewed by the Home School Legal Defense Association, nine states (including Texas) have little-to-no regulation; fourteen states (including California), little regulation; fourteen states, moderate regulation; and eleven states, relatively high regulation (including assessments and, possibly, inspections, although these are rarely enforced). Home-schooling operations are also regarded differently across the states. Lambert (2001) reviewed the legislation, finding state interpretations where operating a home-school is classified in various ways, including: distinctly "not a private school"; possibly a private school or having affiliated status (depending on how the law is interpreted); a nonpublic school; or, in some cases, a public school. These different operational characteristics influence both the regulatory burden and the financing of home-schools. Such diversity is compounded by the lack of information either on how such regulations are enforced or on how legal statutes are applied.[1]

How Many Home-Schoolers Are There?

Of the 55 million school-aged children in the United States in 2002, NCES (2001) estimated that approximately 800,000 to 1 million (1.6–1.8 percent) are being schooled at home. These estimates represent a sizeable increase from the CPS and NHES96 figures for the early 1990s of 0.4–0.6 million (Bauman, 2002; for data on the growth in Florida and Wisconsin since the 1980s, see Isenberg, 2002; on earlier decades, see Knowles et al., 1992). Certainly, the number of home-schoolers is significant, but it is difficult to be precise as to their numbers.

Survey Data

Most research relies on the series of National Household Education Surveys (NHES) of 1999 and 2003 (and earlier in 1996). Although these two surveys sample all households, the numbers of home-schoolers who respond are very small. For the NHES 1999, the actual count was 270–285 individuals. This figure was then aggregated to give the national estimate within the range of 800,000 to 1 million home-schoolers. (However, Isenberg [2002] argues that this figure may be understated by 0.1 million because of the way the NHES 1999 classifies siblings' schooling.) For the NHES 2003, the problem is more acute: because the sample size for this round of the survey series was reduced by 40 percent, the actual count of home-schoolers is even smaller, at 250.

These NHES data may be problematic for a number of reasons. Obviously, the small sample sizes mean that statistical aggregation may be subject to error, such that the national estimate must be expressed as a range. It also means that variation across important characteristics such as family size or income is limited. Subgroup analyses quickly face the problem of cell sizes being too small. A more general concern over categorization is that the NHES definition of home-schooling leaves open the possibility that the majority of a students' education takes place in school. (Home-schooling is identified when a child is being schooled at home and where any public schooling does not exceed 25 hours per week; a child who normally attends public school or who goes to school three days per week is classified as home-schooled.) Finally, because the NHES data are collected through a postal questionnaire, there is little information about how response rates vary between home-school families and those families with children in public and private schools. Information about whether only certain types of home-school families respond is also difficult to obtain (as is information about whether home-school families are more or less likely to have valid postal addresses).

In general, all survey data—such as Gallup poll data indicating that 3 percent of families report that their eldest are home-schooled—must face each of the challenges of the NHES data sets. Other sources for home-school numbers are available, although there are even greater concerns about their validity.

State/District Data

Public officials may be expected to collect data for two reasons. First, educational reforms at the federal and state level now emphasize increased accountability, and yet home-schooling is neglected in these reforms. Second, all children are entitled to an array of educational and child-welfare services; thus, public agencies need to have accurate information on who is eligible and whether the children—in any educational setting—who merit these services are in fact receiving them.

Unfortunately, state and district information on home-schooling is poor. Based on investigation of Web sites of all state education departments, as well as direct e-mail communication, it was possible to obtain data from only 24 states on the numbers of home-schoolers. Combining data across states faces an immediate challenge regarding the comparability of how home-schooling is designated. For example, in California the official term is "independent study (not adults)," which may include many children besides home-schoolers. In some states, families exempt their children from school because of religious preference; this group faces different regulations from the group of families who does not cite religious preference as the motivation to home-school.

State-level data also differ according to how they are collected: in many cases, states rely on a voluntary declaration by parents that their children are being home-schooled. The proportion of parents who comply with this voluntary requirement is unknown. Finally, states are at different stages in their implementation of data collection processes (some states have been collecting data for over a decade); this difference may mean some states identify all home-schoolers accurately, whereas others provide only incomplete counts. Yet, ideally, state-level data are the best source for tracking trends in home-schooling over time.

Using data from state records gives a considerably lower figure for the national population of home-schoolers. Bearing all the measurement difficulties in mind, table 5.1 reports on state-level estimates of home-school numbers across the twenty-four states where data are available (all states were scrutinized for data). This generates a count of 335,465 home-schoolers; when aggregated to national numbers using population weights, the overall estimate is 729,272 home-schoolers. This figure is considerably below those reported in other studies; nationally, it approximates to 1.7 percent of all students being home-schooled. As shown in table 5.1, states vary widely in the proportions of home-schoolers. They also show considerable variations in the proportion of home-schoolers in relation to those in private schools. Taking the average across the twenty-four states, the home-school sector is about one-fifth the size of the private sector (but in Arkansas and Montana, it is almost one-half the size).

Data from the Schools and Staffing Survey (2000) show the limited connection between district-level agencies and home-school families. This survey is a nationally representative questionnaire applied to district officials, public school principals, and teachers; the 2000 survey includes some questions on home-schooling. The responses shed light on why administrative records may be inadequate for research on home-schooling.

In response to the question "Does this district monitor the progress of home-schooled students?" only 38 percent of respondents answered affirmatively (see table 5.2). Thus, only one-third of districts have any information on the academic standing of home-schoolers. For more intensive requirements, the frequencies are even lower. For example, 20 percent of respondents stated that "home-schooled students are required to perform at or above the same specific

Table 5.1 Home-Schooling Estimates by State

	Home-Schoolers	Home-Schoolers as Percent of Public School Students	Home-Schoolers as Percent of Private School Students
AK	724	0.54	11.58
AR	12,474	2.78	46.82
CA[1]	96,337	1.54	15.81
CO	9,719	1.31	18.49
DE	2,290	1.98	9.47
FL	45,333	1.81	16.57
KS	14,249	3.04	35.12
KY[2]	6,208	0.94	9.40
ME	4,595	2.17	26.74
MI	1,033	0.06	0.60
MN	14,610	1.73	16.16
MT	3,788	2.49	45.41
NH	4,319	2.04	20.43
NM	6,487	2.05	33.70
NV	3,903	1.10	30.38
PA	23,903	1.32	6.96
RI	493	0.33	1.97
SD	2,723	2.15	27.80
TN	20,203	2.15	23.87
VA	22,021	1.89	22.40
VT	1,700	1.71	15.71
WA	11,699	1.16	15.20
WI	21,288	2.42	14.90
WV	5,002	1.78	34.17
Across 24 states	*335,465*	*1.70*	*20.88*

Notes: [1] CA uses the term "independent study (not adults)." *Home-schooling sources:* [2]For KY, Houston and Toma (2003); for other states, e-mail communications from state departments and state education department websites (URLs available from author). Home-schooling data are for most recent year (1999–2002). *Public school source:* Data from 2001: http://nces.ed.gov/programs/digest/d02/tables/dt037B.asp. *Private school source: NCES Digest,* 2000, table 64; data for 1999.

level as public school students on state or district achievement tests"; 32 percent affirmed that "home-schooled students in this district are required to meet state or district accountability standards"; and 14 percent reported that "home-schooled students are required to submit evidence of grade level performance other than achievement testing." In addition, these questions do not indicate

Table 5.2 Home-Schooling and District Reporting

	Percent of Districts
District monitors the progress of home-schooled students	38 percent
Home-schooled students are required to:	
Perform at the same level as public school students on state or district achievement tests	20 percent
Meet state/district accountability standards	32 percent
Submit evidence of grade-level performance other than achievement testing	14 percent

Source: Schools and Staffing Survey, 2000.

(a) the proportions of home-schoolers meeting the requirements, even within recordkeeping districts; and (b) the consequences (penalties or supports) for home-school families that do not ensure satisfactory progress. Thus, even where information on the numbers of home-schoolers is available, their academic placement and progress are not easily determinable. (Further review of the data available across nine states classified as imposing "high" regulation of home-schooling yields very limited information. In five states—Washington, Utah, West Virginia, Pennsylvania, New York—home-school students are not required to take state assessments or their results are not recorded. This situation arises because test assessment is often voluntary for these students, tests are administered at the district level and not available from state data, and test results may be returned to parents without being recorded.)[2]

Other Data Sources

Lists of members of home-schooling groups or networks are used for research by advocates. The Home School Legal Defense Association (an advocacy agency) estimates 1.7–2.0 million home-schoolers in 2002, based on its data collection system (see McDowell and Ray, 2000). Such membership lists may yield samples of sufficient size, but they are informative for exploring differences only among home-schoolers and not differences between home-schoolers and public schoolers. Given the predispositions of being a member of any group, it is unlikely that their responses can be compared with responses of families drawn representatively from the national population. Members will understandably tend to respond positively about their home-schooling experiences; they may also give "socially desirable" responses to questions about the merits of home-schooling.

Finally, data on test score performances are available. These, too, should be analyzed with caution. Data from the entire list of SAT test-takers in 2001 show that only 0.5 percent of the test-taking sample indicated that they were home-schoolers. However, test score data at earlier levels also must be sensitively assessed. Even with a norm-referenced test such as the Iowa Test of Basic Skills, there are concerns about the comparability of public school and home-school children. First, home-schoolers have more opportunities to opt out of taking tests; those that do take the tests are likely to be more motivated than the average public school student. Second, home-school students often take tests under different conditions from public school students (often they will take the test at home, rather than under school-based examination conditions). Finally, there is a legitimate question as to whether home-school children should be assessed equivalently with public school students; they may have different goals, and families may place a premium on skills and capacities that are not captured in standardized tests.

The Characteristics of Home-Schoolers

Inevitably, a group this large includes families with many different characteristics and motivations. Nevertheless, a better understanding of these household characteristics may assist in societal acceptance and support for home-schooling, as is desired by the families involved and their advocates (Lines, 2002).

Early adopters of home-schooling have been described as either "ideologues" or "pedagogues" (Nemer, 2002): they either did not agree with what was taught in public schools or felt they could do a better job of educating their children themselves. As the population of home-schoolers grows, other characteristics can be identified. In contrast with public school families, Lines (2002) describes home-schooling families as "more religious, more conservative, white, somewhat more affluent, and headed by parents with somewhat more years of education"; a similar picture emerges from national and state-level data (e.g., Isenberg [2002] finds home-schooling correlated with status as an Evangelical Protestant in Wisconsin; see Rudner, 1999, tables 2.2–2.9). The religiosity of home-schoolers clearly reflects a difference in preferences but may also reflect the greater legal recourse families have in claiming religious freedom from public demands. As well, it is plausible that home-schooling families are in the middle of the distribution of household incomes: when household income falls below a certain threshold, both parents must work; when it rises above a threshold, private-schooling options can be financed more readily. Similarly, more educated parents are likely to feel more competent as educators of their children, but at a certain level of education these parents will be attracted to lucrative employment prospects.

Table 5.3 Characteristics of SAT-takers by School Type (percent)

	Home-School	Public School	Private Independent School	Private Religious School
Student Characteristics				
African American	2.70	10.10	3.84	5.69
Asian	1.94	7.32	5.88	5.28
Hispanic	2.45	7.95	3.05	8.17
U.S. citizen	78.12	83.39	61.55	82.70
First language not English	1.33	6.52	3.40	3.68
Disabled	4.36	6.47	7.73	6.50
Male	46.88	45.24	52.66	49.70
Religious faith (any)	41.80	52.51	36.79	66.69
Religion: Baptist	17.70	11.08	5.08	6.52
Religion: Hindu	0.15	0.60	0.70	0.25
Religion: Jewish	0.60	2.09	4.90	2.06
Religion: Lutheran	1.22	2.48	0.94	1.35
Religion: Methodist	1.86	5.24	3.51	1.45
Religion: Presbyterian	1.78	2.84	3.09	1.45
Religion: Catholic	5.77	18.39	9.32	45.22
Mother's education				
High school	0.01	5.97	1.28	2.49
BA / Graduate degree	32.94	30.86	38.65	38.31
Family income				
<$20K	8	12	5	7
$20K-$40K	28	22	12	17
$40K-$60K	28	21	13	22
$60K-$80K	17	18	13	23
$80K-$100K	8	11	11	19
>$100K	11	16	45	12
Observations	*6,033*	*975,117*	*54,682*	*137,671*

Source: ETS data, 2001; population of test-takers, with exclusion of foreign nationals, missing income, ages 14–24.

To augment this literature, the top panel of table 5.3 reports data on the characteristics of students who took the SAT in 2001, according to school type. These data only relate to students who are college aspirant, but it is useful in comparing home-schoolers who intend to go to college with other school students with equivalent intentions. The home-school cohort is 6,033 (0.5 percent of all test-takers). As found elsewhere, home-schoolers tend to be white, with English as the first language, and without disabilities. However, whereas around half of all public school students and two-thirds of religious school students profess a religious faith, the figure for home-schoolers is just above two-fifths. Yet, a high proportion of these home-schoolers are Baptists: their adherence rate is 17.7 percent, compared with 11.1 percent within the public schools.

The middle panel of table 5.3 shows family characteristics. Home-schoolers are very unlikely to have a mother who has only a high school education, but these mothers are not strongly represented in the upper tail of the education distribution. Similarly, many home-schooling families are in the middle of the distribution of household incomes. Finally, the bottom panel of table 5.3 shows county-level statistics for affluence and childhood deprivation, matched to the residence zip codes. These data show home-schoolers are generally not from affluent counties, even compared with public school students, but they are less likely to live in areas of high child poverty.

The Motivation to Home-School

Although these descriptive data give some indication of the families' motivation, the growth of home-schooling can also be related to social and structural phenomena (on the reasons parents give for home-schooling, see Bauman, 2002). The mother's role is critical in the decision to home-school, and economic studies focus on her efficacy as a teacher and more formally on her time budget (Houston and Toma, 2003; Isenberg, 2002). Labor force participation propensities impact on the decision to home-school. So, whereas 20 percent of mothers whose children attend school do not work, the respective figure for home-schoolers is 50 percent (Isenberg, 2002). Other family-related factors may include a shift toward more intensive investments in fewer children (rather than extensive investments in family size) and an increase in the heterogeneity of preferences for educational curricula, instruction, and pedagogy.

Of policy interest is the relationship between home-schooling and other educational options, particularly given the cost of home-schooling relative to public schooling. (Currently, families who home-school do not receive public funds directly.) A number of reasons for avoiding public schools—besides a preference for religious education—have been offered. (Similar arguments can be applied against private schools: Isenberg [2002] finds home-schooling more common in nonmetropolitan areas with fewer private schools.) One is the inflexibility and lack of responsiveness of provision in the public sector, for example, in districts with large populations or in areas where funding increasingly comes from state sources. A second reason may be greater conformity in public schools, where such conformity fails to accommodate diverse preferences. A third reason (which has not been directly examined) is the increased pressure in public schools for standardized testing. Others may include families' perceptions that public school resources are insufficient or that public schools are dangerous environments. Importantly, many of these motivations suggest that there is a sizeable proportion of middle-class parents who are disaffected by the quality of public schooling.

More generally, the technology of education and schooling may be such that diseconomies of scale set in very early (or productivity growth is slow, relative to other industries). Thus, productivity in home-schools may not be that much lower than productivity levels in schoolhouses. There is reasonably strong evidence that school/district effectiveness is correlated with small size (Andrews et al., 2002), and most large-scale private-school operators are small (Levin, 2001a). Also, there are many advocates of smaller class sizes (Krueger, 1999) and demonstrated benefits from individualized tutoring (Rosé et al., 2003). (Home-schoolers may group together to increase "class sizes" in some cases.) Schools may also face informational costs and high transactions costs (especially when children's safety is involved and when family preferences are varied or idiosyncratic). Home-schooling may allow for families to save on learning materials, uniforms, transportation costs, and contributions to the school; although these are substantial for private schools (e.g., fees), they also may be nontrivial in public schools. Finally, families may obtain some funds, for example, through a cyber/virtual charter school arrangement (Huerta and Gonzalez, 2003), tax credits, or donations from their (religious) community.

A Framework for Evaluating Home-Schooling

Because home-schooling is the ultimate in education privatization, it prompts discussion that is strongly ideological: advocates and detractors may make claims that lack rigor, reflect only one position, or are based on partial evidence. One way to avoid this is to apply the comprehensive framework outlined in Chapters 1 and 2.

Freedom of Choice

Clearly, home-schooling and home-based education represent an expansion of educational options in terms of the technology of schooling. Indeed, all aspects of the educational process—including access, administration, use of teacher and physical resources, and assessment—may be chosen openly by the family, such that the education market is greatly liberalized. Home-based education can combine instructional modes from home and school. (In contrast, private schools often appear technologically similar to public schools; see Benveniste et al., 2003.) Such opportunities will be attractive to some parents, even for a short duration, and especially to families who are able to negotiate with their public school for tailored home-based education. Also, if the broader purpose of education is to create a diverse society, then an array of choices may be socially desirable. Given that home-schooling families do not receive public funds (or receive fewer funds than with full-time enrollment), this promise of independent choice has considerable persuasive power.

However, the desire for choice cannot be regarded as the sole determinant: even when home-schooling is not publicly funded, the state has responsibilities (and expectations) regarding child-rearing, and these must also be acknowledged. Also, an education system that accommodates home-schooling (e.g., through customized programs) will favor some families over others. On current evidence, the families most capable of exercising such choice for a reasonable duration are (typically) two-parent, middle-income families with mothers who are not in full-time employment. Thus, the demand for greater freedom of choice to home-school may not extend to the majority of the population.

Efficiency

The criterion of efficiency can be investigated by looking at expenditures or resources used and the outcomes of home-schooling.[3] From the home-schooling family's perspective, absent irrationality, the practice must be optimal because it is a preferred choice. From the state's perspective, a higher proportion of home-schoolers should result in savings where, as is currently the case in most states, home-schoolers do not receive public funds. However, these savings will be offset where home-schoolers draw on public resources as part of a home-based education plan; home-school families can claim tax credits, tax deductions, and funding through cyber/virtual charter schools; and the state incurs additional regulatory costs. Limited information is available on these costs.[4]

Most studies therefore concentrate on the outcomes of home-schooling. Advocates contend that small class sizes, flexible instruction (without age-tracking), and dedicated parent-teachers should make home-schooling more effective than other forms of education (but Cai et al. [2002] found that home-school teachers use more controlling teaching styles; for a full treatment on home-schooling instruction, see Stevens [2001]). In rebuttal, educational outcomes may be skewed toward those on which the family has competence, and educational progress may be slow if there is no formative assessment or peer pressure to learn (although home-school parents may exert more pressure or have higher expectations as a result of their supervision).

In comparing outcomes from home-schooling with those of public schooling, three empirical issues arise. The first is the common concern over the endogeneity of school choice, that is, different types of families choose the types of schools that their children attend, and little can be inferred about the impacts of schools for students who do not attend them (Neal, 1997). The second is the need to distinguish the absolute performance of home-schoolers from the treatment effect of home-schooling. Given the above-median resources of many home-schooling families, academic performance should be high even if home-schooling itself is not differentially effective. Full controls for family background are needed, however, to identify a treatment effect. Finally, home-schoolers can often choose which tests to take and when to take them (and have parents administer them), introducing other biases. These problems are over and above the practical difficulties of obtaining data on home-schoolers, as already discussed.

Holding these caveats strongly in mind, we report on the available evidence. Ray (2000: 74–75) reviewed mean home-schooling achievement levels from these sources, finding high performance by home-schoolers (see also Rudner, 1999; for a similar approach, Rothermel [2002] reports on the very high academic performance on standardized tests of a sample of 419 home-schoolers in the United Kingdom). Importantly, even where averages are available, school choice endogeneity controls and family background controls cannot be applied, such that a treatment effect can be identified.

Test score data from surveys are becoming available. Rudner (1999) reports average test scores for home-schoolers on the Iowa Tests of Basic Skills or the Tests of Achievement Proficiency by 39,607 students from approximately 22,000 families. The findings refer only to the performance of home-schoolers and not to the treatment effect of home-schooling because no adjustments for any family background characteristics are made and none of the endogeneity corrections are applied (see Welner and Welner, 1999). (Also, in some cases the test was applied in the home, raising issues in regard to test administration.) Using raw averages, home-schoolers post very high scores (above those in public and private schools): the composite scaled scores of home-schoolers range from the 77th to 91st percentile rank across grades K–12; scores are higher in reading, language, math, social studies, and science. (Given selection into test-taking, however, these scores may not indicate how well the average home-schooler performs.)

The SAT may be useful in reflecting final outcomes of schooling; in being applied in a standard manner under test conditions; and in being a high-stakes test, well correlated with future college completion and earnings. However, data on individual SAT scores are unlikely to be indicative of the academic impact of home-schooling, for reasons given above. Rather, SAT results can be useful for looking at relative differences and in providing information on the sizes of possible biases.

Table 5.4 shows the SAT scores of students according to school type from the 2001 test-takers. The first row shows the raw test score, unadjusted for selection effects and family background controls. The importance of endogeneity correction is evident from the bottom rows of table 5.4: home-schoolers make up only 0.5 percent of all SAT test-takers, a proportion considerably below their representation in the student population and lower than any other school type. Observed home-schoolers' scores are likely to be inflated: the negative correlation between test-taking proportions and test scores on the SAT has long been noted (see Behrendt et al., 1986). (For raw scores, home-schoolers obtain high SAT total scores, with a mean of 1093; this is 0.4 [0.2] standard deviations above the public school [private–religious school] scores, but 0.15 standard deviations below those in private–independent schools.) This selection effect means that absolute scores are unlikely to be useful indicators.

Nevertheless, it is possible to make some conclusions in relative terms. Notably, most of the home-schooling premium comes from higher SAT Verbal scores and not the SAT Math scores. (This distinction between Verbal/Reading and Math scores is also found in Rudner's 1999 data.) Insofar as there is a treatment effect (of indeterminate size) from home-schooling, it appears to be much greater for Verbal scores than for Math scores. This discrepancy may reflect greater parental competence across the subject disciplines.

Table 5.4 also reports scores with controls for family background (and a sizeable array of other covariates listed in the table notes, including the state-level SAT test-taking participation rate). After controlling for these covariants, the predicted SAT total scores for home-schoolers and private-independent school students converge toward the mean: the home-school premium over private–religious school students' falls almost to zero.[5] (Also, home-schoolers

Table 5.4 SAT Test-Scores by School Type

	Home-School	Public School	Private Independent School	Private Religious School
SAT Total				
Test score raw:				
Mean	1093.1	1012.6	1123.8	1055.6
(SD)	(198.0)	(205.6)	(213.6)	(196.2)
Test score predicted[a]:				
Mean	1054.5	1021.1	1064.4	1050.5
(SD)	(80.0)	(104.8)	(92.7)	(93.7)
SAT Math				
Test score raw:				
Mean	526.5	510.1	566.9	523.3
(SD)	(106.6)	(111.7)	(113.6)	(108.2)
Test score predicted[a]:				
Mean	527.7	513.4	534.8	528.0
(SD)	(42.3)	(55.4)	(49.2)	(49.6)
SAT Verbal				
Test score raw:				
Mean	566.6	502.6	556.9	532.3
(SD)	(108.9)	(109.0)	(118.3)	(103.0)
Test score predicted[a]:				
Mean	526.7	507.8	529.6	522.6
(SD)	(39.2)	(51.4)	(45.2)	(45.8)
Percent of SAT test-takers	0.5 percent	83.1 percent	4.7 percent	11.7 percent
Percent of all students[b]	1.5 percent	89.4 percent	1.1 percent	8.0 percent
Observations	*6,033*	*975,117*	*54,682*	*137,671*

Source: ETS data, 2001. [a]Predicted test scores based on OLS estimation with SAT test score dependent variables and independent variables of: mother's education (6); father's education (6); gender; grade-level; disability; first language not English (1); ethnicity (4); U.S. citizen (1); religion (10); Higher Education Carnegie class in state; state-level fees; state requires tests; state-level SAT participation rate; state-level participation rate squared; county-level poverty rate; county-level household income; district-level public school percent local funding; district-level per-pupil expenditures in public school; district-level ratio of at-risk students; district-level ratio of instructional expenditures; county-level public school teacher-student ratios. Full specification available from author. [b]NCES Digest of Education and Private School Survey (www.nces.ed.gov).

actually perform worse than would be predicted on SAT Math.) The differences between raw and predicted scores give some indication of the strength of covarying characteristics in explaining test score differences. Lastly, evidence on achievement in non-classroom-based cyber-charter schools may also be pertinent to evaluations of home-schooling. Using California data, Buddin and Zimmer (2003) show that students educated in this way have substantially lower test scores than either classroom-based charter schools or public schools.

Finally, noneducational outcomes have also been considered. One such outcome is child health. Whereas schools undertake preventive health care services (e.g., screening for visual or hearing impairments, inoculations), these services are not regularly provided by pediatricians and so may be less accessible for home-schoolers (see Klugewicz and Carraccio, 1999). An important economic outcome relates to earnings: home-schoolers may graduate without a diploma that serves as a labor market signal, which in turn raises the costs of job search (although diplomas may be obtained through alternative assessment systems). Yet, this consequence will be offset where home-schoolers attend college, and where they do well on academic tests that are correlated with earnings.

The efficiency of home-schooling varies considerably according to whether the family or state perspective is adopted. Given the positive correlation between family wealth and home-schooling, it is likely that families do incur high costs that may be worthwhile where the absolute educational outcomes of home-schoolers are also high (this high-cost and high-effect scenario is evident from cost-effectiveness studies of adult tutoring; see Levin et al., 1987). For states, the efficiency of home-schooling appears to depend in addition on what resources must be allocated to home-schoolers and whether any indirect financing burdens arise (e.g., on other public services).

Social Cohesion

As well as in terms of private academic benefits, home-schooling must be evaluated in terms of the public benefits that are generated. Critics of home-schooling argue that it reduces the socially beneficial outcomes available from school, both for the home-schooler and society at large (see Reich, 2002). It separates children from their peers, impairing "identity formation/choice" and the appreciation of social values and norms if home-schooling becomes "indoctrination" (see Buss, 2000). It may undermine the formation of such social norms; and in exiting the public system, home-schoolers may also undermine the voice needed to reform public schools such that they better accommodate families' preferences (Lubienski, 2000). Public schools have been defended on the grounds that they are best placed to teach social cohesion: they are forums where open debate is encouraged across many social groups and communities (Carnegie Corporation and CIRCLE, 2003). In rebuttal, home-schooling need not be an isolating experience: Isenberg (2002) found that about 50 percent of home-schoolers had siblings attending school; in addition, home-schoolers may be rooted in a religious community. Home-schooling need not be incompatible with public values: some home-schooling parents would like public schools to teach communitarian values more intensely (see Stevens, 2001; Nemer, 2002). Also, where education is intended to create a diverse society, then a plurality of educational options should be promoted (Smith and Sikkink, 1999). The general public is ambivalent: being asked whether home-schooling promotes good citizenship, numbers equally agree as disagree (Rose and Gallup, 2001: 46).

In a review about social outcomes, Medlin (2000) found generally supportive evidence on home-schoolers' behavior: home-schoolers reportedly were more mature and better socialized, participated in activities in their community, and socialized with children of different ages.[6] However, this evidence may not be robust. There are many difficulties in evaluating socialization outcomes, especially from small samples of data drawn from an imprecisely defined population or from a convenience sample. Survey respondents (particularly parents) are likely to give socially desirable responses. Survey measures may be imperfect constructs for socialization over the period of childhood, and survey instruments do not readily allow for comparison between home-schooling and other types of schooling, controlling for family background effects. Many studies report no comparison group and do not indicate whether the effects are substantively significant. Finally, much of the literature considers younger children. (There may also be issues of publication bias: many studies are reported in sympathetic journals.)

Again, the possibility of adverse selection is a concern—those families that feel least inclined to integrate with the rest of society may be the most likely to opt out; these families will not be easily detected in surveys. More fundamentally, almost all the relevant evidence on social cohesion focuses on the individual child, with very little information about how home-schooling impacts on other members of society (and on taxpayer support for public education). (On the political backlash from home-schooling scandals in Spain and France, see Petrie [2001]. On the antagonisms between parents, teachers, and school administrators within the education sector, see Lines [2002].) Evidence from young children is unlikely to yield evidence about the externalities produced from home-schooling, for example. The salient relationship is between home-schooling, religiosity, and social cohesion. Many argue for the separation of religion from public endeavors such as schooling to prevent laws from being viewed through a theocratic rather than a democratic lens; however, others may argue that society should be forged as a "community of communities" where diverse religious affiliations play a role in societal development (Smith and Sikkink, 1999).

Equity

Home-schooling should also be evaluated in terms of equity, an important motivation for state intervention in the education system. Several issues arise, largely as a consequence of the complete transfer of responsibility for a child's education from the state to the individual family.

First, home-schooling clearly weakens the opportunity for a community to guarantee or verify that children obtain a reasonable level of education or personal well-being. Summative assessments may be used to ensure that educational standards are being met, but evaluation of well-being is fraught with measurement error. Generally, the average family's incentives to care for their children are stronger than the state's. There is also evidence that some public schools are dangerous, adversely impacting children's well-being (there were 1.5 million violent incidents in U.S. public schools in 2000; Miller, 2003). From the parental perspective, therefore, home-schooling is associated with improved well-being for the child where the alternatives are dangerous.

But from society's perspective parental preferences cannot be taken as given. Some families do abuse and neglect their children (Child Protective Services receives reports on 3 million children annually, of which over 1,000 involve fatalities; see ACF, 2003), and educational agencies play a significant role in identifying such occurrences. It may be possible to perform a form of calculus on the trade-offs of home-schooling on children's welfare. But no such calculus has been performed and it would be dogged by two difficult issues. The first is that of weighting the welfare of children who may be abused against the welfare of children who are denied the opportunity to be home-schooled. The second is that families who are prone to abuse their children may be the most likely to opt out of schooling to avoid detection (another adverse selection effect). One solution is to allow home-schooling but with greater sanctions on abusive families and more extensive monitoring; however, the efficacy and efficiency of such an approach (including the high infrastructure costs) must be considered.

Second, although family resources are the main determinant of all children's education, for home-schoolers they become almost the only determinant. Home-schooling may therefore entrench intergenerational attributes, such that highly

Table 5.5 SAT Test-Score Gradients by Socioeconomic Status by School Type

	Effect Size Premium Relative to SES Q1 (Lowest Quintile)			
	Home-School	Public School	Private Independent School	Private Religious School
SAT Total				
SES Q2	0.32	0.16	0.21	0.14
SES Q3	0.38	0.26	0.36	0.24
SES Q4	0.60	0.47	0.62	0.45
SES Q5	0.63	0.52	0.70	0.47
SAT Math				
SES Q2	0.12	0.08	0.09	0.07
SES Q3	0.14	0.12	0.16	0.11
SES Q4	0.25	0.22	0.29	0.22
SES Q5	0.27	0.24	0.31	0.22
SAT Verbal				
SES Q2	0.20	0.09	0.12	0.07
SES Q3	0.24	0.14	0.20	0.13
SES Q4	0.35	0.25	0.33	0.23
SES Q5	0.36	0.28	0.38	0.25
Observations	6,033	975,117	54,682	137,671

Source: ETS data, 2001; population of test-takers, with exclusion of foreign nationals, missing income, ages 14–24. OLS estimation as per table 2. All effect sizes are statistically significant at $p < 0.05$.

educated or wealthy families transfer resources to their children most effectively. Educational inequalities and perhaps inequities will be perpetuated as well.

Although these intergenerational transfers may extend to social networks, beliefs, and lifestyles, they can most easily be examined by comparing socioeconomic status (SES) gradients on test scores across school types. These gradients should be steeper for families that home-school. Using the SAT data, these gradients are reported in table 5.5. Splitting the cohort by school type, ordinary least squares (OLS) estimation is applied to the SAT outcome measures. The effect size coefficients on socioeconomic status by quintile are reported, relative to those test-takers in the lowest quintile. In all cases, being in a higher SES quintile is associated with a higher test score. SAT scores increase as SES increases, with evidence of stronger family background effects for home-schoolers. Those in the second quintile score 0.32 standard deviations higher than those in the bottom quintile, the largest of the differentials according to school type. Across the four quintiles, both home-schoolers and private–independent school students show strong family background effects, relative to public and private–religious school students. The effects are evident across math and verbal scores, but the verbal gradients for home-school are steeper.

Given the importance of children's well-being and intergenerational effects, the equity of an education system with a sizeable home-schooling sector bears further scrutiny. Both beneficial and adverse consequences are possible, and some forms of home-schooling may generate significant positive externalities. However, evaluations based on the median home-schooler may mask distributional issues, particularly for those children in families with few resources.

The Impact of Home-Schooling on U.S. Education

Designing Policies for Home-Schooling

Even if the rate of growth of home-schooling slows, the current size of the sector means that education policies need to address the demands of home-schoolers. To design policies for home-schooling, three interlinked instruments need to be considered: regulations, finance, and support services for students.

School regulations relate to durations of attendance in a school, teacher qualifications, curriculum content, reporting/approval, and testing/assessment. From a national review, states' requirements on home-schoolers are often summarized in a relatively short document. The main regulation is that home-schoolers notify the state with a Declaration of Intent (these are often downloaded from state Web sites). Durations of schooling are intended to be equal to a school year (with monthly attendance records to be submitted by the parent), and the curriculum is also expected to correspond to that of public schools (at least in terms of core courses). Parents (or tutors) may be expected to have at least a GED (or college degree, but not necessarily in the subject of instruction). At present, regulations on home-schooling appear very open: almost no instructional mode appears to be proscribed.

However, by law, a state has considerable latitude in regulating private schooling, and in some cases this may extend to home-schooling. Lerner (1995: 373) concludes that such regulation will be defensible when it focuses on educational outcomes (where the state can claim a strong interest). For home-schooling, this means that—even without committing funds—states can impose reporting requirements and mandate test assessments; they might also perform on-site inspections. But home-schoolers may more easily challenge regulations relating to inputs, such as attendance durations, curriculum content, teacher qualifications, and peer inputs.[7]

In conjunction with regulations, states and districts must also stipulate financing terms for home-schooling. Although funds for home-schooling are limited, home-based students do draw on resources from public schools by "opting in" to particular school programs. This raises policy questions as to what resources these students are entitled to and to what extent they should be allowed to negotiate terms with the public school (citing administrative inconvenience, some states may refuse access to public school resources; see Fuller, 1998). If home-schooling conveys positive externalities, then direct funding may be justifiable (e.g., through education tax credits or vouchers). In some states, home-schools can be classified as part of the public school system (thus entitling students to funds, e.g., for those with disabilities; see Lambert, 2001). However, the appropriate amount of funding may be difficult to estimate (absent reliable data on home-schooling costs) and with funding will also come pressure for more regulation.

Finally, states must set out what support services are appropriate for home-schoolers. Typically, because such services include transportation and information on available school choices, the demands of home-schoolers in this respect may be small. (But home-based education does involve transportation to school.) Rather, home-schoolers may need support in accessing health services and educational counselling, as well as in identifying the resources available to them through the public system. Also, education officials must adopt policies for validating courses taken by home-schoolers who wish to enter the public school system.

Yet as Levin (2002a: 164) points out, these policy instruments are useful only if implemented effectively. As noted, test score accountability is irregularly enforced; and there appear to be obvious problems in forcing parents to administer tests or take their children to a testing center and in then designing programs for children based on such assessments. Establishing even a general regulatory framework may be complex: home-schooling is heterogeneous, difficult to classify, and expensive to monitor. States and districts may therefore face considerable difficulty in contriving policy instruments in regard to home-schooling. (For example, some states stipulate that home-school educational programs must be 180 days in length, but this stipulation cannot be enforced without monitoring.)[8] The status quo appears to be a bargain where home-schoolers receive no funds and little regulation is imposed; this serves home-schoolers and state/district officials tolerably well. But it is debatable how well the taxpayer is being served by this arrangement; and as the numbers of home-schoolers rise, and where the opportunity to obtain funds (indirectly) increases, this status quo may be untenable.

The Future of Home-Schooling

Potentially, home-schooling could revolutionize education in the United States: instead of regimented, standardized provision delivered within a detailed set of rules and regulations, learning could be much more diverse, open, and flexibly tailored to a child's requirements and responsive to his or her individual development. Some education will take place in a schoolhouse, but increasing proportions may not, as children become integrated into more adult social settings. Although, currently, high-quality data are sparse, a consensus description of the home-schooling sector emerges; what is less clear are the consequences both for the individual student and for broader society. Undoubtedly, one result would be a rise in the amount of religious education children receive. As well, there could be strong economic repercussions, not only at the individual level but also in regard to the financing of public services. But the diversity of home-schooling is such that generalization is difficult; inference using averages is problematic where the distribution of home-schoolers' characteristics is bimodal. For identifying treatment impacts, however, there is an opposite problem: home-school family backgrounds must be controlled for because these are on average more advantageous than for students in public schools.

Any impacts will become more important if home-schooling grows. Such growth will depend on several factors. First, home-schooling epitomizes freedom of choice as to how education is provided; although full home-schooling is limited to families with substantial home resources, short-term or part-time home-schooling is an option for many. Families may appreciate such freedom. Second, where home-schooling appears to be effective for the individual (either academically or socially), then other families will adopt the practice. (How these families will identify the treatment impact is not obvious.) Third, the growth of home-schooling may depend on social acceptance, which thus far appears to be increasing (albeit in somewhat of an evidentiary vacuum).

Finally, home-schooling may interact with federal education policies as stipulated in No Child Left Behind (NCLB). Home-schoolers may be liable in two ways: (1) home-based education does draw on public resources, some of which may be sourced at the federal level; (2) some state laws classify home-schools as "public schools." NCLB legislation has two components that may relate to home-schooling. One is the expectation that every class will have a "highly qualified" teacher; yet it will be difficult to enforce this for home-schooling families. The second is that NCLB requires a considerable increase in testing accountability (with tests through grades 3–8 in reading and math) to improve school quality. What sanctions might apply to home-schoolers who fail these tests is unclear. In summary, the growth of home-schooling will depend on federal, state, and district policies in terms of regulation, finance, and support services; perhaps more influential will be how these policies are implemented or can be implemented.

Notes

1. Petrie (2001: 483–484), reviewing the law across Europe, found: eleven countries where home education has been accommodated historically; five countries that do not permit home education legally but allow exceptions; and one country (Austria) that had recently legalized home education. However, her review indicates that some countries may be reverting toward restrictions on home education. Similar patterns of family characteristics emerge from this international evidence (on Norway, see Beck, 2001; on Canada, see Arai, 2000), with religiosity (Christian evangelical) an important characteristic. Again, the numbers are extremely difficult to estimate (in the United Kingdom, for example, home-school numbers are not recorded; Rothermel, 2002).

2. For example, in Virginia the Department of Education reports that it "does not compile data on the achievement of children who are taught at home due to the variety of methods available to parents to report such achievement to the local superintendent. No independent data or data generated by the Department of Education is available describing student performance on other assessments such as portfolios, tests administered by correspondence schools, or parent-developed tests" (Supts Memo. No. 140, August 1996).

3. Home-schooling may promote efficiency across the education system, in that it serves as a competition for public schools. However, competitive gains in the education sector are modest (see Chapter 6), and there is not much evidence that home-schooling is a response to the quality of local public schools rather than to differential preferences and characteristics of parents.

4. For the family it may be possible to home-school without a high direct outlay. Rudner (1999, table 12.2) finds the median expenditures on textbooks, lesson materials, tutoring and enrichment services, and testing to be extremely low, at around $400 per year. However, the main cost to the family will be earnings forgone.

5. As one approach to control for unobservable attributes correlated with the decision to home-school, the frequencies and estimations in table 5.3 were performed with the sample restricted to Baptists. Broadly, the results are equivalent (details available from the author).

6. See also Petrie (2001: 493–494). In contrast, based on a survey of pediatricians in Wisconsin and Maryland, Klugewicz and Carraccio (1999) found that 51 percent of pediatricians thought home-schoolers were less mature than their peers (with only 9 percent finding them more mature). As with home-schooling treatment impacts, the same methodological challenges arise here: the average student reported high levels of socialization and civic engagement because of SES (as is found in studies of civic participation; see Belfield, 2003).

7. Legally, home-schoolers have a strong defense against state regulations that force them to mix with other students. As Buss (2000: 1243) concludes, "Whatever the state can do to control the *content* of classroom instruction, the state cannot control *with whom* children are educated.

Parents are given authority over their children's school associations, particularly along ideological lines." However, state proscriptions in other domains may encourage associations.

8. For example, Georgia regulations state, "The law only requires the program to operate the equivalent of 180 days." But to the question "Should officials of the local public school system attempt to monitor the curriculum, the test program, student assessment process, students records or instruction time of home study programs?" the answer is no (www.doe.k12.ga.us/schools/homeschools.asp).

Part II

The Private Market

Chapter 6

The Effects of Competition on Educational Outcomes
A Review of U.S. Evidence

Introduction

Widespread concern with the quality of public education, particularly among schools attended by minority and low-income students, has generated calls for educational reforms that emphasize market competition between schools. Many economists (including the present authors) believe that market competition improves both technical and allocative efficiency in the use of resources: suppliers must strive to be efficient, and demanders will have more choices. Indeed, a substantial corpus of evidence—both across macroeconomic systems and at the microlevel of particular industries or locales—can be adduced to support this belief. However, what is less clear is the generality and scale of these efficiency gains in education. How much and according to what measures of output does increased competition improve educational quality? This chapter offers answers to these questions, based on a detailed review and critical evaluation of the evidence from cross-sectional (point-in-time), large-scale datasets.

The recent focus on the impact of competition on educational production has generated a substantial empirical literature. This chapter reviews systematically the research evidence on the effects of competition on educational outcomes. The chapter is structured as follows. The first section describes the strategy for selecting studies and considers the validity of "competition" as a construct. The second section reports the evidence on the effects of competition on academic achievement outcomes such as test scores. The third section reports on the effects of competition on other measures of schooling quality such as graduation rates, efficiency, and teacher pay. The research is evaluated, and the methodological challenges and sensitivity of the results are considered as well. The fourth section summarizes the results, assesses the substantive significance of this evidence, and draws some inferences for education policy. The last section provides a summary.

Identifying the Evidence on Competition

The Sampling Frame for Review

The sample for review was selected using the following protocol. The Web of Science database was searched from 2001 back to 1972, using "competition," "markets," and "education" as keywords. The relevant papers were then checked for further citations (and two journals were hand-searched: *The Economics of Education Review* and *Public Choice*). The sample analyzed here is on research on schooling (not higher education), and for the United States. Only research with an explicit measure of market competition is included. Essentially, the review focuses on the link between educational outcomes and competitive pressures across large markets, and using large-scale cross-sectional datasets.[1] Studies were only rejected from the sample where no dataset was specified.[2]

There is a substantial body of literature on competition and choice in education, emerging from several strands of research inquiry. So, one might infer that competition and choice are efficacious either if voucher programs are effective, or if private schools are the most efficient, or if decentralization policies improve education systems. As reviewed in Chapter 2 above, there is pertinent literature on each of these arguments. However, the focus here is more specific and fundamental, namely to identify the correlation—net of other influences—between more competition (more choice) and educational outcomes. If the net correlation is believed to be positive, then alternative policy options should be considered. Identification of such a correlation at a broad level is important, because there is some concern over the external validity of small-scale voucher programs (see Goldhaber, 2001); specifically, with small-scale studies of choice, there is a legitimate concern about the effects on those unable to choose or who face highly constrained choices. Also, competition may impact in myriad ways (e.g., input amounts, input mixes, outputs). Large-scale evidence across markets—encompassing the many possible effects of competition—is therefore a powerful evidence base in itself.

For exposition, the evidence is divided across several domains. In Section 3, the effects of competition on academic outcomes—typically standardized test scores—are reported; it is this domain for which most evidence is available, and where more proxies for competition are utilized. Section 4 reports the effects across a range of other educational outcomes including educational attainment, expenditures, efficiency, teacher salaries and conditions, private school enrollments, housing prices, and wages.

Construct Validity and Identification Strategy

Before reviewing the evidence, two concerns are raised here. The first is that of construct validity—the meaning of "markets" and "competition"—and the second is that of estimation—accurately identifying the effects of competition. Two other concerns, of sensitivity and of publication bias, are addressed directly in the discussions of the evidence below.

Fundamentally, inference from the evidence depends on the "education market" and "competition" being valid constructs (see Taylor, 2000). Specifically, an education market exists where parents have a feasible choice set of alternative provision. The choice set has three domains. Parents may choose (1) between public and private schools, (2) among public school districts, and (3) among public schools within a given district (the variants of public-private choice, interdistrict choice, and intradistrict choice).

What is a feasible choice set is not easily identified, however. Ostensibly similar provisions may not always be legitimate components of the choice set: religious and nonreligious schools may not be straight substitutes within a choice set, for example (yet there are nontrivial proportions of nonreligious enrollments at religious schools, particularly in urban areas). More generally, the costs to parents of choosing differ across the variants: parents choosing a private school incur tuition fees; parents choosing a different district typically incur residential relocation costs; parents choosing a different public school may also incur relocation costs, and or costs of appealing to the school district for reassignment (Couch and Shughart, 1995). Thus, particularly for low-income families, private and public schools may not represent a "single market." As well, choice variants may be simultaneously determined (with, for instance, weak public-private choice being offset by strong intradistrict choice). It is not, therefore, possible to identify in a straightforward manner the relative strength of each of the three domains of competition.

Similarly, competition as a construct refers both to the existence of multiple education suppliers within the choice set, and to how these suppliers behave strategically. Competitive pressures from a neighboring public school may differ from those of a neighboring private school; competition may be horizontal (between services) or vertical (for inputs); or competition may impact only at a critical threshold level. The effects of competition might be strongest where there is presently very limited competition, or where the costs of making an alternative choice are relatively high, so choosing an alternative district may be more expensive than choosing an alternative public school. Lastly, the effects of competition will depend on where the locus of control over resource allocation resides. For example, if inputs are mainly allocated at the district level, intradistrict competition is likely to have weak effects (for a case study in Arizona, see Hess et al., 2001).

The school production function model can also be used to predict the effects of competition. Demand-side competition may improve the productivity of student inputs if greater choices mean that students can enroll at a school that better maps to their preferences. Thus, competition may be more beneficial where student preferences are more heterogeneous. Supply-side competition may improve the productivity of schools, leading to a more efficient allocation of inputs (e.g., better teacher selection). Either demand-side or supply-side competition—or both—may be obtained, with different and indeed multiple effects. Either form, it should be noted, would serve to improve student outcomes. But if supply-side competition is important, inputs may be used more efficiently and costs reduced. However, any of the inputs or outputs may be affected by competitive pressures (as illustrated in the case studies in Hess et al., 2001).

Typically, competition is assessed using the Herfindahl Index (HI), the sum of the squares of per-unit enrollments over total enrollments (Borland and Howson, 1992). In this literature, the Index typically relates to public school choices, either interdistrict or intradistrict. Bounded between 0 (full competition) and 1 (monopoly), the Index may be regarded as continuous or may be used to identify a critical competition threshold.[3] Another measure of competition is the private schooling enrollment share. This share may represent competition, but may also be determined by other factors, such as regional religiosity, or community wealth levels. However, neither measure of competition captures how or whether schools or districts compete: some schools may be "dominant firms"; others may collude; niche markets may develop; and schools may respond to competition either by changing their provision or by quitting the market (Hoxby, 1994). In some cases, the competition variable may equate to a distinction between urban and rural areas (Hoxby, 2001). Strictly speaking, in many cases the measure of competition is actually a measure of alternative or ostensible options (a "choice set"), without a conception of actual strategic behavior.

The second substantial caution regarding this evidence base relates to the two estimation problems from simply correlating competition measures with educational outcomes (Dee, 1998). One is the problem of simultaneity. Competition refers to how suppliers behave, holding demand constant; yet available supply and effective private–public schooling demand are simultaneously determined. So, only the equilibrium quantity of supply and demand is observed. Hence, when public schooling is of low quality, the demand for private schooling will rise, creating a negative relationship between public school quality and private schooling enrollment.[4] The other problem is that of omitted variable bias, i.e., when factors that confound the relationship between, say, public school quality and private school supply are omitted from analysis.[5] Ability-omission bias may arise where private schools cream-skim more able students; this will reduce average ability and educational outcomes in public schools. Resource-omission bias may arise where higher demand for private schooling reduces taxpayer support for public schooling. Socioeconomic-omission bias will arise if the demand for private schooling is influenced by local socioeconomic characteristics (such as community income and education levels), but these also have a direct effect on educational attainment.[6] The evidence below sheds light on the importance of each of these problems.

Ideally, then, estimation techniques should identify the supply of alternative schooling and should control for key confounders. For studies using the Herfindahl Index to measure intradistrict public school choice, identification of supply may be straightforward. For studies that use private schooling as the measure of competition with public schools, supply is identified through a source of variation—such as Catholic religiosity in the region—that is held to be uncorrelated with schooling quality. Typically, either two-stage (2SLS) or instrumental variable (IV) approaches are used (e.g., Zanzig, 1997; Borland and Howson, 1992). Evidence from this research survey helps to assess the impact of using these approaches over simple OLS correlations.

All evidence will be assessed in light of these validity and estimation concerns. In addition, both statistical significance and magnitude of findings will be scrutinized. The former will be established when a coefficient is accepted as different from zero at the 5 percent two-tailed level (or above). The magnitude of competitive impact or substantive significance will be established in terms of standard deviation changes to the educational outcome when the amount of competition increases by one standard deviation. These representations allow for comparative and uniform metrics to be applied across different studies and for consistent discussion of how much increases in competition would affect schooling quality. The evidence is summarized below in an overall summary table (6.1).

Competition and Academic Outcomes

Evidence for Academic Outcomes

Evidence from 25 studies on the effects of greater market competition on academic outcomes is given here. A simple appraisal indicates that over one-third (of the 206 separate estimates) report a statistically significant correlation between increased competition and higher public school achievement. A trivial number show more competition impairs public school outcomes; but a sizable minority shows no effect. Here the studies are considered in more detail, divided by the measure of competition used.

Evidence Using the Herfindahl Index

The Herfindahl Index (HI) values in education markets range from .11 to .87, with an approximate average for the concentration level at .35. Broadly, these index values indicate education is highly concentrated compared to other sectors (Barrow and Rouse, 2000). Primary schooling is more competitive (or at least more atomistic) by this measure than secondary schooling.

Using the HI as a continuous variable, most empirical papers report only weak or null effects on academic outcomes. Borland and Howson (1992, 1995) found no statistically significant correlation between the HI and mean test scores across 170 districts in Kentucky. From a scatter plot, Hanushek and Rivkin (2001) discerned no correlation between HI values and school average test score gains across 27 metropolitan areas in Texas. Using regression, Marlow (2000) found mixed results for counties in California: 10 out of 18 estimations are not statistically significant at the 5 percent level; with the strongest effects at eighth grade (but no effects for tenth grade). For the significant results, a one standard deviation decrease in the HI is associated with fourth grade reading scores that are higher by .22 standard deviations and writing scores by .12 of a standard deviation. For eighth grade the figures are .41 for reading, .22 for writing, and .4 for mathematics.

Other studies use the HI to categorize education markets into high or low levels of competition. In general, this categorization yields more statistically significant results. For their data on Kentucky, Borland and Howson (1993) reported a statistically significant but substantively moderate effect above a

Table 6.1 Summary of the Effects of Increases in Competition by One Standard Deviation

Outcome Variable	Statistical Significance Estimations (n)[a]	Competition Measure	Effect of Increasing Competition by One Standard Deviation
Academic outcomes	38% (206)	Herfindahl Index	Outcome scores in public schools rise by 0.1 s.d.
		Private school enrollments	Outcome scores in public schools rise by <0.1 s.d.
		Other proxies for competition	Outcome scores in public schools rise by <0.1 s.d.
Attainment, graduation rates, drop-out rates	42% (52)	Number of districts or schools	Drop-out rates are not affected
		Private school enrollments	Graduation rates are higher by 0.08–0.18 s.d.
Spending	42% +ve	Number of districts in state	Spending is lower by 12%
	22% −ve (33)	Private school enrollments	Spending effect is ambiguous (higher by 0.2–0.4 s.d. or lower by 7%)
Efficiency	66% (64)	Herfindahl Index	Efficiency is higher, only in concentrated markets
		Private school enrollments	Efficiency is higher, by approximately 0.2 s.d.
Teaching quality	60% (30)	Private school enrollments	Teacher salaries rise by 0.1–0.3 s.d. ($400–$1,000) Student-teacher ratios are lower, by at most one student
Private school enrollments	31% (29)	Public school quality	Private school enrollments fall by 0–0.17 s.d.
Wages	41% (17)	Private school enrollments	Wages rise by 0.1 s.d. (1%–4% higher)

Notes: [a] Number of separate studies: academic outcomes, 25; attainment, graduation rates, drop-out rates, 6; spending, 11; efficiency, 13; teaching quality, 8; private school enrollments, 6; wages, 3. Also, the estimations on housing prices are excluded, because the number of studies is too low (1). Final column effects are calculated using all studies, where both significant and insignificant coefficients are reported.

critical threshold HI value: test scores are 3 percent higher when the HI value falls below .5. (This critical threshold—where competition was found to be effective—was determined endogenously in the model). For California, Zanzig (1997) finds consistent effects of competition across two measures. First, where there are less than four local districts, a one standard deviation increase in their number (i.e., .64 extra districts) is linked to district twelfth grade test scores that are about .1 standard deviations higher. Second, where the HI is over .58, a one standard deviation fall in the HI is associated with district twelfth grade test scores that are lower by about .1 standard deviations. However, using individual-level data from NELS, Figlio and Stone (1999) found no clear positive effects across the United States: the test score gap between public and private (religious or nonreligious) schools is unaffected by stratification according to whether the schools are in high or low competition areas.

Finally, the HI can be interacted with other process measures. Hanushek and Rivkin (2001) interacted their HI scores with the percentage of different teachers across 1140 schools and 832 districts in Texas. For this estimation, more competition leads to a smaller between-cohort variance in school average value-added test scores; the latter proxies for teacher quality variance (more competition should reduce the school/district variance in teaching quality, because poor teachers would not be hired, monitoring of teachers would be better, etc.). At the school level, a one standard deviation increase in competition reduces this cohort variance by roughly .09 standard deviations. However, these results are not robust to sample decomposition.[7]

Evidence Using Private School Enrollment

Higher private school enrollments may also serve as a measure of competition for public schools. However, as noted above, this competitive pressure would be anticipated to be weaker than equivalent concentration levels within the public sector. Several studies have used private school enrollments as a measure of competition.

Across districts and counties, the effect of private school competition on public school outcomes is mixed. Couch et al. (1993) correlated county private school enrollments with eighth–twelfth grade algebra test scores for North Carolina: a one standard deviation increase in private school enrollments is associated with an increase in public school test scores by .22 standard deviations. Newmark (1995) replicated this result, and found similar effects. But he also showed that these effects for North Carolina were not robust: from 12 other specifications, none showed a statistically significant relation of private school enrollment and public school test scores. In a similar estimation, Geller et al.

(2001) found no significant effects on academic outcomes employing differenced and lagged values of competition for Georgia (using either the number of private schools or the percent of private enrollments); and Simon and Lovrich (1996) found broadly neutral effects using data on districts in Washington state. Using school-level data, Sander (1999) found no significant effect on math scores within the State of Illinois.

Smith and Meier (1995) found the percentage of public school students passing standardized tests (in the subjects of mathematics and of communications studies) was lower with higher private school enrollment across Florida districts. These effects appear substantively small: for tests in communications, an increase of four percentage points in private school enrollment is associated with a decrease in one percentage point in public school performance in the following year. Moreover, these results are sensitive to the income distribution. In a re-estimation of Smith and Meier's (1995) Florida data, Maranto et al. (2000) split the sample across high- and low-income families. For low-income districts, competition reduces public school test scores (generally, a statistically significant result, as well as substantively important); for high-income districts, competition has ambiguous effects.[8] As well, Wrinkle et al. (1999) follow the approach of Smith and Meier (1995), using data from 73 Texas counties. They find the link between public school performance and percent county private school enrollment to be insignificant.

Several studies use individual, student-level data to test for the effects of private school enrollments on academic outcomes. Using the NELS data, McMillan (2004) found weakly negative effects on public school eighth grade scores (although in the strongest case, a one standard deviation increase in private school enrollment was associated with lower scores for individual public school students by .66 standard deviations). Using High School and Beyond data, Arum (1996) found a positive effect for individuals' twelfth grade test scores. Here, the effects were substantively small: a one standard deviation increase in private schooling was associated with a .01–.02 standard deviation increase in test scores. From the National Longitudinal Survey of Youth (NLSY, 1979–90) and using an Instrumental Variables technique, Hoxby (1994) found that ability scores (the Armed Forces Qualification Test, AFQT) were positively associated with competition, but the magnitude is small with only a one percentile gain for a standard deviation increase in the Catholic enrollment share. Finally, using NELS and NLS72 with 2SLS estimation, Jepsen (2002) regressed standardized mathematics scores against four measures of private school competition. Only one was statistically significant (NLS72, county level competition), and this effect was substantively weak (with OLS estimation yielding no statistically significant results).

Evidence Using Other Measures of Competition

The third set of evidence on academic outcomes uses proxy measures for competition typically for different levels of choice. The proxy measures are idiosyncratic, but have some affinity to Herfindahl Index values.

Using the number of districts/schools per 1000 students, Marlow (1997) found a strongly positive statistical effect on math SAT and eighth grade scores, and (more weakly) verbal SAT scores across the 50 states. The substantive influence of these variables does not appear to be large, however. Using the number of neighboring districts, Blair and Staley (1995) found no effect on district-level achievement test scores in Ohio. However, using the average district test scores of adjacent districts as a proxy for competition there is a positive effect on test scores. Where average adjacent-district test scores are one standard deviation higher, home-district test scores are .41 standard deviations higher. In contrast, using the numbers of neighboring public school districts, Geller et al. (2001) identified no positive effects on academic scores in Georgia (and in one estimation—tenth grade reading—the correlation is negative). Husted and Kenny (2000) report mixed effects, using a proxy for government (monopoly) intervention—the proportions of education expenditures funded at the state level. Using state-average SAT scores, they find that a one standard deviation increase in the proportion of state-level expenditures lowers scores by .02–.08 standard deviations. Husted and Kenny (2000) do report stronger effects when Catholic religiosity is used as a proxy for the competition between public and private schools. A one standard deviation increase in Catholicism is associated with .19–0.27 standard deviation increases in SAT scores, although the effect is only significant in four of the six estimations.

Hammons examines competitive effects in Vermont and Maine, both states having education systems with strong elements of choice. Using two measures of choice (proportion of town-tuitioned students) and competition (distance to all tuition towns within a 7 mile radius), Hammons finds a positive impact on test performance: an increase of one standard deviation in competition raises test scores by .16 standard deviations.

Finally, Hoxby (2001) used as a measure of school choice the share of a district's enrollment in a particular metropolitan area, with an instrumental variable based on the natural boundaries to the formation of school districts. This index variable (range 0–0.97, standard deviation of .27) is higher where there is greater choice. Competition has beneficial effects. Hoxby (2001) reported the effects of going from minimum to maximum amounts of interdistrict choice: but, in terms here of one standard deviation changes, eighth grade reading scores are 1.03 percentile points higher, tenth grade math scores are .84 percentile points higher, and twelfth grade reading scores are 1.56 percentile points higher. When the percentage in private school enrollment is used as a measure of competition, academic scores increase by 2.5–3.7 percentile points when private school choice goes from moderately "low" to moderately "high."

Sensitivity Analysis and Publication Bias

These results are generally consistent in suggesting modest gains in achievement from competition. There were few negative correlations, although a large number were statistically insignificant. However, a general concern regarding mismeasurement still remains. For the dependent variables, the (artificial score) variables may have nonnormal distributions, be compressed or bounded, or be sensitive to outlier results. Many estimates do not explicitly use the student "yield"; that is, the proportions of students taking the test within a given jurisdiction (see Newmark, 1995). Yet, states where educational quality is low may submit fewer students to standardized testing (and in the case of the SAT, students self-select themselves for the test). For the independent variables, the distribution of the Herfindahl Index may be sensitive to outliers.[9]

In checking for robustness of the results, a number of papers do report sensitivity tests. One important set of tests relates to the estimation method, i.e., whether the study compensates for simultaneous determination of the dependent and independent variable. Instrumental variables should be used to address simultaneity, but the value of such estimation depends on the quality of the instruments that are available. Based on comparing results using different estimators among these studies, however, it appears that instrumental variable estimation may not be necessary for generating reasonably precise point estimates. Five contributions explicitly identify no empirical advantage from using 2SLS over ordinary least squares. In contrast, three find an advantage from using 2SLS. When private school supply is used as the measure of competition, 2SLS estimation raises point estimates of the effects.

Another set of sensitivity tests relates to the derivation of the key variables and to omitted variable bias. For example, Newmark (1995) estimates a basic model and then separate models: for seven additional academic subjects; without population density; with private enrollment Census measures (which include home-schooling and exclude kindergarten); with only nonreligious private school enrollment; and with adjustments for student yield. In none of these cases are the simple results from Newmark (1995) and Couch et al. (1993) replicated. Many studies report both significant and insignificant correlations, often for equally plausible specifications. This spread of results suggests that the effects of competition are sensitive to the specification utilized. This raises the possibility of bias whereby a specification is chosen because it shows statistically significant results (see Begg, 1994). Moreover, studies may be more likely to be published where they show statistically significant results (Shadish and Haddock, 1994). Publication bias is of particular concern in areas of inquiry where there are a large number of small-sample studies; where fewer randomized trials are conducted; and where research is ideologically motivated. Overall, there may be a tendency for bias toward discovering a link between competition and outcomes.[10]

Competition and Educational Quality

Evidence for Educational Quality

In addition to academic outcomes, many studies consider the effects of greater competition on other measures of educational quality and performance. The studies use a range of proxies for competition, and are listed here according to the measure of educational quality used as the dependent variable.

Educational Attainment

There are effects of competition on drop-out rates, graduation rates, and college attendance. For drop-out rates, Marlow (1997) found that states with more districts or more schools (per student body size) had lower drop-out rates (although no substantive effect can be determined). For graduation rates, Dee (1998) found private school student numbers raise graduation rates across a sample of almost 4,500 school districts. The elasticity of graduation with respect to private school competition is small, however, at .03; a one standard deviation increase in private schooling raises public school graduation rates by .18 standard deviations (1.7 percentage points). In directly addressing simultaneity, Dee (1998) compared OLS estimation with 2SLS estimation (where Catholic population levels are used to identify supply): OLS estimation appears to understate the positive effects of private school competition. However, using the same model and instrument, Sander (1999) found no statistically significant effect either on graduation rates, or on proportions of college-bound students in Illinois.

For attainment, graduation, and college attendance, Jepsen (2002) used individual level data from NLS72 and NELS and found broadly neutral effects of competition. For attainment, the NLS72 shows no effect of greater competition on years of schooling; and the NELS shows weak results on high school graduation (a one standard deviation increase in competition across zip codes actually reduces graduation rates by .11 standard deviations). For college attendance, similarly weak results are found (with three of four estimations not statistically significant): a one standard-deviation increase in private school share at the county level raises the probability of going to college by at most .14 standard deviations. Generally, these results are invariant to OLS or 2SLS estimation.

For attainment, graduation with a diploma, and college graduation, Hoxby (1994) used the percentage of Catholic/private schools to identify competition, with NLSY data. On attainment, the instrumental variables approach yields a statistically significant positive correlation: an increase of one standard deviation in Catholic or private schooling raises years of education by .08 standard deviations. (Alternatively expressed, a 10 percentage point increase in the share of enrollment in Catholic [private] schools produces an extra .33 [0.35] years of education for public school students.) On graduation with a diploma, and on college graduation, positive (and robust) effects of competition are also identified: a one standard deviation increase in the Catholic enrollment share increases these variables by 1–1.5 percentage points. (These results are found with instrumental variables, but are less evident when FGLS estimation is used.) Using Census data for metropolitan areas, Hoxby (2000a) found positive effects of district choice across subgroups of families: in estimations where the coefficient for choice is statistically significant, an increase of one standard deviation in the choice variable raises attainment by .03–.17 standard deviations.

Educational Expenditures

Competition may influence resource levels. Competition may have conflicting influences here: more efficient enterprises operating in a competitive market may be rewarded with higher subsidies (because they generate more human capital for a given resource level), or may be allocated lower funding (to generate the standard amount of public school human capital).[11] Competition may encourage schools to eliminate ineffectual programs, cutting wasteful costs, or may motivate students (who are better matched to schools of choice). Also, and perhaps more important, the higher the percentage of students in private schools, the larger the public resource base for each public school student. However, the evidence on the link between educational expenditures and competition is mixed.

Using state-level Census data, Kenny and Schmidt (1994) found the least competitive quartile of states (i.e., those with the fewest school districts) had higher state-level expenditures by 12 percent ($336 per student in 2000 dollars). Perhaps this indicates diseconomies of scale from having large districts. For Michigan public school districts, Brokaw et al. (1995) regress total operating expenditure per pupil against the ratio of public to private school students. Where the public monopoly is stronger, operating expenditures rise. The effect is statistically significant, but small (<$10 in 2000 prices).

With large city 1970 Census data, Lovell (1978) reported no effect on public school expenditures from the proportions of private schools. Also using state-level data, Marlow (1997) reported mixed effects on spending by competition levels: where the number of schools per 1,000 students is higher, so is funding; but the number of districts has no statistically significant effect. For California, though, Marlow (2000) reported more conclusively on lower spending where the HI value is lower. At the county level, a decrease in the HI of one standard deviation reduces per-pupil spending by .53–.59 standard deviations. However, using 1980 Census data, Arum (1996) found the percentage of private school enrollment has a positive effect on public school expenditure: increasing private school attendance by one standard deviation raises public school expenditures by .22–.26 standard deviations. This translates into increases of $209 (in 2000 dollars) per student for each four percentage point increase in private school enrollment. With panel data for New York state, Goldhaber (1999) reported greater private school enrollment raises public school expenditures (this is for two of four specifications; the other two are not significant). For New York state, the effect appears large: increasing private school enrollments by four percentage points (i.e., moving it around three-quarters of one standard deviation above other states) raises public school expenditure by 2.73–1.93 standard deviations, or $3304–$2334 (2000 dollars). With MSA Census data, Schmidt (1992) found a higher (predicted) proportion of students in private schools raises per pupil expenditures, although the relationship appears substantively trivial. Also using Census data, Burnell (1991) found that less centralized (i.e., more competitive) school districts in a given county had higher expenditures per pupil.

Hoxby (2000a) used a range of measures of competition to test for changes in spending, and found the results sensitive to the estimation method. With data on 211 metropolitan areas, Hoxby (2000a) found a one standard deviation increase in interdistrict choice (based on enrollment options across districts) reduced spending by 2.1 percent. However, competition from private school enrollment only slightly increased spending per pupil in public schools by .1 percent. Using the NLSY (1979–90), Hoxby (1994) found no statistically significant effects from competition on per-pupil spending, and only very weak negative effects for per-resident public school spending (of .07 standard deviations, or $73 in year 2000 dollars).

Educational Efficiency

Fundamentally, competition should be anticipated to raise efficiency levels in terms of output per unit of cost or cost per unit of output. Indeed, the evidence above is suggestive of greater efficiency: competition appears to raise performance, along with neutral or ambiguous effects on spending. Four studies that directly assess efficiency are reported.

Grosskopf et al. (1999a, b) found efficiency rises with competition among Texas school districts. Again, these competitive pressures—as measured by the HI—are not continuous. The threshold for "low competition" is where the Index value equals 27.61 (with half the metropolitan areas and 20 percent of urban districts in concentrated markets). Below this value, concentration and inefficiency are not correlated; but in districts above the concentration threshold, predicted inefficiency is at least 40 percent higher.

Duncombe et al. (1997) reported mixed evidence on the link between cost efficiency and competitive pressures across New York districts. Neither a greater number nor density of schools increases efficiency. In big city districts—that is, "monopoly" districts—cost efficiency is lower by 6.5 percent; yet, where the number of private school students in the district is greater, cost efficiency is also lower. Both these effects (prima facie, contradictory) appear statistically and substantively significant. Also using New York districts, Kang and Greene find that competition as measured by the Herfindahl Index does raise technical efficiency (using five measures), but that private school enrollments have no effect on efficiency. The effect on efficiency is not consistent, however, and so may be inferred to be small.

Finally, in a substantial study Hoxby (2000a, 2001) estimated productivity as the ratio of academic test scores and (log) per-pupil spending for metropolitan areas. Interdistrict choice has a positive, statistically significant effect on productivity across each grade/subject. However, the effect appears to be substantively small. When interdistrict choice rises by .25 (approximately one standard deviation), school productivity rises by approximately 2.5 percent, or .3 standard deviations.[12] Hoxby's (2000a) evidence on achievement and spending can be combined to interpret the efficiency gains from competition: increasing choice by one standard deviation (0.27 units), achievement is .8–1.5 percentile points higher, but spending is 1.9 percent lower. Together, these appear to be moderate gains. Similarly, competition from private schools also raises productivity, but the effect appears to be very modest: if private schooling increases by 10 percentage points, a metropolitan public school has eighth grade reading scores that rise by only .27 percentile points more for every 100 percent increase in per pupil spending. As private schooling has broadly neutral effects on spending, productivity improvements from competition arise because of higher public school achievement when private school enrollments are higher.[13]

Teacher Salaries and Teacher Quality

Greater competition may also influence how inputs are allocated and rewarded. So, more teachers may be hired (displacing other inputs), and these teachers may face different payment systems. As one possibility, it may encourage districts to hire teachers of higher quality, and put pressure on teachers to deliver education that is more valuable to students (reducing teacher rents); this may raise either teacher numbers or teacher quality per dollar expended.[14] The research on teacher inputs can be summarized, with teacher quality measured in terms of teacher pay, conditions, and hours of instruction.

Several studies report on how teacher pay is influenced by competition. Using district-level data in Ohio, Vedder and Hall (2000), found average teacher salaries were higher either as within-state county private school enrollments rose, or as the number of public school districts in a county increased. However, the effects are substantively small: a one standard deviation increase in private school enrollment would raise average public school salaries by approximately 1 percent ($380); and going from 1 to 12 public school districts in a county raises salaries by 2 percent ($808). Borland and Howson (1993, 1995) found competition raises teacher salaries for districts in Kentucky; but, again, the effect is small, with salaries in low-competition districts reduced by approximately $700. Finally, Hoxby (1994) found a one standard deviation increase in the Catholic enrollment share increased public school teacher pay by .33 standard deviations ($794 in year 2000 dollars), a substantively significant effect.

Teacher conditions may also be influenced by the extent of competition. Marlow (2000) correlated Herfindahl Index values against the student-teacher ratio for California: a one standard deviation reduction in the HI raises student-teacher ratios by .45–.48 standard deviations (although this estimate is sensitive to model specification). Arum (1996) found the student-teacher ratio in public schools was correlated with private school enrollment across the states: for each increase of five percentage points in the private school sector (approximately one standard deviation difference when enrollment is measured across counties), public schools had 1 less student per teacher (.47 of a standard deviation).[15] Also using national data, Hoxby (2000a) correlated interdistrict choice and student-teacher ratios: instrumental variable estimations show a one standard deviation increase in choice (.27) reduces student-teacher ratios by .72 students (0.34 of a standard deviation). (But this result holds only for three of five IV estimations, and for none of the OLS estimations.) Finally, Hoxby (2000b) found more choice leads to more working hours for teachers: a one standard deviation increase in choice (0.27, from Hoxby, 2000a) raises instructional and noninstructional hours by .62 and .3 hours respectively, i.e., around 2–4 percent. The effects on other working conditions for teachers are mixed.[16]

Private School Enrollments

Competition is of course a two-way phenomenon: public schools themselves represent competition for private schools. Thus, the demand for private schooling is anticipated to be lower, when public schools compete against each other.

Smith and Meier (1995) found no relationship between lagged public school performance and private school enrollment for Florida. However, Goldhaber (1999) found that higher public school graduation rates (weakly) reduce enrollments in private schools in New York state. Martin-Vazquez and Seaman (1985) modeled primary/secondary private school enrollment against both district and school-level public competition; they found insignificant coefficients for each form of competition, but the negative sign on the interaction term is (weakly) supportive of higher district-choice reducing private schooling demand. Wrinkle et al. (1999) used data across 73 Texas counties but found that higher public school performance raised private school enrollments (contrary to the hypothesis that competition improves outcomes). They found no correlation between lagged private enrollment and pass rates. Using data from the nineteenth century in California, Downes (1996) correlates the number of students per district with the county private enrollment share, finding that more competition between public schools raises their enrollments relative to the private sector. However, the effect is not statistically significant. Hoxby (2000a) regressed the share of students in private schooling on instrumented measures of district choice: four of the five estimations show greater district choice reduces private school student numbers (again, OLS estimation shows no significant effects). Where district choice increases by one standard deviation, the share of students in private schools falls by .18 standard deviations (1.1 percentage points).

Housing Prices

Given local education funding, house prices serve as a way to capitalize the quality of public schooling. By extension, if competition raises educational quality, it should also raise house prices. One study reports on this relationship (but other models are pertinent, e.g., Brasington, 2000). Using Census data, Barrow and Rouse (2000) model the relationship between state aid for education and house prices, with the sample divided into high, average, and low Herfindahl competition. Increases in state aid positively affect house prices, but most evidently in districts where competition is strong. Hence, more competitive districts may be more efficient, insofar as this is capitalized into house prices.

Wages

Earnings of educated adults may be a useful indicator of education quality (or the extent to which education generates human capital). Using individual-level data from the NLS72, Jepsen (2002) regressed (with 2SLS) log wages against four different measures of private school competition. Only one measure—county-level competition—generates statistically significant effects, with a one standard deviation increase in private school enrollments raising hourly wages by .09 standard deviations, or around 4 percent (no statistically significant effects emerge using OLS). Using NLSY (1979–90), Hoxby (1994) also found a positive (but substantively small) effect on wages from increases in Catholic schooling enrollment: a one standard deviation increase in this competition raises wages at age 24 by 1 percent. Using Census data on metropolitan areas, Hoxby (2000a) found district choice raises wages. Again, the effects appear small: a one standard deviation increase in district choice raises wages by .01–.05 standard deviations; the effect of school choice is not found to be statistically significant for wages.

Sensitivity Analysis

The effects of competition appear to be consistently but not uniformly positive across these diverse education measures. Given the different outcome variables and the range of estimation techniques, this consistency suggests the results are reasonably valid. Nevertheless, tests of sensitivity are appropriate to check for a systematic bias in the evidence. It is not possible to test for publication bias. Plotting effect sizes is not meaningful with small samples (a test proposed by Shadish and Haddock, 1994), and the outcome measures cannot be pooled. Instead, the sensitivity analyses within each study are discussed and the discrepancies across results discussed.

Overall, the sensitivity tests suggest that these results are not typically robust to alternative specifications. There are only a few studies where a correlation showing the beneficial impact of competition cannot be undermined, either by an alternative estimation technique or model specification. For example, Kenny and Schmidt (1994) reported on the sensitivity of their estimation of lower competition on per pupil expenditure. The relationship is statistically significant with the predicted value of "less competition." However, no statistically significant relationship emerges either with "less competition" rederived in two equally plausible ways, or with the actual value of district competition. Martin-Vazquez and Seaman (1985) found no threshold effect for competition; and their sensitivity tests reported weaker results (for example, normalizing the square mileage of the metropolitan areas generates statistical insignificance in all cases). Vedder and Hall (2000) reported five sensitivity tests: adjusting for ability; adding in dummy variables to control for large cities; excluding school districts with greater than 10,000 students; including only disadvantaged students; and including only high socioeconomic status districts. The coefficients on both private school enrollment and competition remain statistically significant, but now vary widely (by factors of 2 and 6 respectively). The lack of robustness reported in these studies is the norm, rather than the exception, across the literature.

A more general critique of the studies may also be offered. Although many studies control for covariates, there is still a possibility that—at this aggregated level—the models are inappropriately specified. However, mis-specification bias may serve to inflate or deflate the point estimate on the measure of competition; there are also no strong theoretical grounds for inclusion of particular covariates. Although the research using instrumental variables appears the most plausible, it is difficult to generalize where different instruments are used. Most of the studies refer to one variant of competition: if there is a correlation between intradistrict and interdistrict competition, the total effects of competition (across the three variants) cannot be estimated. Finally, although there is research across states, counties, and districts, and over reasonable durations, research at the individual student level draws primarily on two surveys—the NELS and NLSY.

Policy Reform and Competition

Competition Policy

The individual results reported suggest (rather than conclusively establish) a potentially important policy: increasing competition—either intradistrict, interdistrict, or from private schools—may raise effectiveness and efficiency, as well as addressing other educational objectives. Although statistically significant, however, the aggregate effects of competition in fact need to be substantively significant. The effects also need to be set within the broader context of educational research and policy.

Economic evidence suggests skepticism about specifying the relationship between inputs and outputs (Hanushek, 1998): efficiency is not easily identified, and the optimal allocation of inputs unclear. Prescriptive policies (e.g., class size reduction, performance-related pay) may therefore be fraught with uncertainties, with possible high deadweight losses. In contrast, the introduction of competition is less prescriptive; it requires policymakers to regulate outcomes, and write effective contracts (requirements for all policies). A procompetitive policy does not require policymakers to make predictions about phenomena that are not easily observed or manipulated, such as the optimal input mix or the preferences of parents; these are determined through the organic interplay of market forces. However, this interplay is hard to prespecify: competition may increase or decrease teacher salaries, for example, and this cannot be predicted *ex ante*. Research on competition may therefore suffer from a kind of "optimistic eclecticism," where any differences are held to be important.[17] In interpreting the research, there is then a danger of "cherry-picking" or publication bias; and although the results are presented as a series, they need not be independent findings. Notwithstanding these caveats, schools might reasonably be considered to optimize academic performance (for which they are most often held publicly accountable), and this has been the main focus in this review. (Also, these performance measures are unlikely to be negatively correlated with other, unspecified but desirable educational outcomes.)

It is also appropriate to be cautious about what policies would follow from a finding that competition improves outcomes. Competition may be promoted in a number of different ways. Schools might be forced to improve their accountability measures, which would allow parents to make a more informed choice. Vouchers might be introduced, or charter schools encouraged. Policies on private schools may be revised: relative to public school choice, however, new private school choice is expensive for parents. Within the business sector, competition may be stimulated through asset divestment; but this is rare in the education sector. The practicalities of each of these policies would need to be thoroughly investigated. In addition, to represent a practical, desirable policy reform, the substantive benefits must be set against any increases in costs that are required to boost competition in education.

The Substantive Benefits of Increased Competition

The substantive significance of competition is summarized in table 6.1, across each of the outcome variables (except housing prices). On a simple vote count, not adjusting for sample size, between 31 percent and 66 percent of estimations are statistically significant and positive; a trivial number of less than 5 percent show competition worsens outcomes. There are benefits from higher competition, but the substantive effects—across the set of outcomes and based on an increase in competition of one standard deviation—appear to be modest.

Educational outcomes are higher in more competitive markets (although column 2 of table 6.1 shows that more than half of all reported estimations were not statistically significant). Using the Herfindahl Index against educational outcomes, a one standard deviation increase in competition would probably increase test scores by approximately .1 standard deviations or about four percentiles.[18] Using either private school enrollments or other proxies as measures of competition, the effect size is probably less than .1, with many fewer results being statistically significant. Somewhat more positive effects are found in studies where simultaneity and omitted variable bias are accounted for, but these too indicate small effects.

Some measures of attainment also appear to be enhanced by competition: using private school enrollments, graduation rates are higher by .08–.18 standard deviations. Spending appears to be ambiguously affected by competition: some evidence (one-fifth of the estimates) suggests more competitive school systems have lower spending, with other evidence (two-fifths) indicating a .2–.4 standard deviation increase in spending. However, efficiency does appear to be positively correlated with competition: this inference is supported both directly by the evidence, and logically from the evidence on achievement and spending. Teacher quality is also affected by competition. Teacher salaries are higher with competition, by approximately .1–.3 standard deviations; but student-teacher ratios are probably lower with competition, up to 1 student lower. Together, these results may indicate reasonably high "full benefits" to teachers from competition; but they also suggest that competition has significant effects on the technology of education (particularly if absolute spending is lower). Finally, student wages are raised by the extent of competition, to the order of approximately 1–4 percent. This wage effect is broadly equivalent to that from one-third to one-half of a year of schooling.

Forms of Increased Competition

Effecting a one standard deviation increase in competition may require substantial (perhaps even nonfeasible) reform. (More speculatively, if internet-learning becomes more available, the education market may rapidly become much more competitive.) Historical evidence gives some indication of the scope for change. Kenny and Schmidt (1994) charted school district numbers and private schooling enrollments for the decades 1949–50 to 1980–81. During this period, the number of school districts fell by 126 percent, 106 percent, and 12 percent; this represents a mean annual change of -8.1 percent. To reverse this sustained trend, and so promote competition, would require substantial structural reform or political commitment. In contrast, the proportions in private schooling have not fluctuated widely over the four decades (at 10.91 percent, 12.13 percent, 9.14 percent, and 9.04 percent). So, for evaluating the effects of tuition tax credits or vouchers, a plausible annual increase in private schooling enrollments might therefore be no more than 2 percentage points (the mean annual change in absolute terms is 1.46 percent). This contrasts with a one standard deviation difference in private schooling at the county level (applied as the metric in the above protocol), of around 7 percentage points.

In summarizing this evidence, the benefits of competition itemized here should not be exaggerated. To repeat, a number of them may in fact be the "same" benefit, but calculated in a different way: the effects of competition on higher test scores, for example, may pass through into higher wages. Although the evidence gains plausibility in that it triangulates well, the effects of competition as represented in table 6.1 cannot be aggregated.

Finally, the equity of increasing competition needs to be considered. The evidence above suggests that competition has the strongest effects for low-income students. The modest gains may therefore be given a higher weight, where they serve a redistributive function. However, there is evidence from voucher programs that higher income families benefit most when choice sets are expanded (Witte, 2000). Also, the cost burden placed on parents will differ depending on whether private school competition or public school competition is encouraged. Evaluation of competition thus depends on who takes advantage of choice, times the payoff to those who are able to choose, and net of the costs of making that additional choice.

The Costs of Increased Competition

The costs of an education system may also change where more competition is being promoted, and such costs may offset the benefits of competitive reforms (for vouchers, see Levin and Driver, 1997). There is limited evidence on how much it costs to foster, regulate, and monitor competition, and on how to maintain competition (over collusion); but, the argument that competition reform is costless in comparing it with other reforms as assumed by Mayer and Peterson (1999, pp. 352–353) is unsubstantiated and implausible.

As well, there are three other important unknowns in interpreting this evidence. One is the duration over which increased competition has effects; another relates to the threshold impact of competition; and the third unknown relates to equity and social cohesion. So, the substantive benefits (e.g., in terms of test scores) may arise only where increased competition has been sustained over a schooling duration. If so, any cost-benefit calculation will have to take account of the long lag before any benefits from competition are realized. Regarding the thresholds, the evidence suggests that competition is nonlinear: the effects are only detectable in highly concentrated markets. Any practical policy would therefore require reform in these very concentrated markets, with little effect being anticipated for markets that are already weakly concentrated. Finally, the notion that competition is equity-enhancing and socially cohesive may be challenged. Market education systems may rank poorly against equity criteria (e.g., with greater segregation and partitioning of student groups, Levin, 1998; Carnoy, 2000). Relatedly, the effects on social cohesion are unknown. Competition may deliver higher technical efficiency, but lower output efficiency, i.e., fail to produce the types of outcomes most valued by society (in deference to those outcomes valued by parents). Where preferences are more readily satisfied, parents may choose education that emphasizes private (individualistic) outcomes, at the expense of education that inculcates the social benefits of education (Manski, 1992). To emphasize, however, these are speculations.

Conclusion

The above evidence shows reasonably consistent evidence of a link between competition (choice) and education quality. Increased competition and higher educational quality are positively correlated. To an economist, this conclusion is highly plausible. However, this simple summary fails to capture another important conclusion from the evidence: the effects of competition on educational outcomes appear substantively modest, between one-third and two-thirds of the estimates lack statistical significance, and the methods applied are often multivariate regressions. This conclusion too might be thought as equally plausible: after all, many factors determine the quality of education provision. Finally, it is the actual benefits—set against any additional induced costs—that must be used to justify specific approaches and policy proposals to generating greater educational productivity.

Notes

1. The two main outcomes that are omitted from this review are changes in parental involvement and measures of satisfaction with schooling. For libertarians, competition is equated with

choice, and choice is an end in itself. Thus, parental involvement and satisfaction are likely to be two useful outcome measures, proxying for the ability to choose.

2. This rejection criterion serves to exclude only one contribution. Specifically, Hoxby (1999b) reports a sizable set of results from market forces. However, the data source for these results is reported as "on author" and may be the same as those estimations attributed to Hoxby in our main text.

3. So, where there are only two schools of 100 students, the HI value is 0.5; where there are 25 equal-size schools, the HI value falls 0.04; where there are 24 schools of 10 students but also one school of 760 students, the HI value is 0.58. One interpretation of the HI is that applied by the Federal Trade Commission. It defines (industrial) markets with HI values below 0.1 as unconcentrated; between 0.1 and 0.18 as moderately concentrated; and above 0.18 as concentrated (Barrow and Rouse, 2000). This definition may have limited pertinence to education markets: based on the results reported below almost all education markets are concentrated.

4. An equivalent argument may be made for intradistrict school choice—low quality districts may stimulate a taxpayer revolt or secession to generate an alternative public school district, i.e., more choice. On changes in the numbers of school districts in the United States since 1960, see Kenny and Schmidt (1994).

5. Relatedly, the precision of the point estimates on the competition measure may also be a function of the level at which competition is measured. As with the literature on resource effects, aggregation to district or regional level may inflate coefficients through omitted variable bias, raising the likelihood of Type I errors (Hanushek et al., 1996; although see Taylor, 2000).

6. Confounding is likely because private schooling will be more affordable to those in wealthier districts (and perhaps because wealthier districts may better lobby for competitive school systems). The income distribution may also influence the demand for private schooling and so the amount of competition: only families above an income threshold will be able to forgo free public schooling (Maranto et al., 2000). As well as the difficulty of controlling for differences in district circumstances, it is also important to establish whether the greatest variation in competition is within or between districts.

7. Mixed results are obtained from sub-samples: no effect of competition is found for schools with less than 25 percent of students eligible for Free School Lunch, but a beneficial effect is found where at least 75 percent of students are eligible. No competitive effects are found at the district-level, however (Hanushek and Rivkin, 2001).

8. In a further adjustment of Smith and Meier's (1995) specification on lagged test scores, Maranto et al. (2000) adjust for inflation in measuring mean district family income. Although the pooled sample shows a negative coefficient, the effect is no longer statistically significant. For the low-income sample, there is a statistically significant negative effect; but there is no effect for the high-income sample. Maranto et al. (2000) run further regressions with additional lags and find more null results. For the negative effects for low-income families, however, the effects appear substantively large: approximately, increasing private school enrollment by one standard deviation reduces the percentage of public school students who pass exams by one standard deviation.

9. In addition, in a non-trivial proportion of the empirical studies the mean and spread of the dependent and key independent variables are not reported. It is therefore not possible to make direct inference on the marginal effects of competition.

10. A full meta-analysis with sensitivity testing is not appropriate for this research: the studies differ in quality and in outcome measures. However, publication may be gauged from a scatter plot of standard errors against respective point estimates. As the effect of competition should not vary with the size of the standard error, this plot should have a line of best that is horizontal: if there is a tendency to report only when the t-ratio is greater than 1.96, as the standard error increases, so must

the coefficient to preserve the ratio greater than 1.96 (see Ashenfelter et al., 1999). Based on 102 point estimates from Table 1, the line of best fit was upward sloping (â > 0, at the 5 percent significance level); this suggests the possible existence of publication bias and so over-statement of the benefits of competition (but is not conclusive because of the different specifications used in the studies).

11. In looking at Tiebout choice, Hoxby (2000a) describes how educational spending may be affected by the demographic mix. Where there is little Tiebout choice for families, then asset-rich and asset-poor families will be mixed into the same district. This will reduce the demand for education by the asset-rich, as they bear a larger burden of public financing of their district's education. But it will raise the demand by the asset-poor. The net effect on spending will depend therefore on the political engagement of these two groups.

12. Hoxby (2000a, 28–29) describes the result thus: "if we compare two schools, the school in the metropolitan area with maximum choice has math scores that rise by more (0.308 percentile points more) for every 100 percent increase in per pupil spending than the school in the metropolitan area with minimum choice." As a summary, when inter-district choice goes from its minimum to its maximum value (from 0 to 1), school productivity rises by 10 percent; achievement is 3.1–5.8 percentile points higher; and spending is 7.6 percent lower.

13. Arum (1996) reports on both student-teacher ratios and expenditure levels (see later in the main text). However, lower student-teacher ratios in states with high private sector enrollment are found to be a result of high expenditures, not greater teachers as a proportion of total staff. Using individual data from High School & Beyond, Arum (1996) finds that competition has a beneficial effect on public school performance primarily because it raises resource levels.

14. Hanushek and Rivkin (2001) argue that a reduction in variance in teacher quality would result from competition, because principals would be able to hire high quality teachers and fire low quality ones (and areas with low competition would also have lower monitoring). Yet, what teacher characteristics raise student performance is not well-identified. As represented in Table 6.1, Hanushek and Rivkin (2001) investigate teacher quality as reflected in the variance in student scores from year to year. Yet, Kane and Staiger (2002) attribute much of the variance in scores to year-on-year random variations, and to variations in sampling.

15. Looking at the gap between public and private school student-teacher ratios, Arum (1996) finds that the larger the private school sector is in a state, the smaller the gap between public and private school student-teacher ratios. When the private school sector is at 10 percent, public school classes are 1.7 students larger. When the private school sector rises to 19 percent, public school classes are the same size as private school classes. This evidence suggests some mimicking of technologies of provision across the public and private sectors.

16. A measure of competition based on private school choice within an area does not produce any statistically significant effects. Plus, Hoxby (2000b) finds no statistically significant correlation between the amount of control and influence that teachers have and either school choice or the share of private school attendance within the metropolitan area. (For other measures of teacher quality, Hoxby, 2000b, does find statistically significant results from greater competition).

17. Thus, the analysis may be incomplete. So, researchers may have (a) missed the benefits and the costs; (b) missed the costs, but found the benefits; (c) missed the benefits, but found the costs; or (d) found both the benefits and the costs. Obviously, if the research is mainly composed of type (b) analysis, then it will show competition as being much more beneficial than, on balance, it really is.

18. The voucher studies of Peterson and Howell (2004) report effect sizes of approximately 0.2. The Tennessee Class Size experiment found effect sizes of approximately 0.2; and the Milwaukee Parental Choice Program found effect sizes of approximately 0.1 (Rouse, 1998).

Chapter 7

School Choice and the Supply of Private Schooling Places
(with Heather Schwartz)

Introduction

In recent years, education reform has focused on increasing school choice. Proponents claim school choice as a "panacea": in liberating suppliers of education (schools) and clients (students and their parents), choice will dramatically improve educational quality (Chubb and Moe, 1990). Inquiry into parents' demand for private schooling is ongoing, but research and evidence about school supply are considerably more limited.[1] Some studies have focused on individual schools or school types (Chubb, 2002), but there has been no systematic review and analysis of the supply function of schooling. Yet, when considering school choice policies and programs, the issue of supply is as important as that of demand. School choice programs rely critically on parents' having options.

There has been limited investigation of the supply function for private schooling, and which types of schools respond to new opportunities. This chapter investigates school supply both generally and through examination of supply behavior as a result of the Milwaukee Parental Choice Program. The following section sets out the ideas underpinning the discussion of the supply of private schooling. It presents national data on private school supply and briefly considers the organizational advantages private schools may have that could affect their supply relative to other school types. This information is considered in relation to the policy instruments used to design a school choice program that would prompt new supply and a review of the extant evidence on the elasticity of private school supply. The next section presents detailed evidence on the changes in supply that have occurred during the operation of the Milwaukee Parental Choice Program. The implications for private school revenues are also considered, in light of changing student compositions. The final section draws policy conclusions.

The Importance of School Supply in Education Reform

Any discussion of the education market must address school supply (as well as parental choice or school demand). The economic, political, legal, and social implications of school choice will depend heavily on which private schools respond to the incentive of new enrollees. (Legislation to encourage charter schools may create more school choice for families [see Gill et al., 2001]. However, charter schools share many characteristics with local public schools, and so their expansion does not have the same implications as the expansion of private schools.) Supporters of vouchers and school choice contend that the availability of publicly funded vouchers will induce new schools to enter the marketplace and existing schools to expand enrollments. A dynamic market will emerge in which the most attractive and effective schools will lead the way, serving as models for other schools.

Which schools and how many schools will respond is a matter of debate. School choice advocates differ on which types of schools will emerge (although a libertarian position would be that any new schooling revealed will be preferred). The first possibility—prompted in part by the perceived inefficiencies of government provision—is that for-profit or secular schools will come forward (Hoxby, 2003b). The second possibility is that religious agencies will come forward to fulfill a demand for faith-based or community-centered schools (Coleman, 1988). In contrast, opponents of school choice argue that the school supply function is inelastic and that few offerings will emerge. Increasing choice will simply mean rising fees at existing schools (Molnar, et al., 1999). An alternative strand of opposition speculates that any forthcoming school supply will either be low quality or doctrinally inappropriate (Ladd, 2002).

If for-profit private schools respond and these schools are more efficient than public schools, then tax savings may be realized (Epple and Romano, 1998). However, for-profit schools may elicit public opposition. If religious schools are supply responsive, then school choice programs may further entangle church and state. This last eventuality may be the most serious if some religiously affiliated or cult schools teach doctrines that undermine social tolerance and civic order. (To others, the expansion of faith-based schooling is a positive development; for a discussion, see Sander, 2001).[2] Also, some schools may be more effective at raising academic achievement (for public-private comparisons, see McEwan [2000]; on charter schools, see Miron and Nelson [2002]; these are reviewed in Chapter 2).

In relation to the debate over school choice, two aspects of private school supply are particularly important. First, current public-private comparisons of achievement and civic attitudes rely on existing distributions of school types (i.e., by religion). If that composition changes, then it will not be legitimate to extrapolate from existing evidence to predict educational outcomes under expanded school choice (on general equilibrium models of school supply, see Nechyba, 2000). Second, supply responsiveness may occur either through expansion of places in existing heterogeneous schools or by the creation of new schools dedicated to voucher enrollees. This distinction is generally neglected in the literature, although it does have significant consequences. If new supply means new schools and not new places, segregation of students by racial, socioeconomic, and religious dimensions may be preserved, or even sharpened. This undermines the argument that vouchers might allow inner-city minority students to enter high-quality suburban schools.

National Data on Private Schools

The national figures for private schooling supply in 1993 and 2000 are given in table 7.1. Over this period the total number of private schools in the United States increased by 4.3 percent, and total enrollment in private schools increased by 6.7 percent.[3] In contrast, total enrollment at public schools increased by 2.3 percent over the 1990s (NCES, 2003). Although the growth rate of private school enrollment was triple that of public school enrollment, the 5.1 million private school students comprise only 11 percent of the nation's elementary and secondary students.

The private school sector has broadly maintained the same proportions of religious and secular schools throughout the 1990s. Religiously affiliated schools consistently comprise 75–78 percent of all private schools and approximately 84 percent of enrollments. But the religious schools as of 2000 encompass a greater range of faiths. Islamic and "Other Christian" schools far outpaced the growth rates of other school types. (The former, still only 0.3 percent of the total private school population, more than doubled throughout the 1990s.) Catholic schools, however, consolidated over the 1990s, yielding fewer schools but a slight increase in total enrollment.

Overall, there has not been a dramatic change in the proportion of children in private schools and this proportion remains low (compared with more than 86 percent of children in public schools). This is critical, because even a 20

Table 7.1 The Growth in Private Schooling across the United States, 1993–2000

Religious Orientation of Schools	Private School Numbers			Private School Enrollments		
	1993–1994	1999–2000	Percent change	1993–1994	1999–2000	Percent change
Nonsectarian	5,542	5,890	6.3	718,661	808,101	12.4
Roman Catholic	8,331	8,102	-2.7	2,448,101	2,511,040	2.6
Christian Evangelical[a]	6,532	6,738	3.2	848,480	957,324	12.8
Other Christian[b]	3,457	4,976	43.9	429,412	631,322	47.0
Other Religious	1,540	702	-54.4	172,771	66,885	-61.3
Jewish	647	691	6.8	171,214	169,751	-0.9
Islamic	71	152	114.1	7,514	18,262	143.0
Total	26,093	27,223	4.3	4,836,442	5,162,684	6.7

Source: National Center for Education Statistics, Private School Surveys 1993–1994, 1999–2000, tables 1 and 2. *Notes:* (a) Christian Evangelical schools: Assembly of God, Baptist, Brethren, Calvinist, Church of Christ, Church of God, Church of God in Christ, Episcopal, Latter Day Saints, Lutheran Church–Missouri Synod, Mennonite, Pentecostal, Presbyterian, Seventh-Day Adventist. (b) Other Christian schools: Amish, Christian (unspecified), Disciples of Christ, Evangelical Lutheran Church in America, Friends, Greek Orthodox, Wisconsin Evangelical Lutheran Synod.

percent expansion in private school supply would reduce the proportion of children in public schools only from 86 percent to 84 percent.

Identification of the Supply Curve

Because national data reflect the equilibrium of supply and demand, to identify the supply curve it is necessary to apply basic economic theory. Such theory can be used to define the supply curve and so to estimate the elasticity of supply of private schools. To empirically identify the slope of the supply curve for a given quality of private schooling, it is necessary to observe shifts in the demand curve, and to ascertain the size and nature of the shift. For example, a shift in the demand curve occurs if a voucher program is introduced. (Other shifts may occur if there is an increase in religiosity, if the quality of public schools deteriorates, or if other forms of school choice are introduced.) A voucher allocated to families of children who attend public schools will reduce the price of attending a private school by the value of the voucher (V). The new demand curve shifts to the right, and the new equilibrium is generated where the market price of private schooling is higher and enrollments are increased. The size of the change depends on the slope of the supply curve, which is the key variable for understanding supply responsiveness.

Typically, voucher advocates assume that the supply of private schooling is perfectly elastic: any shift in demand will be absorbed without an increase in price. But scarce resources such as teachers must be attracted from alternative endeavors, bidding up the prices of these resources, unless there is a complete transfer of these resources from public schools (i.e., perfectly flexible wage contracts and perfectly mobile capital). Equally implausible is the presumption that the supply curve is perfectly inelastic (i.e., any increase in demand is reflected in higher fees without higher enrollments).

Regardless of the degree of elasticity, it is unrealistic to assume that the supply responsiveness of all types of private schooling is homogeneous. A more sensitive depiction of the private schooling market is of multiple markets, such that the supply curve of secular private schools is distinct from the supply curve of religious schools. The supply of new places at existing schools should be distinguished from the supply of new schools. Most analysis of private schools focuses on Catholic schools, but table 7.1 shows the growing importance of schools serving other faiths (it also shows the distinction between the numbers of schools and the numbers of places in schools). To some extent the markets for schools will be linked, insofar as secular private schools are (imperfect) substitutes for religious schools (and public schools are substitutes for each type of private school). The elasticity of supply is therefore identifiable when there are shifts in the demand curve for all private schools or for specific types of schools.

Factors Influencing the Supply Curve

Several factors will influence the slope of the supply curve. For example, the supply curve will be more elastic in the long run than the short run; and supply responsiveness will be greater when an industry is operating below capacity. Also, characteristics that are specific to the private school market, such as student effects and educational technologies, will affect responsiveness.

The most important influence on the supply curve is the technology of private schooling and the elasticity of supply of inputs into private schooling. For example, private schools may possess certain advantages that allow them to expand their facilities or develop new sites relatively cheaply. Not-for-profit schools may also draw on subsidies from donors. Private schools can price student ability and price peer ability, for example, by providing scholarships to low-income, high-ability students, in a way that public schools cannot (Epple and Romano, 1998). Hence, private schools may employ better learning incentives (via scholarships) for students and their peers. Private schools also have advantages in that they can hire uncertified teachers and they face fewer government regulations.

However, most research finds modest advantages to private schools: classroom-based private schools do not function very differently from public schools and so their efficiency advantage is relatively small (see Benveniste et al., 2003).[4] Many parents are risk averse, preferring schooling provision—at least regarding the curriculum—similar to what is available in public schools (Brown, 1992). One robust finding from the literature is that there are few economies of scale in schooling: it is unlikely that a private school will be able to expand enrollments into a large-scale educational corporation without sharply increasing unit costs (Andrews et al., 2002). Different types of schools will also face different constraints on expansion. Religious schools may have a strong advantage in raising funds, more easily obtaining both donations and in-kind resources (such as school facilities located in the church). Yet, a religious school that enrolls large numbers of nonreligious students would have to pay higher salaries to its teachers as the religious mission of the school becomes less prominent (Chambers, 1987). As described fully in Chapter 8, for-profit schools face numerous challenges, not the least of which is establishing brand equity to encourage parents to choose them.

A second influence on the slope of the supply curve relates to the specific design of the school choice program. Voucher and school choice programs can be designed using three policy instruments: regulation, finance, and support services (Levin, 1991, 2002a). A school choice program that is "generous" across these instruments will increase supply by a relatively large amount. If the amount of private schooling increases under a voucher program, then the supply curve is elastic to some extent. However, if a voucher program is generous in financing the full cost of private schooling, and the equilibrium quantity of private schooling is not much increased, then this indicates inelastic supply. (Unfortunately, the stipulations of the program operate either on demand or supply, making inferences about elasticity complex. Some stipulations—such as lowering the costs of provision for private schools by reducing the regulatory burden—will shift the supply curve directly and make calculation of supply elasticity impossible. Other stipulations will affect demand.)

Finally, students are not homogeneous: the average private school student may differ from the marginal student. When deciding to accept a voucher-eligible student, a school must consider the impact on other students (e.g., if the new student is sufficiently pious). These peer effects may be important, particularly for religious schools, and may mean that new supply responses are muted.

Research on Supply Responsiveness

As noted, evidence on the supply responsiveness of private schools is limited.[5] Table 7.2 reviews studies that have estimated the supply elasticity of schooling using regression analysis. The results are mixed. Frey (1983) finds that whereas the elasticity of supply of private primary schooling is 0.2 (inelastic), the elasticity of supply of private secondary schooling is 2.0 (elastic). Using combined data for primary and secondary schooling, Brasington (2000) and Downes and Greenstein (1996) find highly inelastic supply curves not significantly different from zero. Finally, from Goldhaber's (1996) estimation of the determinants of the private school enrollment rate, it is possible to calculate several elasticities. However, one is not significantly different from zero, a second shows an elasticity of (at most) 1.2, and a third estimate is not precisely determined.

One relevant report summarizes survey findings from five hundred private schools regarding their willingness to participate in a transfer program from overcrowded public schools (Muraskin and Stullich, 1998). Aggregate figures indicate that private schools may be supply responsive: if the schools' current policies could be maintained, 77 percent said they would be (definitely or probably) willing to accept public school students. But participation rates drop sharply if additional conditions are placed on the schools. If students were to

Table 7.2 Parameter Estimates for Elasticity of Supply of Private Schooling

	Estimate	*Data*	
		Year	*Source*
Primary/Secondary	0.00	1979	California[a]
	0.01	1991	Ohio[b]
Primary	0.20	1968-78	NCES[c]
Secondary	2.00	1968-78	NCES[c]

[a]Brasington (2000). [b]Frey (1983). [c]Downes and Greenstein (1996).

be randomly assigned to the private school, participation falls to 36 percent; if state assessments were mandated, the rate falls to 33 percent; and if special needs students were to be accepted, the rate falls to 15 percent. For the religious schools, participation propensities were strongly influenced by whether or not a transfer student could be exempt from religious instruction: only 25 percent of schools would participate under such conditions.

However, a majority of surveyed private schools were not operating at full capacity and so may respond to increases in short-term demand. Approximately two-thirds of the private schools surveyed were operating at less than 80 percent capacity. The report estimated that the total private schools in the twenty-two districts could accommodate 185,000 additional students. Schools operating at the lowest levels of capacity (and thus potentially the most responsive to increased demand) tended to be small, secular elementary schools with low tuition levels. Interestingly, 70 percent of private schools with tuition of $8,000 or more were operating at nearly full capacity whereas only 29 percent of schools charging tuition of $2,000 or less were operating at nearly full capacity. Supply responsiveness may therefore be greater at the low-priced schools. The most important conclusion, however, is that a 20 percent increase in private school places nationally—which is far beyond any historical trend—would amount to only one million new places, that is, less than 2 percent of the public school population.[6] Even with very generous vouchers, the majority of students by far would remain in public schools for at least the next decade.

Supply Responsiveness in the Milwaukee Parental Choice Program

Design of the School Choice Program

The Milwaukee Parental Choice Program (MPCP), a long-standing and large voucher program, is a useful case study for estimating the elasticity of the supply of private schooling (see Witte, 2000; Rouse, 1998). It is also considered a generous voucher program according to the three policy design instruments: school eligibility and restrictions, finance, and support services.

Eligibility for the program is limited to students in the Milwaukee Public Schools from low-income families. Initially, the program was restricted to nonreligious schools, but it was expanded in 1998 to religious schools. The number of schools participating in MPCP quadrupled once religious schools were allowed to join, and enrollment has grown steadily, from 341 students in 1991 to 11,156 in 2003.

As regards finance, the Wisconsin Department of Public Instruction (DPI) pays participating schools the lesser of (a) the schools' per-pupil operating and debt service cost or (b) the per-pupil voucher cap.[7] MPCP has raised the cap on its voucher amount from $2,446 in 1991 to $5,783. This 2003 cap amount exceeds almost 40 percent of participating schools' reported costs, suggesting that the voucher amount is generous.

Regulation of MPCP is minimal. The DPI does not require that schools be accredited, serve special education students, perform criminal background checks on employees, or administer specific tests. The state superintendent has requested the state legislature to pass a bill that would increase the DPI's regulatory powers, including prohibiting schools that commit malfeasance in a current year from participating in MPCP in future years. (The press has reported on this phenomenon in some MPCP schools.)

In terms of support services, private schools participating in the program are not required to bus voucher students. The Milwaukee Public School system will provide busing depending on the location of the school relative to the voucher student's home.

Given the generosity of MPCP, a reasonably robust supply response may be expected. To describe the actual responsiveness of the private school sector to the increased demand via Milwaukee vouchers, these questions were posed: (1) How many and what are the characteristics of voucher-participating schools, in terms of religious or other affiliation? (2) How are voucher students distributed across the voucher-participating schools? (3) How quickly did the private school sector respond to the voucher opportunities? (4) What are the characteristics of the secular schools?

Numbers and Characteristics of Voucher Schools

Table 7.3 shows the numbers of schools that participate in MPCP, by religious orientation.[8] Before 1998, the MPCP consisted entirely of secular schools. Opening the program to religious schools in 1998 generated a sizeable increase in private school participation, as the number of participating schools immediately rose from 23 to 85. The total has since grown to approximately 100 schools, where it appears to have stabilized.

Table 7.3 shows that opening MPCP to religious school participation has not displaced the secular schools within the program. The number of secular schools has in fact trended upward slightly to include 31 participating schools by 2002. In contrast, Catholic schools' participation has declined in recent years from a high of 41 schools in 1998 to only 33 schools by 2002. This suggests

Table 7.3 Schools Participating in Milwaukee Parental Choice Program

Religious Orientation of School	Number of Participating Schools per Academic Year						
	1997	1998	1999	2000	2001	2002	2003
Secular	23	25	25	27	28	31	27
Catholic	N/a	41	39	38	37	33	37
Christian Evangelical	N/a	12	14	19	20	16	22
Other Christian	N/a	4	7	15	12	15	17
Jewish	N/a	1	1	1	1	1	1
Islamic	N/a	2	2	2	2	2	2
Total	23	85	88	102	100	98	106

Source: Public Policy Forum Annual Census and WI Department of Public Instruction.

relatively independent demand for secular versus religious schools as confirmed by the overall share of voucher students attending these schools. Participation of Christian schools (evangelical and "other") has grown. One Jewish school and two Islamic schools also participate. These shifts in participation mean that, by 2002, there was a broader spread of religiously oriented schools participating in MPCP than in 1998.

Distribution of Voucher Students

Table 7.4 shows which school orientations the voucher students attend. Since 1998, approximately one-third of voucher students have attended secular schools. Catholic school representation has decreased over time: there has been a drop from 48 percent to 38 percent of voucher students attending Catholic schools by 2002. A fairly stable percentage of voucher students have attended Christian evangelical (13–20 percent), Jewish (1 percent), and Islamic (3 percent) schools over time. However, "Other Christian" schools saw a marked increase from 2 percent to 10 percent of voucher enrollees from 1998 to 2002.

The concentration of voucher students within schools has risen over time for most school orientations. Increasingly, the voucher program predominantly serves a few schools and finances a high proportion of the students at those schools. Table 7.5 details the proportions of voucher students by the religious orientations of participating schools. Despite the increased supply of schools throughout the 1990s, voucher students increasingly tend to cluster at a small number of them. Participating secular schools in particular have become increasingly voucher-concentrated: voucher students comprised 51 percent of total enrollment at participating secular schools in 1998 and 71 percent in 2002. Participating Catholic schools, in contrast, have the lowest concentration of voucher

Table 7.4 Students Participating in Milwaukee Parental Choice Program

Religious Orientation of School	Voucher Enrollees per Academic Year						
	1997	1998	1999	2000	2001	2002	2003
Secular							
Number of Enrollees	1,497	1,843	2,338	2,685	3,284	3,747	3,837
% of Total Voucher Enrollees	100.0	30.7	33.0	28.6	31.5	34.4	30.1
Catholic							
Number of Enrollees	N/a	2,879	3,448	3,829	4,355	4,127	4,940
% of Total Voucher Enrollees	N/a	48.0	48.7	40.8	41.8	37.8	38.8
Christian Evangelical							
Number of Enrollees	N/a	868	1,119	1,862	1,826	1,441	1,968
Percent of Total Voucher Enrollees	N/a	14.5	15.8	19.9	17.5	13.2	15.6
Other Christian							
Number of Enrollees	N/a	146	198	606	529	1,095	1,432
% of Total Voucher Enrollees	N/a	2.4	2.8	6.5	5.1	10.0	11.2
Jewish							
Number of Enrollees	N/a	76	74	89	90	106	96
% of Total Voucher Enrollees	N/a	1.3	1.0	0.9	0.8	1.0	0.7
Islamic							
Number of Enrollees	N/a	184	87	308	343	392	444
% of Total Voucher Enrollees	N/a	3.1	1.2	3.3	3.3	3.6	3.4
Total Enrollees	1,497	5,996	7,085	9,379	10,427	10,908	12,735

Source: Public Policy Forum Annual Census.

students; nevertheless, these schools show a 10 percent increase in concentration since 1998, such that 35 percent of participating Catholic school students had vouchers in 2002. Christian evangelical schools mirrored the secular school trend, and by 2002 71 percent of enrollees at these schools had vouchers. Interestingly, although "Other Christian" schools commanded an increasing share of voucher students from 1998–2002 (see table 7.4), these schools tended to

Table 7.5 Concentration of Voucher Students within Participating Schools in Milwaukee Parental Choice Program

Religious Orientation of School	Voucher Enrollees as Percent of Total Enrollees at Participating Schools				
	1998	1999	2000	2001	2002
Secular	51.4	59.8	61.6	66.7	70.5
Catholic	25.6	28.3	31.5	36.5	35.4
Christian Evangelical	58.6	64.3	71.6	69.9	70.9
Other Christian	79.3	40.8	57.5	25.8	40.9
Jewish	44.4	45.1	49.4	50.0	56.1
Islamic	95.3	86.1	77.6	76.7	82.5

Source: Public Policy Forum Annual Census.

become less voucher-concentrated over time (see table 7.5). This shows that the overall student population at "Other Christian" participating schools expanded more quickly than did voucher students. Finally, the two Islamic participating schools were the most voucher-concentrated, with 77–95 percent of enrollees holding vouchers.

Table 7.6 shows the numbers of schools where over 80 percent of students have vouchers. We define these as "voucher schools." Whereas in 1998, voucher schools were only 28 percent of all participating schools, by 2002 they comprised 40 percent. Indeed, as of 2002, 12 participating schools were composed entirely of voucher-funded enrollees. Secular schools represent the largest portion of voucher schools (17 out of 41 schools in 2002), but religiously affiliated

Table 7.6 Schools Where Voucher Students Comprise 80 Percent or More of School Population

Religious Orientation of School	Number of Schools with at Least 80 Percent Voucher Enrollees				
	1998	1999	2000	2001	2002
Secular	14	13	17	15	17
Catholic	4	3	6	10	8
Christian Evangelical	2	4	9	6	9
Other Christian	1	0	6	4	6
Jewish	0	0	0	0	0
Islamic	2	1	1	1	1
Total	23	21	39	36	41
Percent of Total Participating Schools	28%	23%	39%	35%	40%

Source: Public Policy Forum Annual Census.

schools have shown a dramatic increase in becoming voucher schools. The number of Catholic voucher schools doubled over time, and the number of Christian evangelical voucher schools increased from two in 1998 to nine in 2000. Despite an increased number of participating schools, a voucher student in 2002 is more likely to attend a voucher school.

Private School Responsiveness to Voucher Opportunities

The growth of private schooling in Milwaukee was considerably above the national and state trend. Whereas from 1993 to 2000 the number of private schools in Wisconsin rose at a rate similar to the national average (from 954 to 991 schools, or 4 percent), the number of private schools in Milwaukee grew 18 percent (from 116 schools in 1993 to 137 schools in 2000). There was a corresponding increase of 16 percent in private school enrollment in Milwaukee compared with a 7 percent increase nationally. This suggests a reasonably robust response to the opportunities created by the voucher program.

Table 7.7 shows the ages of the private schools participating in the program, by religious orientation. This more directly shows the link between MPCP and growth in participating private schools: 46 percent of the 105 private schools that have participated over time were founded after the MPCP started in 1991. The rate of change in supply is most accelerated in 1998–2003, when MPCP allowed religious schools to participate. This post-1998 acceleration may be due in part to the 1998 Wisconsin Supreme Court ruling, which increased the certainty of the program's continuation.

Table 7.7 also shows how supply responsiveness varies by religious orientation in terms of new school places. There has been a steady growth in the number

Table 7.7 Age of Participating Schools in MPCP

Religious Orientation of School	Number of Participating Schools by Year in Which Founded			
	Pre-1990	1990–1997	1998–1999	2000–2003
Secular	7	10	9	8
Catholic	28	2	3	2
Christian Evangelical	11	1	5	0
Other Christian	9	2	2	3
Jewish	1	0	0	0
Islamic	1	1	0	0
Total	57	16	19	13

Source: Public Policy Forum Annual Census.

of secular schools since 1990: of the 34 that have participated in the MPCP, 27 were founded after the commencement of the program. This response rate, which is sustained over the entire period 1990–2003, exceeds that of religiously affiliated participating schools. For religious schools, supply was responsive in the short run: from a base of 56 religious schools, 10 new schools opened in 1998–1999. However, in the three subsequent years (2000–2003), only 5 additional religiously affiliated schools opened, suggesting that, after the initial fillip, the supply of religious private schools was relatively flat.

The responses of particular religions are also noteworthy: of the 35 Catholic schools that have participated in MPCP, only 5 had been founded since 1998. There were no new participating Jewish and Islamic schools founded after 1998. Given this disjuncture between the large short-run response by religious schools and the relatively muted medium-run response, any conclusion about the elasticity of supply via religious school start-ups must be hedged. Yet as is clear from table 7.4, religious schools continued to accommodate growing numbers of voucher students by absorbing them into existing schools. In this sense, the long-run expansion of the private-religious sector occurred primarily by making more places available in existing schools, whereas the private-secular sector expanded by making more places available and by opening new schools. However, some schools operating before MPCP began may have received a windfall by declaring students already enrolled to be voucher eligible. This is likely for schools that have not expanded total enrollments by the number of voucher recipients at the school.

Characteristics of the Participating Secular Schools

Religious schools clearly have a cost advantage in the market in being able to draw on donations and resources. Thus it is of interest to know which secular schools participate in MPCP and what is distinctive about their provision.

The majority of the 31 secular schools that have participated in MPCP since 1998 are not-for-profit schools and are not accredited. Only one secular school can be confirmed as for-profit.[9] Of the 21 secular schools for which we were able to obtain information, two were accredited, two additional schools were seeking accreditation, and the remaining 17 were not accredited.

Participating secular schools have a wide variety of missions and pedagogies. To the extent that secular schools have been the most responsive to MPCP (70.5% of secular school students have vouchers; 17 are voucher schools), their diversity of program offerings may reflect the diversity of MPCP parents' tastes. These schools' disparate pedagogies include Afro-centric curriculum,

Montessori, Waldorf, multiple intelligences, traditional education, technology-centric, school-to-work, and bilingual approaches. Before 1998, none of the secular schools served students with special education needs (after 1998 only one of the 113 participating schools did).

At least two secular schools have been subject to investigation, and an additional two schools closed after their MPCP applications were denied by the state. Other changes in the supply of secular schools included two that became charter schools, and three schools that failed to file financial documentation in 2002 requisite to receiving payment for enrolled voucher students.

School Budget Constraints for Participating in MPCP

Basic economics suggests that a sufficient supply of new schools will be forthcoming if the profits (or surpluses) from operating a voucher school are high enough; it is simply a matter of how high such profits would have to be and whether the taxpayers are willing to bear the expense. However, data on the costs of private schooling are extremely difficult to obtain: there is only limited reporting of fees (and these are often "sticker prices"); in addition to fees, private schools receive charitable donations, share facilities (e.g., with churches), and receive in-kind contributions from parents. Without such information about the costs of private schooling, school districts may offer vouchers that are either overly generous or insufficient, such that no new supply is forthcoming (see PFAW, 2000). Unfortunately, our analysis using information from MPCP is inconclusive: it is not possible to trace the implications for the budget constraints of schools without information on the average fees private schools would charge.

Conclusion

The intent of this chapter, after reviewing the research on school supply and analyzing recent data from the Milwaukee Parental Choice Program, is to inform debates about school choice. Several conclusions are notable.

First, the size of the private school sector would require seismic growth to impinge on the public school system. Even a doubling of the private school sector would still leave three-quarters of all students in the public school system. That said, there is a growing trend for private schools that serve different religious groups, perhaps reflecting a greater differentiation of tastes for education.

Second, evidence on school supply responsiveness is not easy to interpret. Published studies are decades old, and there are likely to be many changes to demand and supply, making identification of the supply curve very difficult. It is this challenge that suggests that examining supply in response to a specific program would be informative.

Third, MPCP data indicate that about 30 percent of participating schools are secular, with the remainder religiously affiliated. When MPCP was first expanded to include religious schools in 1998, the number of participating schools quadrupled, from 23 to 85. Since then the number has leveled out to approximately 100 schools. Although most of the religious schools are Catholic, this number is falling over time, meaning that an expanded range of schooling options for families is being created. MPCP therefore promotes considerable freedom of choice for parents, both for religious and secular education.

Fourth, voucher student enrollments in MPCP are increasingly a majority within these schools: by 2001, 40 percent of participating schools had more than 80 percent of their students who claim vouchers. This consolidation of voucher students within schools may raise concerns about the sorting of students into particular communities, leading to social segregation. Consolidation may also place schools at risk by relying on one funding source: the Wisconsin DPI. Even if the annual budget allocations and the voucher amount remain stable, such voucher schools may be subject to regulatory capture.

Fifth, the supply of new schools appears reasonably elastic: 46 percent of participating schools, a mix of secular and religious, were founded after the program was introduced. For some schools in existence before the introduction of MPCP, however, the voucher funding appears to act as a windfall payment (where fee-paying students have become voucher students). Moreover, although school supply response is reasonably robust, it is worth noting that the Milwaukee program is considerably more generous than other voucher programs (e.g., in Cleveland).

Sixth, explaining private school supply behavior in terms of revenue functions is complex. Ideally, the design of a school choice program should take account of the revenue functions facing schools, along with the willingness of families to pay. However, very limited, imprecise data are available on the budgets of private schools. Also, voucher students may create peer effects within a school that vary according to the characteristics of the school; these peer effects may impact significantly on all revenue sources for a school. This phenomenon may also be related to schools that are able to claim voucher funds for those who were previously fee-paying students. Data from MPCP indicate that many schools report costs above the value of the voucher (suggesting that they subsidize these students from other revenue sources) and costs only weakly converging to the voucher amount. (Plausibly, schools with higher proportions of voucher students do track their costs more closely to the value of the voucher.)

Finally, evidence from MPCP is nonetheless relevant for predictions about the characteristics of an education system with a large-scale voucher program. Several types of supply—secular and religious (but not for-profit)—are responsive to the voucher, suggesting that an expanded sector might have roughly the same composition of secular and religious schools as there is currently. However, the degree of responsiveness appears somewhat larger than what typically emerges from general equilibrium models (see Nechyba, 2003). The religious schools represent a broader array of faiths; and the secular schools appear to offer diverse curricula, rather than mimicking those of public schools. These findings give credence to general equilibrium models that emphasize product differentiation in the choice of school. Given the expansion of schools rather than places, there may be questions about segregation by ethnicity, religion, or socioeconomic status. In addition, only one of approximately 100 participating schools in Milwaukee offers special education services, suggesting there may be very limited private school supply for students with special needs. Finally, the limited understanding of private school financing may cause problems in ensuring voucher students' access and in funding. In some areas of the country (e.g., rural), access to school may be constrained because of high costs that are not captured in the voucher value. And, in some cases, vouchers may offer windfalls to students who would have enrolled in private schools regardless and, therefore, increase the funds required to operate a large-scale voucher program.

Notes

1. There is growing evidence that parents' and students' satisfaction levels rise as they become more active in choosing education (see Peterson and Hassel, 1998; Teske and Schneider, 2001; Witte, 1999). There is also some debate as to whether there is a large untapped demand by public school students for private school education (on high satisfaction levels with existing public schools, see Moe, 2001; on the waiting lists for private vouchers, see Peterson et al., 2002).

2. The types of religious schools that would promote socially undesirable activities may be hard to identify. Coleman (1988) argues that private–religious schools may effectively link generations of families and communities. Godwin et al. (2001) find that nonfundamentalist private schools promote slightly greater amounts of tolerance and support for democratic norms than public schools (see also Campbell, 2001). For a general discussion, see Levinson and Levinson (2003).

3. These increases may be overstated somewhat as NCES experienced lower survey response rates in 1993 than in 2000.

4. Glomm et al. (2005) map out the influences on the locations of charter schools, finding that charter schools are located in areas of greater demographic diversity; Henig and MacDonald

(2002) find that charter schools are more likely to locate in areas with high proportions of African American and Hispanic families but where income levels are moderate (not low).

5. On very little evidence, Howell and Peterson (2002) speculate that a universal voucher program would attract 10–15 percent of all existing public school students; that is, it would double the current size of the private sector. See also the discussion by Hoxby (2003b).

6. Other studies and commentaries compare the sticker price fees at private schools with the average per-pupil expenditure in the local public schools (Salisbury, 2003). Where the private school sticker price is below public school expenditures, under a voucher program it is concluded that the private school supply would be highly (perfectly) elastic. Such a conclusion critically depends on: (1) the accuracy of the sticker price to represent the cost of private schooling; (2) equivalent costs to educate the voucher student as to educate the original private school student; and (3) surplus capacity of inputs into private schooling. Each of these assumptions is unrealistic.

7. The MPCP is unique among voucher programs as it reimburses participating schools for per-pupil expenditures (up to the voucher cap) rather than for the tuition rate (PFAW, 2000).

8. Two sources are available about participation in MPCP: the Wisconsin Department of Public Instruction and the Public Policy Forum in its annual census. There is a slight discrepancy between the numbers declared by these two sources, but this discrepancy does not materially alter the conclusions drawn here. We primarily use the census data because it gives information on the religious orientation of the schools.

9. It is possible that there are additional for-profit secular schools as there is no information about the profit type of 9 out of the 24 secular schools that participated in 1998 or later.

Chapter 8

The Potential of For-Profit Schools for Educational Reform

Introduction

Private schools preceded public schools in American history. Although schooling was often a cottage industry in colonial times in which an adult might provide tutoring for children in a private household, private schools as organized institutions were not set out to yield profits. These schools were likely to be church-affiliated and dedicated to particular educational, philosophical, and religious values. Only at the beginning of the nineteenth century do we see the rise of the common or public school, as each of the states adopted education as a constitutional responsibility.

Towards the end of the nineteenth century, a system of Catholic schools was established to shield Catholic students from the Protestant bias found in public schools and to provide religious instruction (Tyack, 1974, 84–86). In terms of sheer numbers of schools and enrollments, the Catholic schools soon outnumbered the other independent schools in enrollments, as presently. At the same time, public schooling continued to expand, and by the turn of the twentieth century almost all states had compulsory schooling laws. A major controversy arose over whether independent or private schools could meet compulsory attendance requirements. This issue was resolved by the U.S. Supreme Court in 1925 in *Pierce vs. Society of Sisters* which declared that compulsory schooling laws could be met in any independent school approved by the state.

What is notable in this brief historical flow is the absence of a significant presence of for-profit schools in the development of the U.S. educational system. This raises the question as to whether there is something about education that does not lend itself well to for-profit operations. There are undoubtedly a relatively small number of family-run schools that provide a living for these families. However, even these are not common, and there is very little evidence of substantial returns on investment. In general, long hours and constant attention to a specific clientele seem to be needed to make these schools succeed.

The last decade has seen the rise of for-profit companies in elementary and secondary, but few of them own schools. Rather, they have established businesses for contracting with school districts or charter schools, functioning as Education Management Organizations (EMOs). These schools continue to function as public schools, even as they are serviced by EMOs. As charter schools have grown in numbers, EMOs have grown along side them. Reinforcing this link, charter schools also turn to EMOs because (before 2002) charter funding structures tend to disadvantage schools that do not have access to capital funds. EMOs may provide access to start-up funds.

In addition, EMOs have been active in contracting with school districts to operate specific schools within those districts, usually schools with poor educational results and many challenges. The district provides a certain amount of funding, which may be above the amount allocated to public schools if the EMO does not have to provide services which are organized at the district level. (In some cases, EMOs have been able to get additional funding from philanthropic organizations because of their commitment to school reform.) One advantage of contracting directly with the districts is the availability of facilities and a ready cohort of students. In contrast, the establishment of new charter schools requires a search for and financing of a proper facility.

Given this history, it is legitimate to examine whether for-profit EMOs have the potential to reform public education. This leads to two further questions: (i) Can EMOs succeed as a business, and under what conditions? (ii) Are EMOs likely to stimulate changes in elementary and secondary schools that will improve educational outcomes? Clearly, if EMOs are not adequately profitable, they are unlikely to have an educational impact in the long run. Even if they prosper, though, they may not be any different from—in terms of innovation and organization—the public schools.

Can For-Profit EMOs Be Profitable?

It is useful to begin by setting out the early expectations of both the founders of EMOs and the investment community as to why this looked like a promising opportunity. In the early 1990s, the climate for privatizing public services had been well-established. The Reagan and Bush administrations had criticized government as the problem rather than the solution and had praised the private sector, deregulation, and tax reduction as the solution to inadequate public services. The Clinton administration followed up this appeal with an agenda of "Reinventing Government" (e.g., privatizing health care through HMOs).

The specific appeal to the investment community for privatizing elementary and secondary education was a sector spending almost $1 billion per day, the largest government sector that has been untouched by privatization. Wall Street firms went to their investment communities with glossy presentations showing declines in test scores, poor test results relative to other countries, rising educational expenditures, and particular educational challenges in the inner cities (Merrill Lynch, 1999). Many of these critiques were overstated, and the causes of the shortcomings were oversimplified as being the fruits of leaving education to government bureaucracies. It was asserted that funds were being spent inefficiently, with too little being allocated to the classroom and too much to central administrative headquarters of school districts. The investment industry argued that if the education sector were privatized, its performance would rise, and the returns would be substantial because of the gains in efficiency across such a large system. Indeed, such investments were referred to as opportunities to do well (high returns) by doing good (improving education); they were both economically and morally justified.

This argument had one major weakness. Few of those who decided to enter the business of education had studied carefully the economics or politics of education. They failed to look carefully at resource allocation in the public schools and the underlying justification, primarily in the belief that whatever was being done must be inefficient and could be easily improved on. They believed that there were large economies of scale in running schools, so that a large company could prosper in many school districts. Moreover, they did not appreciate the politics of education and the fact that when public funds are being allocated there must be political decisionmaking.

What was not appreciated sufficiently was: (1) education is a tough business because it is regulated, monitored, and subject to the demands of multiple agencies and audiences and layers of government funding; (2) EMOs must incur high marketing costs that public schools do not face; (3) relatively short-term contracts (e.g., of 3–5 years) are risky in amortizing investment at school sites, whether or not the EMO performs efficiently; (4) the economies of scale that were anticipated do not exist; and (5) a uniform educational model akin to a single business model cannot be easily applied, particularly when quality control is not performed within the local district.

Education Is a Tough Business

Ideally, a business would like to provide a concrete product or service with as few restrictions as possible and delivered under stable conditions to a predictable clientele. Risk, change, and uncertainty are all costly. Education is characterized by multiple goals and authorities with constant shifts in the relative importance of each as political, demographic, and social trends intervene. Multiple goals include establishing schools as safe and disciplined environments accommodating a wide variety of student needs, ranging from those of gifted students to those of handicapped students. The goals are not limited to academic study of a wide range of subjects, they also include development of creativity, character, problem-solving, personal health and hygiene, patriotism, and citizenship. From the standpoint of any productive enterprise, this is a complicated production process because it is one in which many products must be produced simultaneously and with limited resources that require continuous trade-offs among goals. Furthermore, student capabilities, motivations, and expectations have a profound influence on educational outcomes, factors that are often beyond the control of schools.

Schools are subject to interventions and pressures of three government bodies and the demands of their clientele. For example, contracted schools within school districts are governed by federal, state, and local laws, regulations, and policies. These strictures and guidelines are voluminous and often difficult to interpret or understand because of their multitudinous details and complexity. As noted above in Chapter 3, these regulations are numerous. Federal reauthorization of the Elementary and Secondary Education Act ("No Child Left Behind") must be translated into specific procedures and regulations by federal agencies for transmission to the states; each state will interpret these details and apply them to local districts, providing hundreds of new regulations and thousands of pages of interpretation for school authorities. Three levels of government monitor contract schools in each district.

As well, the clientele and potential clientele for these schools apply pressure in a variety of ways. For charter schools and contract schools, families have the prerogative of choice and will leave if they believe that the charter school has not delivered what they want. These families also have access to the charter school board, its directors, and individual staff to press for the services they want for their child. Finally, teacher and other professional organizations often set restrictions on hiring and working conditions based upon either their collective bargaining agreements or their political power.

The result of all of the government regulation and scrutiny and that of the choice options and demands of clientele is that the EMO is subject to competing pressures and changes from many sides, with little stability over time. It must somehow find a way to balance a large number of competing claims, a phenomenon that does not lend itself well to a standard schooling process that will allow substantial uniformity across different sites. Yet, most of the EMOs seek to establish national and regional brands that promote a uniform model, one that is highly consistent from site to site, which confers a brand image and which allows for the exploitation of economies of scale.

Marketing and Contracting Costs

EMOs face costs that do not have to be borne by local school districts. The most important of these are the marketing costs that are required to attract and sign charter schools and districts to contracts. Not only are the EMOs competing against other EMOs, but there is an overall resistance by many citizens and educators to delegating schools to for-profit management. To many, the disagreement is fundamental, the view that profits will come from squeezing services rather than from greater efficiency. They believe that such schools have incentives to select students who will be least problematic and require few services outside of routinized instruction, leaving the more costly students to the regular public schools. The result is that EMOs must engage in substantial promotion and marketing activities, from advertising to participating in the regional and national conventions of education associations, and also to direct marketing of the EMO concept and services to school districts. The last of these may consist of direct appeals to administrators and schools boards through expensive retreats at which the potential decisionmakers are approached.

Marketing activity requires substantial personnel who solicit school districts and potential charter school organizers or even offer to do all of the preparation of applying for charter school status. For every contract that is obtained, the EMO may have to solicit intensively among a much larger number of potential districts or charter school sponsors. Even when there is overall agreement on establishing a contractual relation, the details must be worked out. Both of these marketing and contracting costs must be funded ultimately from the operational revenues received from states or school districts; these are excess expenses that are not intrinsic to school districts that operate their own schools. Moreover, these actions are unlikely to improve the informational exchange between the school and the parents (in comparison to the argument that advertising conveys product information to demanders).

Short-term Contracts

Typical contracts between EMOs and charter schools or school districts are only three to five years. This means that overhead costs for establishing the contract and gearing up to operate the school must be amortized over a relatively short period of time, especially given the risks of contract nonrenewal. Contracts may not be renewed for poor performance, and many argue that it does take at least five years to turn around a failing school or to get a new charter school on its feet. This means that the EMO faces the possibility of losing contracts before it can amortize appropriately its start-up expenses. But the situation is also precarious if the EMO succeeds. Districts seek for-profit EMOs to operate schools that are dysfunctional and performing poorly, not their better schools. Often these dysfunctional schools have poor leadership, unqualified teachers, disruptive students, high pupil mobility, and community factionalism. If the EMO is able to turn the school around within five years, the school district may then have an incentive to take the school back into its own operational fold.

Elusive Economies of Scale

Among the most seriously erroneous assumption built into the business models was that there are substantial economies of scale in education (e.g., Chubb, 2001). The thinking seemed to be as follows. The establishment of a for-profit company will entail a large fixed expenditure but the amount that will be received for each student—multiplied across many students—will generate a fairly large surplus of revenues over costs at the school site. It was thought that there is considerable waste at the school site in conventional public schools, although where the substantial savings were to be realized was never specifically identified. In contrast, private sector enterprises were held to be a model of efficiency and the drive to provide the best quality service. To offset the high fixed costs of a central headquarters, it was only necessary to contract with enough schools such that these fixed costs would be spread across enough schools. This meant that the high costs of getting started and establishing EMOs were to be expected, with large initial infusions of capital in the early period and attendant losses in operations.

But, this thinking suffered from one major weakness. Not only had no one demonstrated the economies of scale that were to be counted on, but the economics of education literature finds that economies of scale set in at fairly low enrollments at both school sites and in school districts. In their full review of economies of scale, Andrews et al. (2002, 255) conclude: "sizable potential cost savings may exist by moving from a very small district (500 or less pupils) to a district with circa 2000–4000 pupils, both in instructional and administrative costs. Per pupil costs may continue to decline slightly until an enrollment of roughly 6,000, when diseconomies of scale start to set in." Operations at the minimum efficient scale are therefore likely to generate annual revenues of less than $60 million.

By 2002, many EMOs had already expanded much beyond the most efficient scale. The reason for this low scale being optimal is that schools have high variable costs. Each new school requires a new facility, administrators, teaching/support staff, equipment and supplies, maintenance, utilities, and other resources. Since schools are labor intensive, virtually the only way to reduce costs substantially is to employ lower-cost teachers and introduce labor-saving technology. But, teachers are not highly paid relative to their responsibilities and to other professional groups, so savings are limited even if there is a large untapped teacher supply at lower rates of pay. Also, the qualifications and performance of the teacher is one of the relatively few attributes of a school that parents can discern, and they will oppose undermining the quality of the teaching and instruction. Moreover, educational technology has historically represented an added cost at school sites rather than a guaranteed way to substitute capital for labor; indeed, EMOs proclaim how much more "high-tech" their administration and assessment systems are, relative to the public schools. There is also little evidence in the research that such technology raises the quality of education (Cuban, 2001).

In practice, EMOs have pursued three strategies for saving costs at the school site. First, they have tried to hire less experienced teachers. However, the problem with this strategy is that younger teachers have lower attachment to their jobs (e.g., they leave to start families, return to college, etc.). This turnover creates additional costs in recruitment and training, and these may completely offset the salary advantage (the industry standard for the costs of losing a teacher are one-third of the salary of the new hire, SBEC, 2000). Second, EMOs have implemented standard operating procedures and low-cost educational strategies that minimize the need for ancillary personnel and provide a bare-bones pedagogy in which all teachers follow a standard script of instruction at each grade level. This approach has raised teacher resignations (particularly amongst teachers who seek more creative opportunities with greater professional autonomy), although it does reduce the costs of teacher turnover in terms of academic disruption (continuity is established through the script, not the individual teacher). However, the approach is less appropriate for higher level courses, where students have advanced beyond the mastery of basic skills. Third, EMOs try to recruit students who are less demanding in terms of resources—specifically, they do not accommodate students with moderate or severe learning disabilities (and they may discourage students with even modest behavioral problems). Some EMOs have argued that they are teaching disadvantaged children (Chubb, 2001). However, such EMOs have two practical advantages over public schools. One is that they may maintain strict requirements on parental participation, discouraging single parent families and those who face difficulties in taking on additional responsibilities. This means that even as the students enrolled are from low-income or low-SES families, these families are motivated and have the capacity to support their children's education. The other advantage is that strict discipline policies can be used to suspend or expel disruptive students. However, expulsions both undermine public relations and simply raise the public costs of education elsewhere in the system.

Overall, the strategy of large-scale expansion before becoming profitable is not a promising one based on the research evidence. Given that the minimum efficient scale is approximately 6,000 students, Edison Schools (one of the largest EMOs) appears to be operating well above this point: in the Spring of 2002 it operated approximately 130 schools with 75,000 students; by 2004, it operates 157 schools across 20 states and has developed a curriculum assessment program and summer school program. Yet, by 2002 it had accumulated losses of approximately $200 million since its founding. This is despite its present size being more than ten times the estimated size for an efficient school district. Moreover, school districts are geographically concentrated, easing supply lines and reducing monitoring costs. A national chain of schools incurs higher costs in these respects. The company's stock was traded on the NASDAQ from 1999 to 2003: although the share price climbed to over $30 in 2001, it fell dramatically over the next two years and the company was taken private in a buyout at $1.75 per share. The financial situation of the company is no longer publicly disclosed. However, with limited potential for growth in the operations of its schools, Edison Schools has branched out into offering peripheral services such as summer schools, supplemental tutoring services, and learning diagnostic tools. These appear to be more lucrative than the direct operation of schools.

A Uniform Product

The business plans of the EMOs push for a uniform educational product across their school sites. This push is motivated by several factors. First, costs may be controlled by standardizing the use of curriculum, pedagogy, and school inputs.

Such standardization means that the procedures for establishing and operating schools, selecting and training personnel, and purchasing equipment and supplies can be routinized throughout the network. Personnel can be allocated to different sites without disruption because they are familiar with the model and the operations across the sites. In purchasing a common set of equipment and supplies for each school, EMOs can benefit from competitive bidding and discounts for large purchases. Second, the uniformity of the educational product contributes to the notion of a recognized brand of education for a particular company. With national or regional aspirations, each EMO seeks to establish brand identity based on product differentiation.

However, educational needs can differ immensely from one district to another. In some cases a majority of students are immigrants speaking a first language that is not English. Differences in home backgrounds, handicaps, ethnicity, poverty, and cultures can create large variance in the types of educational programs and materials that will be most appropriate for different groups of students. Differences in local customs and communities may also be important. States and school districts also set different criteria among subjects to be taught and tested, so adjustments must be made to meet these standards. Demographic characteristics of students change over time, sometimes very rapidly. All of these factors undermine the expectation that a standard model, representing a branded approach that changes little from site-to-site and year-to-year is a sound business goal.

A Viable Business Model

Thus, there are a number of reasons to be skeptical of the claim that a standardized business model run by a for-profit firm will outperform the public school provision. The claim is based upon more generic assumptions of private sector efficiency than it is upon a direct analysis of the specific features of school operations. Virtually all of these assumptions violate what is known about the economics and politics of local schools. Moreover, even as a number of economic studies have pointed out the waste, inefficiencies, and corruption of the public sector (Segal, 2004; Brasington, 2002), few of these studies have suggested specific, practical ways for private sector firms to avoid being mired in the same organizational culture and to avoid facing the same constraints. Rather than a stable business context, schools must deal with multiple governments with conflicting priorities and constantly shifting objectives.

Although some of the EMOs have tried to adapt over time, most have held to models that are based on these assumptions. The result is that large operating

172 ▼ *Chapter 8*

losses have been continuing, and several have been unable to get continuous access to capital to finance their operations and cover their losses (e.g., Advantage Schools, Learn Now, Tesseract/EAI) and have either gone out of business or merged with others. In other cases, much attention has been paid to the time when EMOs might reach the break-even point. But, this is not a criterion for economic success: the real issue is whether these enterprises can earn a substantial return on capital. At this point, the viability of the predominant model for privatizing entire school operations—the EMO model—seems highly dubious.

Finally, it is difficult to attribute these poor results to inadequate reimbursement from the district or state. In the case of charter schools the EMOs are working with contracts based on the same remuneration formula as the non-EMO charter schools. The evidence on the funding of charter schools indicates that the operating resources they receive are equivalent to what such a school would receive if it was directly in the public school system (although in the 1990s there was limited funding for facilities for charter schools, more funding was made available as part of No Child Left Behind, see Miron and Nelson, 2002, 62–68; for cost comparisons in Baltimore, see Richards et al., 1996, Chapter 2).

Do EMOs Contribute to Educational Reform?

Even if the existing business models of the EMOs do not suggest economic viability, one can still examine their educational approaches to ask if they contribute to educational reform. There are two paths by which EMOs could stimulate educational reform. The first is to operate schools that make organizational or pedagogical breakthroughs that might lead to their success and to emulation by public schools. The second is to create competition between EMOs and public schools that will stimulate public schools to improve their operations. It is also possible that just the potential threat of EMOs, as opposed to direct competition, will spur the public schools to be more responsive to their clientele.

No careful survey has been made of the strategies of the EMOs, but descriptions of their schools are available (e.g., Miron and Nelson, 2002). Also, observational data is available, although not a systematic survey.

Pedagogical Approaches

There is little evidence of major new pedagogical approaches practiced by EMOs. Many EMOs emphasize a back-to-basics approach that is heavy on traditional drill and practice or what is called direct instruction. There are at least three reasons for reliance on this traditional approach. The first is that there is at least some evidence that direct instruction provides achievement gains in basic skills. Second, many school districts that are contracting with EMOs or charter schools are seeking traditional approaches and test score gains in basic skills. And, third, this approach keeps down costs for the EMOs because it is truly a no-frills method without enrichment and often with minimal instruction in the arts or areas outside of basic skills. Edison Schools, the largest of the EMOs, rely largely upon standard curricula that can be purchased by any school district, although it has developed some applications for its technology and has incorporated other subjects. Edison Schools relies heavily on a combination of direct instruction and other approaches. Many of the other EMOs rely on a "cookie-cutter" approach to the 3 R's (Miron and Nelson, 2002). There is no evidence of "revolutionary" breakthroughs by EMOs with respect to curriculum, instructional strategies, or use of technologies in the classroom. (Although there are some advances in Management Information Systems and assessment systems, it is hard to establish their consequences for student performance.) Virtually every aspect of their pedagogical approaches can be found somewhere in existing public schools, and in many cases, in a large number of public schools. (Brown [1992] provides an economic analysis of why private schools deviate so little from public schools in their basic features.)

Personnel and Organization

In the areas of personnel and organization, EMOs do operate differently from public schools. In particular, many of the EMOs seem to do a more systematic job than the average public school in creating an overall system of personnel selection and training and curriculum consistency across the entire school. According to our observations and inquiries, the EMOs place more effort on selecting their school-site administrators and teaching personnel and evaluating both. In some cases they also provide more training and greater performance incentives. There is a greater focus on accountability of site administrators and school staff through sanctions and rewards. The EMOs view schools as a system that appears to exist in public schools, where departments or initiatives often lack coordination and "new" approaches are adopted helter-skelter.

This difference is especially notable in some of the inner-city environments, where traditional public schools are chaotic with high teacher and administrative turnover, high student mobility, frequent shifts in curriculum approaches and pedagogies, uncoordinated staff development, and haphazard use of educational technologies. Even the appearance of the facility is unkempt and in need of repairs and renovations. In contrast, the EMOs have a good record of attempting to select staff and immerse them in a more systematic pedagogical approach with articulation from grade to grade. Staff are evaluated on their success in implementing the curriculum and pedagogy and on student success, to the degree that it is possible to measure the latter.

Perhaps the greatest visible strength is the ability of EMOs to accomplish the logistics of school maintenance. In many cases, the EMOs are able to physically transform school facilities that have been unsightly, damaged, and compromised for years. Facilities are painted and repaired, and custodial work is taken seriously. School appearance does not necessarily improve test scores, but it is an important symbol of how seriously the school authorities value educating the local population. The EMOs seem to have a major advantage in this area relative to the standard district administration.

Do EMOs Outperform Conventional Schools?

For a good number of years in which the EMOs were making claims about the effectiveness of their approach there was little evidence with which to adjudicate. Some EMOs had reported superior results, but without the documentation to substantiate these claims. Typically, they reported that test scores had risen in most of their schools, but the specifics of which tests, how tests were administered, and which students were included was not given. Moreover, public schools have also raised test scores in this new era of "standards" and high-stakes testing. So, the real issue is whether the test scores have risen in EMO schools at a faster rate than in comparable public schools. (This leaves aside whether test scores should be the appropriate benchmark for comparison; they are clearly not the only benchmark, but there is even less evidence on other indicators.)

Two studies offer initial information on this issue. In their study of early Edison schools, Miron and Applegate (2000) found about the same pattern in test scores between Edison schools and matched public schools. In their study of EMOs in Michigan, Miron and Nelson (2002, 143–145) found that the non-EMO charter schools outperformed those operated by EMOs.

Do EMOs Spur Competition?

Even if EMOs do not directly create breakthroughs in educational practices and results, they do offer an additional alternative to parents. Moreover, they may also spur competition with public schools and non-EMO charter schools by creating a more competitive environment. It is possible that they spur competition and improve results for the education system, although there is no direct evidence related to these specific types of school. Hess (2002) found that with more intense concentrations of charter schools and other alternatives, there is at least some emulation by the public schools of practices that might attract students. But the overall results are fairly nominal, with only a "revolution at the margins." More comprehensively, the review of the effect of competition in Chapter 6 above suggests that EMOs are unlikely to spur competition significantly.

What Has Been Learnt?

What we have learnt in the first decade of EMOs is that, contrary to the facile claims of their investment promoters, privatizing operations of public schools is not a business that is easily convertible to profitability. Whatever the flaws of the existing public school management and its poor performance in many urban areas, it does not appear that privatization via for-profit enterprises is the answer. For-profit EMOs have generally not been profitable, nor is there any evidence of any breakthrough in educational results. And, there is virtually no evidence that the quest for larger scale operations will address this critical feature.

Of course, this does not mean that for-profit EMOs or for-profit firms in elementary and secondary education must fail. Ultimately, the market test is a categorical one: firms that make profits survive and firms that do not will go out of business once the capital runs out. What this discussion does suggest is that the present model is unlikely to be the answer and that alternative approaches may be tried.

First, it should be acknowledged that smaller firms with a few schools are more consistent with the literature on economies of scale in education. Schools can be more easily managed and adapted to local conditions and can focus on improving effectiveness in a situation of high variable costs. A single, for-profit school may hold promise for those committed to educational entrepreneurship. Close monitoring of costs and the needs of clientele are essential to make a profit in this industry, and so moderate expansion may be possible if there is sufficient control.

Second, in the case of multiple schools, cost controls for central administration are important. The claims of some EMOs were that they could do a better job educationally at lower cost by avoiding the waste of central administration in public schools. The paradox is that their costs are considerably higher because of generous staffing, salaries, and benefits in the central headquarters—but with stringent cost control at the school sites. Multiple-school companies must reverse this situation, and yet still ensure that the school brand is well defined. Greater flexibility in school-site operations is required to adapt to different needs and contexts—while focusing the brand identification on goals and concepts rather than the uniformity of operations.

Third, it is crucial to contain marketing and promotional costs. One strategy is to create outstanding demonstration schools and to recruit new schools on the basis of these. This strategy would call for a slow rate of growth of expansion, but it would allow marketing costs to be reduced.

Fourth, it is important for EMOs to seek longer contracts, perhaps with performance benchmarks for each year on which payments (or a fraction of payments) will be based. The contract should be long enough for the company to amortize fixed costs of starting up at a site, while providing reasonable assurance of completing the contract. In some cases the EMO might set its costs on the promise of a "turnkey" operation in which a dysfunctional or low-performing school is returned to the district as a functional one; the EMO would then be responding to a different set of performance criteria and incentives.

Fifth, EMOs may find that niche markets offer the highest rate of return (e.g., private tutoring, after school programs, summer school programs). This is the case in higher education, where for-profit providers such as Apollo and the University of Phoenix division have targeted older and fully employed workers with modular courses of a standardized nature, practitioner teachers at a low cost from within the community, an ambitious approach to evaluation and quality control, and conveniences (such as parking). De Vry has developed a profitable niche market in training individuals for careers in technology. The niche consists of filling a market that is currently underserved; it is not an attempt to compete with the conventional providers. This alone reduces the amount of political opposition that a for-profit company will inevitably engender.

These niche markets may allow for considerable expansion of the for-profit sector. Special education, for example, might be such a niche market and for-profit companies have been able to provide services in this area. Other groups might be definable and targeted by for-profit companies, such as high-school drop-outs. Other services might be after-school services, counseling, and administrative support. These are less ambitious than the EMO schoolhouse operation, but they can be highly profitable (e.g., the provision of textbooks for schools and universities).

More generally, two facts should give pause to those who may continue to believe that there is scope for a large for-profit network of EMO schools. The first is the dearth of for-profit schools that have ever successfully entered the market over the last two centuries, even within the market of independent schools. Elite private schools in large cities charge tuition that is over $20,000 per year, which is 2–3 times what is spent in the local public schools. Yet, the for-profit sector has not been able to show a presence. Second, in addition to tuition, almost all independent schools engage in considerable fund-raising, with the highest tuition schools raising the most additional funding. The for-profit schools have not been able to break into this market either.

To conclude, it is important to appreciate that this analysis is predicated on the existing method of financing education. It is not clear how this might change if educational vouchers or tax credits were introduced and were of reasonable size. It is possible that parents would switch to for-profit schools, although this too may be unlikely: many of the challenges that the for-profit schools face are on the costs side of the ledger, they are not on the revenues side. Increasing revenues will help, but it won't reduce marketing costs, for example. Certainly, this is the lesson from countries where vouchers are widespread (e.g., in Chile, see Carnoy and McEwan, 2001). In those countries, no corporate entity has become a major factor in the private education market.

Chapter 9

Postcompulsory Entitlements
Vouchers for Life-Long Learning

Introduction

Virtually every country has a coherent system of compulsory education in which the structure, purpose, and financing are clear and consistent. Even with regional and local differences and the presence of independent schools, there is an overall order and logic to the institutional structure and financing of compulsory schooling. In contrast, postcompulsory schooling is characterized by large differences in purpose, function, duration, sponsorship, and financing of educational opportunities. Postcompulsory schooling includes all of the formal learning opportunities that are provided by government and the private sector after compulsory education is completed such as colleges and universities, short training courses, apprenticeship programs, retraining institutes, and so on. That these offerings are sometimes referred to as a system of recurrent education or lifelong learning is a highly imaginative use of the term "system."

It is no puzzle that postcompulsory training and educational opportunities are so diverse in purpose, origin, sponsorship, and financing. Each type of education and training arose for different reasons and was initiated by different sponsors in both public and private sectors. The result is that what we might think of as postcompulsory educational and training opportunities are varied in almost every respect. Much of this variety makes sense in reflecting the diversity of opportunities that address different societal and individual needs as well as the historical conditions under which they arose.

The multitude of forms of institutional sponsorship and financing arrangements can lead to both inefficiency and inequity and great inconsistencies in funding among offerings with similar goals. The focus of postcompulsory educational policy is determined by the mix of goals of the institutions offering specific types of education and training and their unique methods of finance rather than on the needs and capabilities of the clientele who must choose among them. That is, these offerings have purposes that are based more upon the histories of the institutions or the government branches that sponsor them than on the demands of the postcompulsory population or social priorities. Levels of subsidy and enrollments often depend upon institutional traditions and the political power of training and education sectors to obtain government subsidies rather than on fairness and efficiency across different types of education and training.

Vouchers for Postsecondary Education

In major respects educational vouchers seem to be more closely suited to postsecondary education than to the elementary and secondary levels. One of the key arguments of supporters of educational vouchers is their potential role in stimulating greater diversity of offerings and choice. Opponents point out that elementary and secondary education require some uniformity for the common preparation of all students for the knowledge requirements and values of citizenship. Indeed, the compulsory nature of the lower levels of education is to provide a common experience required for democratic participation. But, at the end of compulsory schooling these goals are expected to be met, and the arguments for choice outweigh those for uniformity. Thus, it is somewhat surprising that the focus of educational vouchers has not become prominent beyond elementary and secondary levels. The purpose of this presentation is to present the concept of postcompulsory entitlements, a voucher system for financing education and training opportunities beyond secondary school. The spirit of the presentation will be to provide a basis for further discussion rather than a specific plan or design.

In contrast to the supply orientation of most postcompulsory education and training, postsecondary entitlements provide a demand-oriented system of finance. Postcompulsory entitlements or PCEs refer to the provision of a government-sponsored account for every individual that can be used for education and training purposes in the postcompulsory period. A basic entitlement of grants and loans would be stipulated for each individual to use for further education and training. This amount could be applied to any education or training investment approved by the government. As will be shown below, PCEs have major advantages over the existing system in that they can be designed to be more equitable and efficient by building on their inherent comprehensiveness and flexibility.

Postsecondary or postcompulsory entitlements are not a new idea. Almost thirty years ago the U.S. National Institute of Education sponsored research for proposing voucher-type funding for postsecondary education. The Organization for Economic Cooperation and Development (OECD) in Paris and the U.S. government supported various forms of this work and sponsorship of two conferences in 1980 and 1983 featuring entitlement-financing (Levin, 1973, 29–33; Levin, 1977; Levin, 1983; Rehn, 1983). The U.S. project even focused on the development of a detailed design for such entitlements. What follows draws heavily on the earlier discussions and debates. It is also important to note that this brief introduction to PCEs can only provide a skeletal understanding of the concept and its application. More detailed discussions can be found in the earlier publications. Application of the PCE approach to specific countries will require that the concepts be translated into specifics that meet the needs of those entities.

Specifying Postcompulsory Entitlements

Every person would become eligible for a financial entitlement by the government for further training and education at the end of the compulsory schooling period. These entitlements could be applied to further education and training in any program that meets the eligibility requirements set out by the government. Such programs could be sponsored by governments, nonprofit agencies including trade unions and religious institutions, or profit-seeking firms. They could include virtually all of the existing postsecondary institutions such as colleges, universities and training programs, as well as apprenticeship and on-the-job training programs. It is important to note that not all education and training would be eligible for entitlement grants, although most would be eligible for entitlement loans.

Government would set out criteria for both eligibility of particular education and training offerings as well as the size of the entitlement for different groups of individuals. Institutional eligibility to redeem student entitlements would be based upon standards such as educational and training content, financial accountability, procedures for handling disputes with participants, and the provision of sufficient and accurate information on program content and student success (e.g., program completions, employment status of graduates).

The size of entitlements would depend upon PCE goals. Equity aims suggest larger entitlements for those from "disadvantaged" backgrounds. Entitlements could be divided between grants and low-interest or income-contingent loans (Oosterbeek, 1998). In general, the grant portion would be higher for those who came from low-income families and for study in fields considered to have a high social priority. Students could use the entitlement for any combination of eligible training or education programs up to the maximum amount of the entitlement. Also, the entitlement could be used over a considerable period of time both prior to entering the workforce and during the working period. Unused portions of any grant entitlement could be permitted to accumulate interest as an incentive for the participant to consider carefully the recurrent and continuing education and training possibilities that will exist over the life cycle. Unused portions could be redeemed at retirement age as part of the social security retirement system.

Most government subsidies of education and training programs would be accomplished indirectly through the entitlement program rather than through direct institutional subsidies. That is, programs would compete for students and their entitlements, and new offerings that meet eligibility standards would arise in response to emerging education and training needs and demands. Ideally, existing sources of public funding would be coordinated into one overall system of financial support to replace the present confounding diversity of funding programs.

A public information system would be developed that would make entitlement recipients aware of particular education and training programs as well as opportunities that are available in different fields. Much of this could be placed on a "PCE website" that would not only provide information to entitlement holders on the status and size of their remaining entitlements; but would also provide access to all education and training opportunities by field and location of training as well as specific information on the programs and their success. Systematic provision of information would also keep potential providers of programs informed about which areas are in high demand and which are declining.

The Properties of Postcompulsory Entitlements

To summarize, a system of postcompulsory entitlements or PCEs would have the following general properties.

1. Public support for postsecondary education and training would be provided to students in the form of a promissory note or entitlement.

2. The PCE would obligate the government to provide a specified amount of grants and loans that could be used for participating in education and training programs that met eligibility requirements.
3. The PCE could be used over the lifetime of the student, and the unused portion would draw interest.
4. The amount of the entitlement and its composition between grants and loans would be determined by the family resources of the student and other pertinent factors such as the social benefits and priorities of training (as opposed to the private benefits which should be borne by the individual).
5. Any education or training program approved as eligible by the government could accept and redeem entitlements for cash from the government treasury. Such institutions would probably include most existing colleges, universities, training institutes and training programs of trade unions, government, and industry. New programs would be eligible to participate by meeting specified eligibility requirements.
6. Government would sponsor an information and regulatory agency that would provide data for participants on training alternatives and their costs as well as program descriptions and job prospects among different occupations and training specializations. The agency would also set out the specific eligibility regulations to determine both the conditions of student and trainee participation on the one hand, and the requirements that must be satisfied for program eligibility on the other.

Evaluating Postcompulsory Entitlements

Obviously, there is no point in considering a sweeping change in the financing of postcompulsory education and training unless there are substantial benefits to doing so. PCEs are a form of educational voucher. In studies of educational vouchers at the elementary and secondary levels we have suggested four criteria for comparing them with more traditional forms of educational finance: freedom of choice, productive efficiency, equity, and social cohesion (Levin, 1998). On the basis of their greater comprehensiveness and flexibility, it will be argued that PCEs have the potential for much greater freedom of choice, higher productive efficiency, and more equitable participation and outcomes than the existing methods of organizing and providing postcompulsory education. We will not address social cohesion because there is wide agreement that this is a principal purpose of compulsory education rather than of postcompulsory experiences.

Comprehensiveness

PCEs replace the present complex system of financing for postcompulsory education and training with a unified approach. On the basis of the PCE system, each individual is certified for a specific amount of entitlement eligibility. Continuous accounting on the use of the entitlement and the remaining amount is provided through easily accessible records. The amount of government subsidy is shifted from the politics of institutional subventions that may be highly inequitable across different types of institutions and programs. PCEs enable a complete integration of existing forms of postcompulsory education and training as well as emerging ones, since the entitlement is neutral with respect to these alternatives, although a supplement could be added to an entitlement to study or train in areas of unusually high social priority.

Under more conventional forms of financing, educational and training institutions can only establish programs with government support by getting direct financing commitment from the government, an act based upon political persuasion rather than student demand. This means that the provision of new opportunities that allow government financial assistance must depend upon the acquisition of government support, creating cumbersome requirements for establishing new offerings and a lack of government support for private and nonprofit sponsors. In contrast, the entitlement approach enables adults to use their education and training subsidies directly, whether for traditional university education or any other eligible postcompulsory alternative. The financing mechanism is generally neutral with respect to types of education or training, so that new offerings can be considered on their own merits rather than on whether or not they fit a more traditional system of direct institutional subsidies. Entitlements can provide grant subsidies to target training that has social externalities (particular benefits to society beyond those to the individual), while avoiding the more "piecemeal" approaches that characterize subsidies in the present system. And, they can easily encompass future alternatives that are not yet on the drawing board. The comprehensiveness encompasses the possibility of many different paths to lifelong learning as does the flexibility of PCEs.

Flexibility

The PCE maximizes the flexibility and adaptability of further education and training since the subsidy can be used for any combination of training and educational opportunities selected. Flexibility in timing especially encourages a lifelong learning approach "on-demand" as needed. The entitlement can be partially utilized before entering the labor force and partially utilized intermittently during the individual's career. Or, the individual can apply the entitlement to a university education immediately following completion of secondary school. Alternatively, the use of the PCE could be deferred for several years until after the recipient establishes a career. All of these patterns can be accommodated without special arrangements, and the possibility of interest payments on the unused portion of the entitlement neutralizes the pressure to use it immediately.

This flexibility also extends to the supply of offerings. Given the neutrality of funding, the incentives to undertake particular types of education and training will be determined by demand patterns. Of course, as we will note below, the government can increase entitlement grants for certain types of education and training if it is believed that these have a higher social priority. New offerings can enter the marketplace as long as they meet the eligibility requirements. This means that new approaches are likely to arise more quickly and creatively in the marketplace than when left to existing subsidized institutions that have a "monopoly" on particular types of training. There will be a strong pressure to meet the needs of students and trainees to attract adequate enrollments.

Additional flexibility is afforded by the fact that specific policy goals with respect to equity or special educational needs can be targeted in a more effective manner than with existing subsidies to institutions. Equity considerations among different populations or regions can be addressed through providing compensatory PCEs that will promote education and training for groups that have traditionally been underrepresented or have received the least investment. The entitlement can be "pro-poor" in providing more resources for education and training to those who have the least ability to finance preparation for their own careers and who lack other advantages that enhance adult opportunities. This combination of comprehensiveness and flexibility can be related to the criteria of freedom of choice, productive efficiency, and equity.

Freedom of Choice

With respect to freedom of choice, it seems obvious that PCEs will provide a larger and more varied and accessible set of options than the traditional approaches, dominated by institutional finance. Both the comprehensiveness of the PCE approach and its flexibility mean that providers will have incentives to study market potential carefully and to provide alternatives in both variety and form that meet participant demand to a much greater degree than the present system. Whether part-time or full-time or classroom or distance education or area of study and training, a market-based system is poised to respond with more options than a politically based system. Freedom of choice depends on the variety of alternatives and their accessibility, but also on their responsiveness to demand. On all of these, a market is likely to be more responsive.

Efficiency

One can also make a strong argument that a postcompulsory system of education and training that is funded through PCEs will be more efficient than the present system, provided that social externalities are addressed. The efficiency claims arise from the comprehensiveness and flexibility referred to above as well as the competitive incentives of the marketplace. Comprehensiveness means that it is easier for the student to move from one type of training or education to another and to take the combination that is desired. It also means that market competition among suppliers will reduce overlap and duplication, and, particularly, offerings of lower quality. Flexibility means that market response will be higher on both the demand and supply sides with newer forms of education and training and expansion of high-demand subjects and types responding quickly to client pressures rather than being subject to institutional constraints and political obstacles. Finally, the fact that students will be using their own valuable resource, a PCE which has many alternative uses, means that PCE recipients will have incentives to make better choices and to be more demanding of themselves and those providers to whom they allot their PCEs. These incentives are muted under present systems of finance.

As suggested below, market solutions do not necessarily account for external benefits such as equity in participation. But, these issues can be addressed in the design of the system such as adjusting PCEs according to student need and merit. Other social benefits can be addressed through regulation and information. With respect to costs, it would appear that the costs of a unified system of postcompulsory finance would be more efficient than one that requires many government agencies to establish sources of funding for separate and overlapping services. Although the public costs of a voucher system at the elementary and secondary level were found to be high, this was primarily because of the substantial costs of publicly borne transportation costs and the additional costs of absorbing students in private schools who would be eligible for the government subsidy (Levin and Driver, 1997). These cost factors are not features of a postcompulsory system of education and training since adults can provide their own transportation and since many of the present subsidies would be replaced by income-contingent loans rather than grants.

Equity

It is important to note that traditionally, more-advantaged persons have been overly represented in universities and, especially, in the most lucrative fields of study, and that further education and training also has favored those from relatively advantaged social origins (OECD, 1994).[1] There are three reasons that the PCE approach, generally, and its comprehensiveness and flexibility, specifically, will increase access to productive investments in education and training for the less-advantaged. The fact that each person will become aware that they will be awarded an entitlement for postcompulsory education and training will increase the likelihood that they will use this award. It will also raise motivation to study harder in the compulsory period of schooling to take advantage of later opportunities. Under the present approach, only those persons who have the resources for further educational and training opportunities—generally the more advantaged and better-informed—are more fully aware of those options and secure in their ability to finance them. Thus, postcompulsory options will be an accepted fact for everyone with an incentive to prepare and take advantage of them.[2]

Second, under PCEs there will be incentives by providers to create education and training choices that will be more accessible and responsive to the needs of those who were traditionally underrepresented, as providers seek to attract the "new clientele." Government, not-for-profit, and for-profit providers will be challenged with how to capture potential increases in enrollments, in many cases, among persons who undertook little or no postcompulsory education and training in the past.

Third, under a system of postcompulsory entitlements, it is possible to tailor the size of the entitlement and the conditions of its use to favor persons from less advantaged backgrounds. In contrast, existing systems of postcompulsory finance provide subsidies to institutions according to educational and training costs, often the programs most accessible to those who are better off (such as the most intensive and remunerative fields of study in the university and the most prestigious and costly universities, see Leslie and Brinkman, 1988). To the degree that PCEs provide grant subsidies, they will be determined largely on the basis of need rather than on the basis of the cost of educational options with income-contingent loans being available to pay any balance of costs.

Design Issues

In order to implement a system of PCEs, a number of design issues must be addressed. Evaluation of educational vouchers for use at elementary and secondary education levels has focused on three types of policy tools for such design: finance, regulation, and support services. Regulatory issues include such matters as eligibility of participants and providers, and support services include information and adjudication. Each will be discussed briefly, although more information can be found in other sources (Levin, 1983; Rehn, 1983).

Finance Issues

Finance issues include the issue of public subsidy, sources of funding, size of entitlements, and composition between loans and grants. In his classic treatise on the role of the state in education, Milton Friedman has argued that the benefits of postsecondary education are mostly vocational in nature and are captured by the individuals receiving the education rather than being broadly distributed to society as external benefits (Friedman, 1962). Accordingly, Friedman concluded that the individual and family should pay for the educational investment rather than society. In contrast to Friedman's position, the argument for public support for postcompulsory education generally rests on the view that there are benefits to society as a whole beyond those to the individuals being educated. Friedman accepted this view for elementary and secondary education, but found no parallel role for "higher schooling." At the earlier levels of education, a major purpose is to mold a society that is equitable and democratic and shares a common set of institutional values. Friedman argued that the costs of postsecondary education should be paid for by the beneficiary of the education through taxation on a portion of the additional lifetime income that is conferred by such education and training (one version of this is the graduate tax, e.g., in Australia, see Chapman, 1997). He suggested the use of income-contingent loans that can be paid during one's working life through the income tax.

However, a strong case can be made that postcompulsory education has external benefits for society as a whole that merit subsidies (Leslie and Brinkman, 1988; Bowen, 1977; McMahon, 1998). Certainly, equity considerations suggest subsidies to encourage those from less-advantaged backgrounds to participate more fully in postcompulsory education. Greater social equity is an important component of a democratic society that yields social benefits in the provision of fairness and in reducing the potential for conflict as well as diminishing the demands for publicly supported health, public assistance, and other services. In recent years the many sources of social benefits that have been asserted for postcompulsory education have been augmented by endogenous economic growth theory in which the ability to benefit from improved technology and work organization is heavily tied to the aggregate capabilities of the workforce. According to endogenous growth theory, continuous educational investments beyond compulsory education may benefit the entire society by generating technological advances through a more adaptable workforce that is able to accommodate new technologies, organization, and work methods (Romer, 1994). Postcompulsory education and continuing education enables societies to capitalize quickly on new knowledge through a higher level of general technical literacy, information flows that provide quick access to the latest developments, and widespread research and inquiry that can generate technical advance.

The foregoing does not mean that every postcompulsory education and training activity should be subsidized by PCE grants, nor does it suggest the level of subsidy. Individuals often find it lucrative to undertake additional education and training, even in the absence of government subsidies (Cohn and Addison, 1998). In those cases, costs are more than compensated by substantial increases in earnings. Many enterprises also face substantial financial incentives to provide training to adapt to new production and market realities with high returns.

Subsidies through grants should be provided only in those situations where there are compelling social externalities or social benefits. An argument for general subsidies for some portion of postcompulsory education and training costs can be made on the basis of endogenous growth theory. Unfortunately, the empirical magnitude of this effect is difficult to calculate because the effects are so widely diffused. Equity arguments suggest creating greater subsidies for those from less-advantaged backgrounds to compensate for lower capacities of families to invest in human capital. The need to accelerate adjustment to emerging or future labor force demands from shifts in economic activity (e.g., caused by globalization) might also be an argument for subsidies for particular types of training or for particular regions suffering from unemployment or underemployment. Some assessment must be made for each country in determining subsidy policies based upon unique social benefits in excess of the benefits to the participant which would result in grant entitlements for particular types of training or for persons in particular regions or from particular social circumstances. These subsidies would be reflected in the grant portion of the entitlement.

Sources of Funding

The underlying idea for the finance of PCEs is to take the many piecemeal provisions of funding and to combine them into a more comprehensive approach. This could be done using a broad-based tax approach such as that of income, sales, or value-added taxes. Arguments have been made for a payroll tax, because educational leave and educational sabbaticals might be an important component of postcompulsory and lifelong learning. Such a tax is usually levied on both employers and employees. However, because it is a tax on wages and salaries (often with a ceiling on the level that is taxed) and omits taxation on dividends, interests, rents, and other forms of nonlabor income, it is a highly regressive tax (Pechman and Okner, 1974).

The challenge is how to take many different tax and expenditure sources and to combine them to as great a degree possible into a single fund for use for entitlements. These sources might include taxes supporting present subsidies for universities, vocational training and retraining, and even unemployment compensation. Surely it is better to use a portion of the latter funds as a preventative device to prepare those whose industries or occupations are declining or who need skill upgrading to maintain employment rather than waiting until they have lost employment and must be supported while looking for work. Further, the fact that individuals can decide when to use their entitlements for this purpose means that many will make that adjustment in advance of job loss as they observe the possibility of preparing for expanding segments of the economy.

Overall, the solution is to consolidate to the greatest degree possible the various sources of funding of existing postcompulsory opportunities into a comprehensive system of finance. This process is likely to be one that requires considerable negotiations with the present sources of funding and programs, and the transition may have to be done in stages, by types of education and training. For example, the university sector might be transformed initially with entitlement funding, followed by agreements with other sectors to convert part or all of institutional subsidies to entitlements. At the same time, the use of income contingent loans for all eligible investments will provide access to capital for individuals who have financial need above the grant portions of their entitlements.

Size of Entitlements

A PCE will be provided for each person who reaches the postcompulsory period. The PCE will be composed of two parts, a grant and a loan capability. The grant portion will be a direct subsidy for the individual based upon a universal criterion, family resources, and special considerations on course of study. With respect to the universal criterion, each society needs to place a value on the social benefits of postcompulsory education. This amount will be given to all PCE recipients as an entitlement grant. In addition, an equity adjustment would suggest that those with families with the least resources by virtue of parental education, income, and wealth would be eligible for larger entitlements to compensate for the lower capacities of their families to invest in human capital.[3] Finally, specific types of education and training investments that have particular social benefits such as those accelerating the transitional training or retraining from declining to rising occupations and industries or investing in training of local populations for economic development in regions of high priority might all be a basis for larger grant entitlements. In the cases of the universal and equity criteria, the grant portion would be built into the PCE. In the latter cases of special social priority, the grant would be added to the PCE if the participant undertook the specialized education or training that carried the extra subsidy.

In addition, participants would be eligible for income-contingent loans for all approved investment categories and expenses. Such loans would be repaid out of the higher income generated over the individual's lifetime.[4] In this way, every participant would have the capability of investing in further education and training with no time urgency since the built-in grant would generate interest for the unused portion, and the loan would have no cost until it was obtained and used to generate additional income. Clearly, the exact parameters for the scheme would have to be established by each society.

Regulatory Issues

Regulations for operation of the PCE system would be embodied in the laws establishing the system as well as a government regulatory agency that would administer the law. Among regulatory functions, the law would establish both the eligibility of participants to receive the vouchers and the conditions under which they could be used. It would determine the size of the entitlement and the division between loans and grants according to the criteria set out by the law. The agency would initiate and maintain detailed PCE accounts for each participant with detailed information on account status that would be accessible to the participant through the Internet.

Based upon the law, the agency would also determine the eligibility of educational and training institutions to receive PCEs in payment for services. The agency would invite applications from providers to evaluate and certify their eligibility. Providers would be monitored through periodic reporting requirements as well as inquiries in response to complaints or reported irregularities. Financial accountability and information reporting by eligible providers would be mandatory.

Support Services

The regulatory function would also be responsible for the provision of two support services to assist the PCE approach to function efficiently, an information system and an adjudication system. An information system would be designed and operated by the agency to collect and disseminate accurate information to both individuals and institutions on educational and training alternatives. This would probably best be done through an extensive website. The information system would contain data on each provider including the length, type, and cost of training; the curriculum, delivery system, and scheduling options; qualifications of teaching staff; record of program completions; placement services and performance measures including employment of graduates; and numbers and details of complaints as well as disposition by regulatory agencies. This information system could be organized by types of training, location, cost, flexibility of studies, and other criteria to make it easy to access for the potential participant by a PCE search engine. It would also provide pertinent data on providers for potential suppliers to use in making decisions about establishing new training centers or expanding or closing existing ones.

An adjudicatory mechanism would be maintained by the regulatory agency for resolving disputes that might arise between program sponsors and enrollees. This mechanism would be used if the participant believed that there were issues of provider misrepresentations to the information system. The regulatory agency would have the power to challenge the validity of the complaint or to require the participant to provide a refund of the entitlement or some other remedy. Data on such violations would also be recorded on the information system for guiding prospective participants in the future. For the most extreme infractions, the agency could cancel eligibility for the provider.

Can PCEs Work?

It may appear that PCEs are an interesting idea, but that they deviate so much from present financing approaches that they carry great risk. In the U.S. we have had experience with two types of voucher or entitlement programs in higher education. Pell Grants are provided from the federal government to students from low income families. However, they are very modest relative to the full costs of postsecondary education and limited in duration and application (for example, the maximum Pell Grant was only slightly more than $3,000 a year in 2000–01). According to analyst Tom Kane, they have not seemed to have a major effect on equity in redistributing participation in higher education (see his recommended changes to Pell Grants, Kane, 1999). By contrast, the GI Bill of Veterans' Education Benefits Program in the U.S. suggests that larger and less restricted entitlements are a highly workable approach to the financing of postcompulsory education and training and lifelong learning that can have strong equity effects. The GI Bill was established in 1944 to assist military veterans to adjust to a changing economy.[5] A monetary allowance was provided for paying college tuition and other educational costs at approved institutions that included most colleges and universities as well as secondary schools and vocational training programs. The magnitude of the program is substantial with at least $70 billion having been spent on it since its inception.

At the present time veterans receive from $672 to $800 per month for full-time studies for up to four academic years.[6] The allotments will rise to $985 a month in 2003 for a maximum of almost $36,000 for the four academic years. (GI Bill students who select public institutions are still beneficiaries of subsidies beyond the GI Bill entitlement, so the entitlement component represents only part of the overall subsidy received by the participant). Veterans are able to receive benefits for enrollment at almost any educational and training program, but not for apprenticeships or on-the-job training or courses offered outside of the U.S. Eligibility of institutions is based upon educational, legal, financial, and information reporting criteria. Almost 18 million veterans have participated in the GI Bill, and the program has accounted for about half of the U.S. federal support for postsecondary education and training. Veterans have a period of a decade to use their benefits and have wide latitude in the choice of programs, although, historically, about three-fourths have chosen colleges and universities according to a study of the Congressional Budget Office (U.S. Congressional Budget Office, 1978). This study also found that about one-tenth were studying in vocational and technical institutes and another tenth in on-the-job and farm training programs which are no longer eligible for coverage. The remainder chose correspondence schools, flight instruction, and high school completion programs. Although benefits for part-time study are proportionately lower, either part-time or full-time study is permissible. Benefits are received as long as the student attends regularly and performs satisfactorily. It is clear that the program is both comprehensive and flexible as described above.

The program also encourages potential participants to take advantage of further education and training. O'Neill and Ross found that over three-fifths of veterans were likely to use their benefits in the early 1970s (O'Neill and Ross, 1976), and a study in 1996 found that 95 percent of eligible military recruits enrolled in the educational program (Kane, 1999). The Congressional Budget Office found that one-third of all veteran students would not have undertaken training and education in the absence of the GI Bill benefits.[7] Although in the overall population, enrollment rates of blacks in postsecondary education is considerably lower than that of whites, blacks actually showed higher rates of enrollment (O'Neill and Ross, 1976, p.53). After adjusting for test scores and prior educational attainments, the participation rate for blacks was found to be some nine percentage points higher than for equivalent whites.[8] There were also considerable earnings advantages relative to similar populations that had not participated in the GI Bill.

This evidence suggests that at least one system of PCE-type arrangements was better able to increase participation and equity, and that its comprehensiveness and flexibility suggest increased efficiency as well. Almost 50 years of experience with the GI Bill also supports the view that PCEs do not require excessive regulation or meddling with institutions, and there is little evidence of serious administrative problems or corruption.

Conclusion

Postcompulsory education and training have shifted from a focus on immediate postsecondary education and universities to lifelong education through recurrent patterns of education and training over the lifecycle, so-called lifelong learning. This shift means that potential educational and training needs are no longer as predictable as they have been in the past and opportunities must adapt rapidly to new demands as they arise. These demands are characterized by much greater diversity of timing and types of educational and training offerings as well as future directions that have not yet been realized, including much greater use of distance education and the Internet. Such an approach requires a much more flexible and encompassing approach to education, and one that is more comprehensive with an integrated funding approach. The development of a system of postcompulsory entitlements seems to be an appropriate response that meets criteria of efficiency and equity of result.

Notes

1. In the U.S. the proportion of persons with university education who take adult education courses is about three times that of those who fail to complete secondary school according to the National Center for Education Statistics. See K. Kim and S. Creighton, *Participation in Adult Education in the United States: 1998–99*, (Washington, D.C.: National Center for Education Statistics, 2000). At http://nces.ed.gov/pubs2000/qrtlyspring/6life/q6–1.html.

2. Kane (2001) implicates inaccurate expectations and lack of planning by parents as one of the causes of low participation rates for the less advantaged. See his "Assessing the U.S. Financial Aid System: What We Know, What We Need to Know," *Ford Policy Forum, 2001* (Cambridge, MA: Forum for the Future of Higher Education, 2001), pp. 25–34.

3. Kane notes that in the U.S. after controlling statistically for differences in examination scores, high school grades, and schools attended, much of the difference in attendance patterns in higher education in favor of higher income families remains. See T. Kane, "Assessing the U.S. Financial Aid System: What We Need to Know," *Ford Policy Reform 2001* (New York: The Ford Foundation 2001), pp. 25–34.

4. Income-contingent loans would have to be restricted to an age range for each type of education and training that would provide an adequate time horizon to recoup the loan from the returns on the investment.

5. This brief description is taken from *West's Encyclopedia of American Law: Government Agencies and Programs* under the heading of "GI Bill" as found at http:www.wld.com/conbus/weal/wgibill.htm.

6. The Veterans Education and Benefits Expansion Act of 2001 was enacted on December 27, 2001. Details are found at http://www.gibill.va.gov/Education/News/PL107103.htm.

7. U.S. Congressional Budget Office, 1978, pp. 12–13. More recent econometric analyses have found the GI-Bill stimulation to be about 20 percent. See M. Stanley, "The Mid-Century GI Bills and Higher Education," (Cleveland: Department of Economics, Case-Western Reserve University, 2002). S. Turner and J. Bound also find positive effects on enrollments for whites and blacks outside of the South.

8. In a related work, it was found that blacks in the South did not share proportional benefits because of the relative lack of higher educational opportunities for southern blacks in the latter 1940s. S. Turner and J. Bound, "Closing the Gap or Widening the Divide: The Effects of the GI Bill and World War II on the Educational Outcomes of Black Americans," Draft paper presented at Annual Meetings of the American Educational Research Association, Seattle (April 2001).

References

ACF (Administration for Children and Families). 2003. *Child Maltreatment, 2001.* http://www.acf.hhs.gov/programs/cb/publications/cm01/outcover.htm.

Alexander, KL, Entwisle, DR, and LS Olson. 2001. Schools, achievement, and inequality: A seasonal perspective. *Educational Evaluation and Policy Analysis,* 23(2), 171–191.

Andrews, M, Duncombe, W, and J Yinger. 2002. Revisiting economies of size in American education: Are we any closer to a consensus? *Economics of Education Review,* 21, 245–262.

Apple, M. 2001. *Educating the "Right" Way: Markets, Standards, God and Inequality.* New York: Routledge and Farmer.

Arai, B. 2000. Reasons for home schooling in Canada. *Canadian Journal of Education,* 25, 204–217.

Arum, R. 1996. Do private schools force public schools to compete? *American Sociological Review,* 61, 29–46.

Ashenfelter, O, Harmon, C, and H Oosterbeek. 1999. A review of estimates of the schooling/earnings relationship, with tests for publication bias. *Labour Economics,* 6, 453–470.

Barrow, L, and C Rouse. 2000. "Using market valuation to assess the importance and efficiency of public school spending." Annual Meeting of the American Educational Finance Association.

Bast, JL, and HJ Walberg. 2004. Can parents choose the best schools for their children? *Economics of Education Review,* 23, 431–440.

Bauman, KJ. 2002. Home-schooling in the United States: Trends and characteristics. *Education Policy Analysis Archives,* 10(26).

Beck, CW. 2001. Alternative education and home schooling in Norway. *Childhood Education,* 77, 356–359.

Begg, CB. 1994. Publication bias. In Hedges, LV, and H Cooper (eds.), *Handbook of Research Synthesis.* New York: Russell Sage.

Behrendt, A, Eisenach, J, and WR Johnson. 1986. Selectivity bias and the determinants of SAT scores. *Economics of Education Review,* 5, 363–371.

Belfield, CR. 2003. Democratic education across school types: Evidence from the NHES99. Working Paper, http://www.ncspe.org/list-papers.php.

———. 2004. Modeling school choice: Comparing public, private, and home-schooling enrollment options. *Educational Policy Analysis Archives,* April.

Belfield, CR, and HM Levin. 2002. The effect of competition on educational outcomes: A review of the U.S. evidence. *Review of Educational Research,* 72, 279–341.

———. 2003. The economics of tuition tax credits for U.S. schools. *NTA Proceedings,* 95th Annual Conference on Taxation, Orlando, Florida, November 14, 1–15.

Belfield, CR, Levin, HM, and HL Schwartz. 2003. School choice and the supply of private schooling places: Evidence from the Milwaukee Parental Choice Program. Working Paper, http://www.ncspe.org/list-papers.php.

Bennett, WJ. 1987. *The Book of Virtues.* New York: Simon and Schuster.

Benveniste, L, Carnoy, M, and R Rothstein. 2003. *All Else Equal. Are Public and Private Schools Different?* New York: Routledge Falmer.

Bernstein, B. 1971. *Class, Codes, and Control.* London: Routledge and Kegan Paul.

Bifulco, R, and HF Ladd. 2003. The impacts of charter schools on student achievement: Evidence from North Carolina. Working paper. Durham, NC: Duke University.

Bishop, J. 1996. Incentives to study and the organization of secondary instruction. In Becker, WE, and WJ Baumol (eds.), *Assessing Educational Practices.* Cambridge, MA: MIT Press.

Blair, JP, and S Staley. 1995. Quality competition and public schools: Further evidence. *Economics of Education Review,* 14, 193–198.

Block, JH, Everson, ST, and TR Guskey. 1995. *School Improvement Programs.* New York: Scholastic.

Bok, D. 2000. *The Trouble with Government.* Cambridge, MA: Harvard University Press.

Borland, MV, and RM Howson. 1992. Students' academic achievement and the degree of market concentration in education. *Economics of Education Review,* 11, 31–39.

———. 1993. On the determination of the critical level of market concentration in education. *Economics of Education Review,* 12, 165–169.

———. 1995. Competition, expenditures and student performance in mathematics: A comment on Crouch et al. *Public Choice,* 87, 395–400.

Bourdieu, P, and J-C Passeron. 1977. *Reproduction in Education, Society and Culture.* London: Sage.

Bowen, HR. 1977. *Investing in Learning: The Individual and the Social Value of Higher Education.* San Francisco: Jossey Bass.

Bowles, S, and HM Levin. 1968. The determinants of scholastic achievement. *The Journal of Human Resources,* 3, 3–24.

Brasington, D. 2000. Demand and supply of public school quality in metropolitan areas: The role of private schools. *Journal of Regional Science,* 40, 583–605.

Brint, S, MF Contreras, and MT Matthews. 2001. Socialization messages in primary schools: An organizational analysis. *Sociology of Education,* 74, 157–180.

Brokaw, AJ, JR Gale, and TE Merz. 1995. Competition and the level of expenditures: K through 12 public schools in Michigan. *Journal of Economics,* 21, 99–103.

Brown, B. 1992. Why governments run schools. *Economics of Education Review,* 11, 287–300.

Buckley, J, and M Schneider. 2003. Shopping for schools: How do marginal consumers gather information about schools? *Policy Studies Journal,* 31, 121–145.

Buddin, R, and R Zimmer. 2003. A closer look at charter school achievement. Working paper, November 2003, APPAM.

Burnell, BS. 1991. The effect of school district structure on spending. *Public Choice*, 69, 253–264.

Buss, E. 2000. The adolescent's stake in the allocation of educational control between parent and state. *University of Chicago Law Review*, 67, 1233–1289.

Cai, Y, J Reeve, and DT Robinson. 2002. Home schooling and teaching style: Comparing the motivating styles of home school and public school teachers. *Journal of Educational Psychology*, 94, 372–380.

Camilli, G, and K Bulkley. 2001. Critique of "An Evaluation of the Florida A-Plus Accountability and School Choice Program." *Education Policy Analysis Archives*, 9, 7.

Campbell, DE. 2001. Making democratic education work. In Peterson, PE, and DE Campbell (eds.), *Charters, Vouchers and American Education*. Washington, DC: Brookings Institution.

Kane, T. 1999. Reforming subsidies for higher education. In MH Kosters (ed.). *Financing College Tuition*. Washington, DC: AEI Press.

Carnegie Corporation and CIRCLE. 2003. *The Civic Mission of Schools*. http://www.civicyouth.org/whats_new/index.htm.

Carnoy, M, 1997. Is privatization through vouchers really the answer? *World Bank Research Observer*, 12, 105–116.

———. 1997. School choice? Or is it privatization? *Educational Researcher*, 29, 15–20.

Carnoy, M, and HM Levin. 1985. *Schooling and Work in the Democratic State*. Stanford, CA: Stanford University Press.

Carnoy, M, and P McEwan. 2001. Privatization through vouchers in developing countries: The cases of Chile and Colombia. In Levin, HM (ed.), *Privatizing Education*. Boulder, CO: Westview.

———. 2003. Does privatization improve education? The case of Chile's national voucher plan. In Plank, DN, and G Sykes (eds.), *Choosing Choice: School Choice in International Perspective*. New York: Teachers College Press.

Center for the Study of Public Policy. 1970. *Education vouchers: A report on financing elementary education by grants to parents*. Cambridge, MA: Author.

Chambers, J. 1987. Patterns of compensation of public and private school teachers. In James, T, and HM Levin (eds.), *Comparing Public and Private Schools. Volume 1*. New York: Falmer Press.

Chapman, B. 1997. Conceptual issues and the Australian experience with income contingent charges for higher education. *Economic Journal*, 107, 738–751.

Chubb, JE. 2001. The profit motive: The private can be public. *Education Matters*, 1(1), 6–14.

———. 2002. A supply-side view of student selectivity. In Hill, PT (ed.), *Choice with Equity*. Stanford, CA: Hoover Institution.

Chubb, J, and T Moe. 1990. *Politics, Markets, and America's Schools*. Washington, DC: Brookings Institution.

Cohen-Zada, D, and M Justman. 2003. The political economy of school choice: Linking theory and evidence. *Journal of Urban Economics,* 54, 277–308.

Cohn, E, and JT Addison. 1998. The economic return to lifelong learning. *Education Economics,* 6, 253–308.

Coleman, JS. 1988. Social capital, human capital, and schools. *Independent School,* Fall, 9–16.

Coleman, JS, et al. 1966. *Equality of Educational Opportunity.* Washington, DC: U.S. Department of Education, U.S. Government Printing Office.

Cookson, PW. 1992. *The Choice Controversy.* New York: Sage.

Coons, JE, and SD Sugarman. 1978. *Education by Choice: The Case for Family Control.* Berkeley: University of California Press.

Coons, JE, SD Sugarman, and WH Clune. 1970. *Private Wealth and Public Education.* Cambridge, MA: Harvard University Press.

Couch, JF, and WF Shughart. 1995. Private school enrollment and public school performance: A reply. *Public Choice,* 82, 375–379.

Couch, JF, WF Shughart, and A Williams. 1993. Private school enrollment and public school performance. *Public Choice,* 76, 301–312.

Coulson, AJ. 1999. *Market Education: The Unknown History.* New Brunswick, NJ: Transaction Publishers.

Cuban, L. 2001. *Oversold and Underused: Computers in the Classroom.* Cambridge, MA: Harvard University Press.

Dearing, E, E McCartney, and BA Taylor. 2001. Change in family income-to-needs matters more for children with less. *Child Development,* 72, 1779–1793.

Dee, TS. 1998. Competition and the quality of public schools. *Economics of Education Review,* 17, 419–427.

Dee, TS, and H Fu. 2004. Do charter schools skim students or drain resources? *Economics of Education Review,* 23, 259–271.

Downes, TA. 1996. Do differences in heterogeneity and intergovernmental competition help explain variation in the private school share? Evidence from early California statehood. *Public Finance Quarterly,* 24, 291–318.

Downes, TA, and SM Greenstein. 1996. Understanding the supply decisions of nonprofits: modelling the location of private schools. *Rand Journal of Economics,* 27, 365–390.

Duncan, GJ, and J Brooks-Gunn (eds.). 1997. *Consequences of Growing Up Poor.* New York: Russell Sage Foundation.

Duncombe, W, J Miner, and J Ruggiero. 1997. Empirical evaluation of bureaucratic models of inefficiency. *Public Choice,* 93, 1–18.

Edmonds, R. 2002. Effective schools for the urban poor. *Educational Leadership,* 37, 15–24.

Ensign, J. 2000. Defying the stereotypes of special education: Home school students. *Peabody Journal of Education,* 75, 147–158.

Epple, D, and R Romano. 1998. Competition between private and public schools, vouchers, and peer-group effects. *American Economic Review,* 88, 33–62.

Epstein, JL. 2001. *School, Family, and Community Partnerships.* Boulder, CO: Westview Press.

Evans, WN, and RM Schwab. 1995. Finishing high school and starting college: Do Catholic schools make a difference? *Quarterly Journal of Economics,* CX, 941–974.

Fairlie, RW, and AM Resch. 2002. Is there "white flight" into private schools? Evidence from the National Educational Longitudinal Survey. *Review of Economics and Statistics,* 84, 21–33.

Figlio, DN, and J Ludwig. 2001. Sex, drugs and Catholic schools: Private schooling and adolescent behaviors. Working Paper #30, http://www.ncspe.org/list-papers-php.

Figlio, DN, and JA Stone. 1999. Are private schools really better? *Research in Labor Economics,* 18, 115–140.

Finn, JD, and CM Achilles. 1999. Tennessee's class size study: Findings, implications, misconceptions. *Economic Evaluation and Policy Analysis,* 21, 97–109.

Fiske, EB, and HF Ladd. 2003. School choice in New Zealand: A cautionary tale. In Plank, DN, and G Sykes (eds.), *Choosing Choice: School Choice in International Perspective.* New York: Teachers College Press.

Frey, D. 1983. *Tuition Tax Credits for Private Education. An Economic Analysis.* Ames: Iowa State University Press.

Friedman, M. 1962. The role of government in education. In Friedman, M, *Capitalism and Freedom.* Chicago: Chicago University Press.

———. 1993. Public schools: Make them private. *Education Economics,* 1, 25–45.

Fuller, DW. 1998. Public school access: The constitutional right of home-schoolers to "Opt in" to public education on a part-time basis. *Minnesota Law Review,* 82, 1599–1630.

Gamoran, A. 1996. Student achievement in public magnet, public comprehensive, and private city high schools. *Educational Evaluation and Policy Analysis,* 18, 1–18.

Geller, CR, DL Sjoquist, and MB Walker. 2001. The effect of private school competition on public school performance. Working Paper, http://www.ncspe.org/list-papers.php.

Gill, B, PM Timpane, KE Ross, and DJ Brewer. 2001. *Rhetoric Versus Reality: What We Know and What We Need to Know about Vouchers and Charter Schools.* Washington, DC: The Rand Corporation.

Glomm, G, D Harris, and T-F Lo. 2005. Charter school location. *Economics of Education Review,* forthcoming.

Godwin, K, Z Deng, V Martinez, P Wolf, and S Wood. 2001. *Comparing Tolerance in Public, Private, and Evangelical Schools.* Denton, TX: Department of Political Science, North Texas State University.

Godwin, RK, and FR Kemerer. 2002. *School Choice Trade-offs.* Austin: University of Texas Press.

Goldhaber, D. 1999. An endogenous model of public school expenditures and private school enrollment. *Journal of Urban Economics,* 46, 106–128.

———. 2002. The interface between public and private schooling: Market pressure and the impact on performance. In Monk, DH, HJ Walberg, and M Wang (eds.), *Improving Educational Productivity.* Greenwich, CT: Information Age Publishing.

Gorard, S, and J Fitz. 2000. Investigating the determinants of segregation between schools. *Research Papers in Education,* 15, 115–132.

Greene, JP. 2001. An evaluation of the Florida A-Plus Accountability and School Choice Program, Working Paper. New York: The Manhattan Institute.

Greene, JP, PE Peterson, and J Du. 1998. School choice in Milwaukee: A randomized experiment. In Peterson, PE, and BC Hassel (eds.), *Learning from School Choice.* Washington, DC: Brookings Institution.

Grissmer, DW, A Flanagan, J Kawata, and S Williamson. 2000. *Improving Student Achievement: What State NAEP Scores Tell Us.* Santa Monica, CA: The Rand Corporation.

Grogger, J, and D Neal. 2000. Further evidence on the benefits of Catholic secondary schooling. *Brookings-Wharton Papers on Urban Affairs.* Washington, DC: Brookings Institution.

Grosskopf, S, K Hayes, LL Taylor, and WL Weber. 1999. Allocative inefficiency and school competition. *Proceedings of the 91st Annual Conference on Taxation.* Washington, DC: National Tax Association.

Gutmann, A. 1987. *Democratic Education.* Princeton, NJ: Princeton University Press.

Hammons, CW. 2001. School@home. *Education Next,* Winter, 48–55.

Hanushek, EA. 1994. *Making Schools Work.* Washington, DC: Brookings Institution.

———. 1998. Conclusions and controversies about the effectiveness of schools. *Federal Reserve Bank of New York Economic Policy Review,* 4, 1–22.

———. 2004. What if there are no "best practices"? *Scottish Journal of Political Economy,* 51, 157–172.

Hanushek, EA, and SG Rivkin. 2001. Does public school competition affect teacher quality? Mimeograph.

Hanushek, EA, J Kain, and S Rivkin. 2003. New evidence on the impact of charter schools on academic achievement. APPAM, November 2003.

———. 2004. Disruption versus Tiebout improvement: The costs and benefits of switching schools. *Journal of Public Economics.*

Hanushek, EA, SG Rivkin, and LL Taylor. 1996. Aggregation and the estimated effects of school resources. *Review of Economics and Statistics,* 78, 611–627.

Hart, B, and T Risley. 1995. *Meaningful Differences in Everyday Parenting and Intellectual Development in Young American Children.* Baltimore: Brookes.

Haveman, RH, and BL Wolfe. 1984. The role of nonmarket effects. *Journal of Human Resources,* XIX, 377–407.

Heath, SB. 1983. *Ways with Words.* New York: Cambridge University Press.

Hedges, LV, and A Nowell. 1998. How and why the gap has changed. In Jencks, C and M Phillips (eds.), *The Black-White Test Score Gap.* Washington, DC: Brookings Institution.

Henig, JR. 1994. *Rethinking School Choice: Limits of the Market Metaphor.* Princeton, NJ: Princeton University Press.

Henig, JR, and JA MacDonald. 2002. Locational decisions of charter schools: Probing the market metaphor. *Social Science Quarterly,* 83, 962–980.

Henig, JR, and SD Sugarman. 1999. The nature and extent of school choice. In Sugarman,

SD, and FR Kemerer (eds.), *School Choice and Social Controversy: Politics, Policy and Law.* Washington, DC: Brookings Institution.

Hess, F. 2002. *Revolution at the Margins: The Impact of Competition on Urban School Systems.* Washington, DC: Brookings Institution.

Hess, F, R Maranto, and S Milliman. 2001. Small districts in big trouble: How four Arizona school systems responded to charter competition. *Teachers College Record,* 103, 1102–1124.

Heubert, JP, and RM Hauser (eds.). 1998. *High Stakes: Testing for Tracking, Promotion, and Grade Retention.* Washington, DC: National Academy Press.

Hirsch, ED, Jr. 1987. *Cultural Literacy: What Every American Needs to Know.* New York: Houghton Mifflin.

Hirschman, AO. 1970. *Exit, Voice, and Loyalty.* Cambridge, MA: Harvard University Press.

Hochschild, JL, and N Scovronick. 2003. *The American Dream and the Public Schools.* New York: Oxford University Press.

Hoover-Dempsey, KV, AC Battiato, JMT Walker, RP Reed, JM DeJong, and KP Jones. 2001. Parental involvement in homework. *Educational Psychologist,* 36, 195–209.

Houston, RG, and EF Toma. 2003. Home-schooling: An alternative school choice. *Southern Economic Journal,* 69, 920–935.

Howell, WG, and PE Peterson. 2002. *The Education Gap. Vouchers and Urban Public Schools.* Washington, DC: Brookings Institution.

Hoxby, CM. 1994. Do private schools provide competition for public schools? Working Paper 4978. NBER.

———. Where should federal education initiatives be directed? In Kosters, MH (ed.), *Financing College Tuition: Government Policies and Educational Priorities.* Washington, DC: AEI Press.

———. 2000a. Does competition among public schools benefit students and tax-payers? *American Economic Review,* 90, 1209–1238.

———. 2000b. Would school choice change the teaching profession? Mimeograph. Cambridge, MA: Harvard University.

———. 2001. If families matter most, where do schools come in? In Moe, T (ed.), *A Primer on America's Schools.* Stanford, CA: Hoover Institution.

———. 2003a. School choice and school productivity (or could school choice be a tide that lifts all boats?) In Hoxby, CM (ed.), *The Economics of School Choice.* Chicago: University of Chicago and NBER Press.

———. 2003b. *The Economics of School Choice.* Chicago: University of Chicago and NBER Press.

Huerta, L, and M-F Gonzalez. 2004. Cyber and home school charter schools: How states are defining new forms of public schooling. Working Paper, http://www.ncspe.org/list-papers.php.

Husted, TA, and LW Kenny. 2000. Evidence on the impact of state government on primary and secondary education and the equity-efficiency trade-off. *Journal of Law and Economics,* 43, 285–308.

————. 2002. The legacy of *Serrano*: The impact of mandated equal spending on private school enrollment. *Southern Economic Journal,* 68, 566–583.

Isenberg, E. 2002. Home schooling: School choice and women's time use. Working Paper. Washington University, St. Louis, Missouri.

James, E. 1987. The public/private division of responsibility for education: An international comparison. In James, T, and HM Levin (eds.), *Comparing Public and Private Schools.* New York: Falmer Press.

————. 1993. Why do different countries choose a different public-private mix of educational services? *Journal of Human Resources,* 28, 571–592.

James, T, and HM Levin. 1983. *Public Dollars for Private Schools: The Case of Tuition Tax Credits.* Philadelphia: Temple University Press.

Jepsen, C. 2002. The role of aggregation in estimating the effects of private school competition on student achievement. *Journal of Urban Economics,* 52, 477–500.

Jordan, C, E Orozco, and A Averett. 2002. *Emerging Issues in School, Family, and Community Connections.* Annual Synthesis 2001, National Center for Family and Community Connections with Schools. Austin, TX: Southwest Educational Development Laboratory.

Kagan, SL, and B Weissbourd (eds.). 1994. *Putting Families First: America's Family Support Movement and the Challenge of Change.* San Francisco: Jossey-Bass.

Kane, PR. 2003. Interview with Milton Friedman. Working paper, http://www.ncspe.org/list-papers.php.

Kane, PR, and CJ Lauricella. 2001. Assessing the growth and potential of charter schools. In Levin, HM (ed.), *Privatizing Education.* Boulder, CO: Westview Press.

Kane, TJ, and DO Staiger. 2002. The promise and pitfalls of using imprecise school accountability measures. *Journal of Economic Perspectives,* 16, 91–114.

Karsten, S. 1994. Policy on ethnic segregation in a system of choice: The case of the Netherlands. *Journal of Education Policy,* 9, 211–225.

Katz, MB. 1971. *Class, Bureaucracy, and Schools: The Illusion of Educational Change in America.* New York: Praeger.

Kenny, LW, and AB Schmidt. 1994. The decline in the number of school districts in the U.S.: 1950–1980. *Public Choice,* 79, 1–18.

Klugewicz, SL, and CL Carraccio. 1999. Home schooled children: A pediatric perspective. *Clinical Pediatrics,* 38, 407–411.

Knowles, JG, SE Marlow, and JA Muchmore. 1992. From pedagogy to ideology: Origins and phases of home education in the U.S., 1970–1990. *American Journal of Education,* 100, 195–235.

Kohn, ML. 1969. *Class and Conformity: A Study in Values.* Dorsey, IL: Homewood.

Krueger, AB. 1999. Experimental estimates of education production functions. *Quarterly Journal of Economics,* CXIV, 497–532.

Krueger, AB, and P Zhu. 2004a. Another look at the New York City school voucher experiment. *American Behavioral Scientist,* 47, 658–698.

————.2004b. Inefficiency, subsample selection bias, and nonrobustness: A response to Paul E. Peterson and William G. Howell. *American Behavioral Scientist*, 47, 718–728.

Kupermintz, H. 2001. The effects of vouchers on school improvement: Another look at the Florida data. *Education Policy Analysis Archives*, 9, 8.

Lacerino-Paquet, N, TT Holyoke, M Moser, and JR Henig. 2002. Creaming versus cropping: Charter school enrollment practices in response to market incentives. *Educational Evaluation and Policy Analysis*, 24, 145–158.

Ladd, HF. 2002. School vouchers: A critical view. *Journal of Economic Perspectives*, 16, 3–24.

Lambert, SA. 2001. Finding the way back home: Funding for home school children under the Individuals with Disabilities Education Act. *Columbia Law Review*, 101, 1709–1729.

Lareau, A. 2000. *Home Advantage*. New York: Rowman and Littlefield.

Lee, VE, and DT Burkam. 2002. *Inequality at the Starting Gate: Social Background Differences in Achievement as Children Begin School*. Washington, DC: Economic Policy Institute.

Leichter, H. 1975. *Families as Educators*. New York: Teachers College Press.

Lemon v. Kurtzman. 1971. U.S. Supreme Court, 403 U.S. 602.

Lenti, L. 2003. New wave of voucher programs? The Colorado Opportunity Contract Pilot Program. Occasional Paper, http://www.ncspe.org/list-papers-php.

Lerner, JS. 1998. Protecting home schooling through the Casey Undue Burden standard. *University of Chicago Law Review*, 62, 363–392.

Leslie, LL, and PT Brinkman. 1988. *The Economic Value of Higher Education*. London: Macmillan.

Levin, HM. 1991. The economics of educational choice. *Economics of Education Review*, 10, 137–158.

———. 1992. Market approaches to education: Vouchers and school choice. *Economics of Education Review*, 11, 279–286.

———. 1998. Educational vouchers: Effectiveness, choice and costs. *Journal of Policy Analysis and Management*, 17, 373–392.

———. 1999. The public-private nexus in education. *American Behavioral Scientist*, 43, 124–137.

———. 2001a. High stakes testing and economic productivity. In Orfield, G, and ML Kornhaber (eds.), *Raising Standards or Raising Barriers?* (pp. 39–50). New York: The Century Foundation Press.

———. 2001b. The profit motive: Bear market. *Education Matters*, Spring 2001, 6, 9, 11, 13, 15.

———. 2001c. *Privatizing Education. Can the Market Deliver Freedom of Choice, Productive Efficiency, Equity and Social Cohesion?* Boulder, CO: Westview Press.

———. 2001d. Thoughts on for-profit schools. Occasional Paper, National Center for the Study of Privatization in Education, http://www.ncspe.org/list-papers.php.

———. 2002a. A comprehensive framework for evaluating educational vouchers. *Educational Evaluation and Policy Analysis,* 24, 159–174.

———. 2002b. Issues in designing cost-effectiveness comparisons of whole-school reforms. In Levin, HM, and P McEwan (eds.), *Cost-Effectiveness and Educational Policy: 2002 Yearbook of the American Educational Finance Association.* Larchmont, NY: Eye on Education.

Levin, HM, and CR Belfield. 2005. Education vouchers: When ideology trumps evidence. *American Journal of Education,* forthcoming.

Levin, HM, and C Driver. 1997. Costs of an educational voucher system. *Education Economics,* 5, 303–311.

Levin, HM, G Glass, and GR Meister. 1987. Cost-effectiveness of computer-aided instruction. *Evaluation Review,* 11, 50–72.

Levinson, M, and S Levinson. 2003. "Getting religion": Religion, diversity, and community in public and private schools. In Wolfe, A (ed.), *School Choice: A Moral Debate.* Princeton, NJ: Princeton University Press.

Lines, P. 2000. Home-schooling comes of age. *The Public Interest,* 140, 74–85.

———. 2002. Support for home-based study. *Eric Clearinghouse on Educational Management.* University of Oregon.

Lott, JR. 1987. Why is education publicly provided? A critical survey. *Cato Journal,* 7, 475–501.

Lovell, MC. 1978. Spending for education: The exercise of public choice. *Review of Economics and Statistics,* 40, 487–495.

Lubienski, C. 2000. Whither the common good? A critique of home schooling. *Peabody Journal of Education,* 75, 207–232.

Manski, CF. 1992. Educational choice, vouchers and social mobility. *Economics of Education Review,* 11, 351–369.

Maranto, R, S Milliman, and S Stevens. 2000. Does private school competition harm public schools? Revisiting Smith and Meier's "The case against school choice." *Political Research Quarterly,* 53, 177–192.

Marlow, ML. 1997. Public education supply and student performance. *Applied Economics,* 29, 617–626.

———. 2000. Spending, school structure, and public education quality: Evidence from California. *Economics of Education Review,* 19, 89–106.

Martin-Vazquez, J, and BA Seaman. 1985. Private schooling and the Tiebout Hypothesis. *Public Finance Quarterly,* 13, 298–320.

Martinez, V, K Godwin, and F Kemerer. 1996. Public school choice in San Antonio: Who chooses and with what effects? In Fuller, B, and R Elmore (eds.), *Who Chooses? Who Loses? Culture, Institutions, and the Unequal Effects of School Choice.* New York: Teachers College.

Mayer, SE, and PE Peterson. 1999. *Earning and Learning: How Schools Matter.* Washington, DC, and New York: Brookings Institution and Russell Sage Foundation.

McDowell, SA, and BD Ray. 2000. The home education movement in context, practice, and theory: Editor's Introduction. *Peabody Journal of Education,* 75, 1–7.

McEwan, PJ. 2000. Comparing the effectiveness of public and private schools: A review of evidence and interpretations. Occasional Paper, National Center for the Study of Privatization in Education, http://www.ncspe.org/list-papers.php.

———. 2001. The potential impact of large-scale vouchers. *Review of Educational Research,* 70, 103–149.

———. 2003. Peer effects on student achievement: Evidence from Chile. *Economics of Education Review,* 22, 131–141.

McEwan, PJ, and M Carnoy. 2000. Effectiveness and efficiency of private schools in Chile's voucher system. *Educational Evaluation and Policy Analysis,* 22, 213–240.

McMahon, WW. 1998. Conceptual framework for the analysis of the social benefits of lifelong learning. *Education Economics,* 6, 309–346.

McMillan, R. 2004. Competition, incentives, and public school productivity. *Journal of Public Economics,* 88, 1872–1892.

Medlin, RG. 2000. Home schooling and the question of socialization. *Peabody Journal of Education,* 75, 107–123.

Merrill Lynch. 1999. *The Book of Knowledge: Investing in the Growing Education and Training Industry, In-depth Report.* New York: Merrill Lynch.

Metcalf, KK, SD West, NA Legan, KM Paul, and WJ Boone. 2003. *Evaluation of the Cleveland Scholarship and Tutoring Program,* Summary Report 1998–2002. Bloomington: Indiana University School of Education.

Miller, AK. 2003. *Violence in U.S. Public Schools: 2000 School Survey on Crime and Safety.* National Center for Educational Statistics, http://www.nces.ed.gov/pubsearch/pubsinfo.asp?pubid=2004314.

Miron, G, and B Applegate. 2000. *An Evaluation of Student Achievement in Edison Schools Opened in 1995 and 1996.* Kalamazoo, MI: The Evaluation Center, Western Michigan University.

Miron, G, and C Nelson. 2002. *What's Public about Charter Schools?* Thousand Oaks, CA: Corwin Press.

Moe, TM. 1995. *Private Vouchers.* Stanford, CA: Hoover Institution.

———. 2001. *Schools, Vouchers and the American Public.* Washington, DC: Brookings Institution.

Molnar, A, P Smith, J Zahorik, A Palmer, A Halbach, and K Ehrle. 1999. Evaluating the SAGE program: A pilot program in targeted pupil-teacher reduction in Wisconsin. *Educational Evaluation and Policy Analysis,* 21, 170–171.

Mortimore, P. 1998. The vital hours: Reflecting on research on schools and their effects. In Hargreaves, A, A Lieberman, M Fullan, and D Hopkins (eds.), *International Handbook of Educational Change, Part One.* Boston: Kluwer Academic Publishers.

Muraskin, L, and S Stullich. 1998. *Barriers, Benefits, and Costs of Using Private Schools to Alleviate Overcrowding in Public Schools.* Washington, DC: U.S. Department of Education, Planning and Evaluation Service.

Murray, SE, WN Evans, and RM Schwab. 1998. Education-finance reform and the distribution of education resources. *American Economic Review,* 88, 789–812.

National Center for Education Statistics (NCES). 2001. *Homeschooling in the United States: 1999.* http://www.nces.ed.gov.

―――. 2003a. *Digest of Educational Statistics 2002.* http://www.ed.nces.gov.

―――. 2003b. *Trends in the Use of School Choice: 1993 to 1999.* http://www.ed.nces.gov.

―――. 2003c. *A Brief Portrait of Private Schools.* http://www.ed.nces.gov.

―――. 2005. *America's Charter Schools: Results from the NAEP 2003 Pilot Study.* Washington, DC: NCES 2005–456.

Neal, D. 1997. The effects of Catholic secondary schooling on educational achievement. *Journal of Labor Economics,* 15, 98–123.

Nechyba, T. 2000. Mobility, targeting, and private-school vouchers. *American Economic Review,* 90, 130–146.

Nemer, MK. 2002. Understudied education. Toward building a home-school research agenda. Working Paper, http://www.ncspe.org/list-papers.php.

Newacheck, PW, JJ Stoddard, and M McManus. 1993. Ethnocultural variations in the prevalence and impact of childhood chronic conditions. *Pediatrics,* 91, 1031–1038.

Newmark, CM. 1995. Another look at whether private schools influence public school quality: Comment. *Public Choice,* 82, 365–373.

O'Neill, DM, and S Ross. 1976. *Voucher Funding of Training: A Study of the GI Bill.* Arlington, VA: Public Research Institute.

OECD. 1994. *The OECD Jobs Study,* Parts I and II. Paris: OECD.

Oosterbeek, H. 1998. Innovative ways to finance education and their relation to life-long learning. *Education Economics,* 6, 219–252.

Pechman, JA, and BA Okner. 1974. *Who Bears the Tax Burden?* Washington, DC: Brookings Institution.

Peshkin, A. 1986. *God's Choice: The Total World of a Fundamentalist Christian School.* Chicago: University of Chicago Press.

Peterson, PE, and BC Hassel (eds.). 1998. *Learning from School Choice.* Washington, DC: Brookings Institution.

Peterson, PE, and W Howell. 2004. Efficiency, bias and classification schemes: A response to Alan B. Krueger and Pei Zhu. *American Behavioral Scientist,* 47, 699–717.

Petrie, A. 2001. Home education in Europe and the implementation of changes to the law. *International Review of Education,* 47, 477–500.

Pierce v. Society of Sisters. 1925. U.S. Supreme Court, 268 U.S. 510.

Pindyck, D, and R Rubinfeld. 2000. *Microeconomics* (5th ed.). New York: Macmillan.

Public Agenda. 1999. *On Thin Ice.* New York: Author.

Ray, BD. 2000. Home schooling: The ameliorator of negative influences on learning? *Peabody Journal of Education,* 75, 71–106.

Rebello Britto, P, AS Fuligni, and J Brooks-Gunn. 2002. Reading, rhymes, and routines: American parents and their young children. In Halfron, N, M Schuster, and K McLean (eds.), *The Health and Social Condition of Young Children and Their Families.* New York: Cambridge University Press.

Reich, R. 2002. The civic perils of homeschooling. *Educational Leadership,* 59, 56–59.

Roback Morse, J. 2002. Competing visions of the child, the family, and the school. In Lazear, EP (ed.), *Education in the Twenty-first Century*. Stanford, CA: Hoover Institution.

Romer, PM. 1994. The origins of endogenous growth. *Journal of Economic Perspectives*, 8, 3–22.

Rosé, CP, K VanLehn, and NLT Group. 2003. *Is Human Tutoring Always More Effective than Reading?* Proceedings of AIED Workshop on Tutorial Dialogue Systems: With a View Towards the Classroom, Washington, DC.

Rose, LC, and AM Gallup. 2001. *The 33rd Annual Phi Delta Kappa/Gallup Poll of the Public's Attitudes Toward the Public Schools*. http://www.pdkintl.org/kappan/kimages/kpoll83.pdf.

Rothermel, P. 2002. Home-education: Aims, practices, and outcomes. Mimeograph. Durham, UK: University of Durham.

Rothstein, R. 1996. Finance fungibility: Investigating relative impacts of investments in schools and non-school educational institutions to improve student achievement. *A Volume Exploring the Role of Investments in Schools and Other Supports and Services for Families and Communities*. Washington, DC: Center on Education Policy.

———. 2004. *Class and Schools*. Washington, DC: Economic Policy Institute.

Rouse, CE. 1998. Private school vouchers and student achievement: An evaluation of the Milwaukee Parental Choice Program. *Quarterly Journal of Economics*, 113, 553–602.

Rudner, LM. 1999. Scholastic achievement and demographic characteristics of home-school students in 1998. *Education Policy Analysis Archives*, 7, 8.

Ryan, J, and M Heise. 2001. The political economy of school choice. *Yale Law Journal*, 2043.

Sander, W. 1999. Private schools and public school achievement. *Journal of Human Resources*, 34, 697–709.

———. 2001. The effects of Catholic schools on religiosity, education, and competition. Occasional Paper, National Center for the Study of Privatization in Education, http://www.ncspe.org/list-papers.php.

Schauble, L, and R Glaser (eds.). 1996. *Innovations in Learning*. Mahwah, NJ: LEA Publishers.

Schmidt, AB. 1992. Private school enrollment in metropolitan areas. *Public Finance Quarterly*, 20, 298–320.

Schneider, M, P Teske, and M Marschall. 2000. *Choosing Schools: Consumer Choice and the Quality of American Schools*. Princeton, NJ: Princeton University Press.

Scott-Jones, D. 1995. Parent-child interaction and school achievement. In BA Ryan (ed.). *Family-School Connection: Theory, Research, and Practice*.

Segal, LG. 2004. *Battling Corruption in America's Public Schools*. Boston: Northeastern University Press.

Shadish, WR, and CK Haddock. 1994. Combining estimates of effect size. In Hedges, LV, and H Cooper (eds.), *Handbook of Research Synthesis*. New York: Russell Sage.

Simon, CA, and NP Lovrich, Jr. 1996. Private school performance and public school performance: Assessing the effects of competition upon public school student achievement in Washington state. *Policy Studies Journal,* 24, 666–675.

Smith, C, and D Sikkink. 1999. Is private schooling privatizing? *First Things,* 92, 16–20.

Smith, KB. 2003. *The Ideology of Education: The Commonwealth, the Market, and America's Schools.* Buffalo, NY: State University of New York.

Smith, KB, and KJ Meier. 1995. Public choice in education—markets and the demand for quality education. *Political Research Quarterly,* 48, 461–478.

Somerville, S. 2001. Legalizing home-schooling in America: A quiet but persistent revolution. Mimeograph. Home-school Legal Defense Association, http:www.hslda.org.

Sosniak, L. 2001. The 9% challenge: Education in school and society. Teachers College Record, http://www.tcrecord.org/content.asp?contentid=10756.

Steinberg, LD. 1996. *Beyond the Classroom: Why School Reform Has Failed and What Parents Need to Do.* New York: Simon and Schuster.

Stevens, ML. 2001. *Kingdom of Children: Culture and Controversy in the Home-Schooling Movement.* Princeton, NJ: Princeton University Press.

Stipek, DJ, and RH Ryan. 1997. Economically disadvantaged preschoolers: Ready to learn but further to go. *Developmental Psychology,* 32, 492–504.

Sugarman, SD. 2002. Charter school funding issues. *Education Policy Analysis Archives,* 10(34), http://www.epaa.asu.edu.

Sullivan, DJ. 1974. *Public Aid to Nonpublic Schools.* Lexington, MA: Lexington Books.

Taylor, D. 1999. *Family Literacy.* Woburn, MA: Heineman.

Taylor, LL. 2000. The evidence on government competition. *Federal Reserve Bank of Dallas Economic and Financial Review,* II, 1–9.

Teske, P, and M Schneider. 2001. What research can tell policymakers about school choice. *Journal of Policy Analysis and Management,* 20, 609–632.

Tiebout, C. 1956. A pure theory of local expenditures. *Journal of Political Economy,* 64, 416–424.

Tsang, M. 2002. Comparing the costs of public and private schools in developing countries. In Levin, HM, and PJ McEwan (eds.), *Cost-effectiveness and Educational Policy.* Larchmont, NY: AEFA Yearbook, Eye on Education.

Tyack, DB. 1974. *The One Best System: A History of American Urban Education.* Cambridge, MA: Harvard University Press.

U.S. Congressional Budget Office. 1978. *Veterans' Educational Benefits: Issues Concerning the GI Bill.* Washington, DC: Author.

Vedder, R, and J Hall. 2000. Private school competition and public teacher salaries. *Journal of Labor Research,* 21, 161–168.

Viteritti, JP. 1999. *Choosing Equality.* Washington, DC: Brookings Institution.

Weiher, GR, and KL Tedin. 2002. Does choice lead to racially distinctive schools? Charter schools and household preferences. *Journal of Policy Analysis and Management,* 21(1), 79–92.

Weiler, D. 1974. *A Public School Voucher Demonstration: The First Year at Alum Rock.* Santa Monica, CA.

Wells, AS, and R Crain. 2005. Where school desegregation and school choice policies collide: Voluntary transfer plans and controlled choice. In Scott, J (ed.), *The Context of School Choice and Student Diversity.* New York: Teachers College Press.

Welner, KM, and K Welner. 1999. Contextualising home-schooling data: A response to Rudner. *Education Policy Analysis Archives*, 7, 13.

Wenglinsky, H. 2002. How schools matter: The link between teacher classroom practices and student academic performance. *Education Policy Analysis Archives*, 10(12).

West, EG. 1965. Tom Paine's voucher scheme for public education. *Southern Economic Journal*, 33, 378–382.

———. 1991. Public schools and excess burdens. *Economics of Education Review*, 10, 159–169.

Willms, JD. 1996. School choice and community segregation: Findings from Scotland. In Kerckhoff, A (ed.), *Generating Social Stratification: Toward a New Research Agenda.* Boulder, CO: Westview Press.

Witte, JF. 2000. *The Market Approach to Education.* Princeton, NJ: Princeton University Press.

———. 2003. Charter schools in Wisconsin: Assessing form and performance. APPAM, November 2003.

Wolfe, A (ed.). 2003. *School Choice: The Moral Debate.* Princeton, NJ: Princeton University Press.

Wrinkle, RD, J Stewart, and JL Polinard. 1999. Public school quality, private schools, and race. *American Journal of Political Science*, 43, 1248–1253.

Zanzig, BR. 1997. Measuring the impact of competition in local government education markets on the cognitive achievement of students. *Economics of Education Review*, 16, 431–441.

Zelman vs. Simmons-Harris, 00–751, U.S. Supreme Court Ruling, 2002.

Zimmer, R, and R Buddin (eds.). 2003. *Charter School Operations and Performance: Evidence from California.* Santa Monica, CA: The Rand Corporation.

Zimmer, R, and E Toma. 2000. Peer effects in private and public schools across countries. *Journal of Policy Analysis and Management*, 19, 75–92.

Index

Academic achievement, 65
    competition and, 18, 124
    expenditures and, 133–134, 143(n12)
    parental involvement and, 71(t), 72
    private versus public schools and, 46–47
    school supply and, 147
    socioeconomic status and, 69–70, 70(t), 71–72(t), 72
    See also Educational attainment
Academic outcomes. *See* Outcomes
Accelerated School, Los Angeles, 77(n1)
Accountability, home-schooling and, 97–98, 99(t)
Achievement tests, home-schooling and, 98, 99(t). *See also* SATs; Test scores
Adequate Yearly Progress (AYP), 53, 54
Adverse selection, home-schooling and, 109
AFQT. *See* Armed Forces Qualification Test
Apollo, 175
Apprenticeship programs, 179
Arizona, 5
Armed Forces Qualification Test (AFQT), 127
Asia, 2
Assisted activities, contracts and, 75
Australia, 2
Austria, 115(n1)
AYP. *See* Adequate Yearly Progress

Breakfast Programs, 67

Bronx Preparatory Charter School, 77(n1)
Bush administration, 165
Business model, standardized, and education management organizations, 171–172

California, 5, 24, 95, 97, 124, 126, 132, 134
Capacity constraint, 74
Catholic schools
    civic education and, 52, 53(t)
    establishment of, 163
    outcomes of, 13, 46, 47(t)
    school choice and, 80
    See also Religious schools
Charter schools, 4(t), 5, 22, 27–28
    education management organizations and, 7, 11, 164, 166
    funding of, 9, 164, 172
    governance of, 7
    locations of, 161–162(n4)
    outcomes of, 13, 46, 48(t), 58(n10)
    production of, 11
    sponsorship of, 6
    See also Magnet schools
Child abuse, home-schooling and, 110
Child health, home-schooling and, 108
Child Protective Services, 110
Chile, 32, 43
Christian schools, 13. *See also* Religious schools
Church and state entanglement, and religious schools, 146

Civic attitudes, school supply and, 147
Civic education, 52, 53(t), 58(n16)
Civic order, religious schools and, 146
Class size
    competition and, 143(n18)
    home-schooling and, 103
Cleveland Scholarship and Tutoring
    Program, 25, 48
Clinton administration, 165
Colleges, 179
Colorado Opportunity Contract Pilot
    Program, 26
Community, school choice and, 88(t),
    89, 90
Competition, 17–18, 65
    academic achievement and, 18, 124
    benefits of, 125(t), 138–139, 140
    class size and, 143(n18)
    construct validity and, 121–122, 123–
        124
    costs of, 140–141
    educational attainment and, 125(t),
        130–131, 139
    educational expenditures and, 131–
        133, 143(n11)
    education management organizations
        and, 174–175
    education quality and, 141
    effects of increases in, by one standard
        deviation, 125(t)
    efficiency of, 125(t), 133–134
    enrollment and, 121–123
    equity and, 140
    estimation and, 121, 123–124,
        142(n5)
    forms of increased, 139–140
    housing prices and, 135–136
    markets and, 31–32, 43–45
    measures of satisfaction and, 141–
        142(n1)
    measuring effects of, 120–130
    outcomes of, 119, 120, 123, 124–130,
        125(t), 139
    parental involvement and, 141–
        142(n1)
    policy, 137–138

    private school enrollment and, 126(t),
        135, 143(n6)
    production of, 119
    publication bias and, 121, 129–130
    SATs and, 128
    school choice and, 120, 121
    sensitivity analysis and, 121, 129–130,
        136–137, 142–143(n10)
    supply and demand and, 121, 122,
        123, 142(n6)
    teacher quality and, 126, 134–135,
        143(n14)
    teacher salaries and, 134–135,
        143(n14)
    test scores and, 44–45, 45(t), 126–128,
        139, 142(n8)
    wages and, 125(t), 136
    See also School choice
Comprehensiveness, postcompulsory
    entitlements and, 184
Compulsory attendance, 1–2
Conformity, home-schooling and,
    103
Construct validity, 121–122, 123–124
Contracts, 66–67
    assisted activities and, 75
    capacity constraint and, 74
    enforcement of, 76
    external support and, 75
    families and, 68–69, 72, 73–76
    family activities and, 76
    implementation of, 73–76
    incentives and, 73–74
    information and, 74–75
    knowledge base and, 75–76
    parental role and, 72, 77(n1)
    short-term, education management
        organizations and, 168, 176
    See also Metaphorical family
        contract
Contract schools, 166. *See also*
    Education management
    organizations

Declaration of Intent, 112
Democracy, education and, 34–35, 56

Economics of Educational Review, 120
Economies of scale, education
 management organizations and,
 168–170, 175
Edison Schools, 46, 170, 173, 174
Education
 as common experience, 34–36
 conflicting goals of, 34–35
 democracy and, 34–35, 56
 home-schooling impact on, 112–115
 public and private purposes of, 2
 quality of, and competition, 141
Educational attainment, 62–64
 competition and, 125(t), 130–131, 139
 See also Academic achievement
Educational expenditures, competition
 and, 131–133, 143(n11)
Educational outcomes. *See* Outcomes
Education management organizations
 (EMOs), 19, 28
 charter schools and, 7, 11
 competition and, 174–175
 costs of, 167, 168–170, 175–176
 early expectations of, 164–165
 economies of scale and, 168–170, 175
 education reform and, 172–175
 family pressure and, 166–167
 niche markets and, 176
 pedagogical approaches and, 172–173
 personnel and organization and, 173–174
 problems of, 175–177
 profit and, 165, 175
 public schools and, 8, 11, 174
 regulation and scrutiny of, 166, 167
 school district contracting and, 164
 school maintenance and, 174
 short-term contracts and, 168, 176
 special education and, 176
 standardized business model and,
 171–172
 uniform educational product and,
 170–171
 See also For-profit schools
Efficiency
 competition and, 125(t), 133–134

home-schooling and, 104–108,
 115(n3)
 postcompulsory entitlements and,
 183, 186–187
Eligibility, postcompulsory entitlements
 and, 181, 184
EMOs. *See* Education management
 organizations
Endogenous growth theory, 189
England, 77(n1)
Enrollment
 competition and, 121–123
 in private schools, 126–128
 in private schools, and competition,
 126(t), 135, 143(n6)
Equity
 competition and, 140
 home-schooling and, 110–112
 markets and, 49–51, 58(n12),
 58(n13)
 postcompulsory entitlements and,
 182, 183, 185, 187, 188, 190–191,
 194(n1), 194(n2), 195(n3)
 tuition tax credit and, 50
 vouchers and, 35, 38–39, 50, 58(n12)
Estimation, 121, 123–124, 142(n5)
Europe, 2; home-schooling in, 115(n1)
Evangelical schools, 58(n16). *See also*
 Religious schools
Exit, 32
Exit, Voice, and Loyalty (Hirschman),
 32
Expenditures, academic achievement
 and, 133–134, 143(n12)
Externalities, markets and, 32–33,
 57(n8)
External support, contracts and, 75

Families
 activities, contracts and, 76
 background, home-schooling and,
 106
 contracts and, 68–69, 72, 73–76
 freedom of choice and, 42–43
 home-schooling and, 16–17
 outcomes of, 61

Families *(continued)*
  pressure of, and education
    management organizations, 166–
    167
  resources, home-schooling and, 110–
    111
  role of, 10–11
  school choice and, 61, 79
  and schools, balance between, 62, 63,
    66–68
  and schools, preoccupation with, 64–66
  socioeconomic status and, 68–70, 70–
    71(t), 72
  values, markets and, 33–34
  See also Parental involvement
Family-run schools, 164
Federal laws, 66
First Amendment, 11
Florida, 127
Florida Opportunity Scholarship
    Program, 25–26, 48, 67
For-profit private schools, 163–164
  markets and, 46–47
  supply responsiveness and, 146
  See also Education management
    organizations; Private schools
Freedom of choice
  families and, 42–43
  home-schooling and, 104, 114
  markets and, 41–43
  postcompulsory entitlements and,
    183, 185–186
  vouchers and, 35, 38
  See also School choice
Free School Lunch, 142(n7)
Friedman, Milton, 19, 23–24, 33
Friedman voucher plan, 40
Fundamentalist Christian schools, 13.
    See also Religious schools

Georgia, 116(n8), 127, 128
GI Bill, 19, 193–194, 195(n6), 195(n7),
    195(n8)
Governance, 3, 4(t), 6–8, 21
Government subsidies, postcompulsory
    entitlements and, 182, 188–189

Grade-level performance, home-
    schooling and, 97–99, 99(t)

Heath, Shirley Brice, 73
Herfindahl Index (HI), 122, 124, 125(t), 126
HI. *See* Herfindahl Index
High School and Beyond, 127
Hirschman, Albert, 32
Home-based education, 94
Home-schoolers
  characteristics of, 100–102
  number of, 94, 95–100, 98(t)
Home-schooling, 3, 4(t), 94–95
  accountability and, 97–98, 99(t)
  achievement tests and, 98, 99(t)
  adverse selection and, 109
  child abuse and, 110
  child health and, 108
  class size and, 103
  conformity and, 103
  cost of, 102–103, 104, 115(n4)
  definition of, 83, 96
  diversity of, 94–95
  duration of, 94–95, 113, 116(n8)
  efficiency of, 104–108, 115(n3)
  equity and, 110–112
  in Europe, 115(n1)
  evaluation of, 103–112
  families and, 16–17
  family background and, 106
  family resources and, 110–111
  freedom of choice and, 104, 114
  funding of, 8–9, 113
  future of, 114–115
  governance of, 6–7
  grade-level performance and, 97–99,
    99(t)
  growth and development of, 79–80
  growth of, 112, 114
  home-based education and, 94
  household income and, 100, 101(t)
  impact of, on U.S. education, 112–115
  mother's role and, 102
  motivation for, 102–103
  No Child Left Behind Act and, 114–
    115

outcomes of, 12, 104–105
parental preferences and, 110
parents' education and, 100, 101(t), 102
production of, 11
productivity and, 103
public schools versus, 102–112
regulation of, 95, 112–114, 115(n1), 115–116(n7)
religion and, 94, 100, 101(t), 109–110, 114
SATs, socioeconomic status and, 111–112, 111(t)
SATs and, 99–100, 101(t), 102
school choice, community and, 88(t), 89, 90
school choice, household, mothers and, 84–85, 86(t), 90
school choice, students and, 85, 87(t), 89, 90
school choice and, 80–83, 82
social acceptance and, 114
social cohesion and, 108–110, 115(n6)
sponsorship of, 6
standardized testing and, 103
standards and, 110
state and district information on, 96–99, 98(t), 99(t), 115(n2)
support for, 94
support services and, 113
technology and, 104
test scores and, 99–100, 105–106, 107(t), 108, 113
Home-schooling movement, 94–103
Home School Legal Defense Association, 95, 99
Household characteristics, school choice and, 84–85, 86(t), 90
Housing prices, competition and, 135–136
Hyde School, 77(n1)

Illinois, 127, 130
Incentives, markets and, 31
Income
  home-schooling and, 100, 101(t)
  school choice and, 82
Income-contingent loans, 19;
  postcompulsory entitlements and, 191, 195(n4)
"Independent study (not adults)," 97
Information, contracts and, 74–75
Iowa Test of Basic Skills, 100, 105

Jencks voucher plan, 40

Kentucky, 124, 126, 134
Knowledge base, contracts and, 75–76
Knowledge constraint, 74
Kohn, Melvyn, 73

Latin America, 2
Lemon v. Kurtzman, 11
Lifelong learning, 179, 194

Magnet schools, 22, 46
  civic education and, 52, 53(t)
  See also Charter schools
Maine, 24, 128
Market approaches, prospects for, 53–55
Market reforms, 23–28
Markets
  competition and, 31–32, 43–45
  definition of, 28
  equity and, 49–51, 58(n12), 58(n13)
  externalities and, 57(n8)
  failure and externalities of, 32–33
  family values and, 33–34
  for-profit schools and, 46–47
  freedom of choice and, 41–43
  incentive and, 31
  production of, 30–31
  productive efficiency of, 43
  regulation of, 31
  school choice and, 31, 32, 33–34
  social cohesion and, 51–52, 58(n14), 58(t)
  supply and demand and, 28–31, 29(f), 30(f)
  teachers' unions and, 32, 56–57
  vouchers, and choice, evidence on, 41–52
  vouchers, experience and, 54

Maternal characteristics, school choice and, 84–85, 86(t), 90
McKay Scholarship, 26
Metaphorical family contract, 68–69, 73–76. *See also* Contracts
Michigan, 5, 174
Milwaukee Parental Choice Program, 18–19, 24–25, 48, 52, 143(n18)
  ages of schools participating in, 157, 157(t)
  costs of, 158, 160–161
  design of, 152–153
  finance and, 153
  number of religious versus secular schools participating in, 153–154, 154(t), 156(t), 157(t), 158–159, 160
  per-pupil expenditure at, 153, 162(n7)
  private school responsiveness to voucher opportunities in, 157–158, 157(t), 160
  regulation of, 153
  school budget constraints for participating in, 159
  school supply and, 145, 146
  special education services in, 161
  supply responsiveness and, 152–161
  support services and, 153
  voucher students in, distribution by religious orientation and, 154–157, 155(t), 156(t), 160
Minimum standards, 33

National Center for the Study of Privatization in Education (NCSPE), 15–16
National Household Education Surveys (NHES), 95–96
National Longitudinal Survey of Youth (NLSY), 127
NCLB. *See* No Child Left Behind Act
NCSPE. *See* National Center for the Study of Privatization in Education
NELS, 127
Netherlands, 58(n13)
New York, 99, 132, 133
New Zealand, 58(n13)

NHES. *See* National Household Education Surveys
NHES99. *See* National Household Expenditure Survey
NLSY. *See* National Longitude Survey of Youth
No Child Left Behind Act (NCLB), 11, 53–54, 66, 114–115, 172
North Carolina, 126
North Star Academy Charter School of Newark, 77(n1)

OECD. *See* Organization for Economic Cooperation and Development
Ohio, 25, 128, 134
Organization for Economic Cooperation and Development (OECD), 181
Outcomes, 3, 4(t), 12–13
  Catholic schools and, 13, 46, 47(t)
  charter schools and, 13, 46, 48(t), 58(n10)
  competition and, 119, 120, 123, 124–130, 125(t), 139
  families and, 61
  home-schooling and, 12, 104–105
  private schools and, 12–13
  public schools and, 13

Paine, Thomas, 23
Parental involvement, 61
  academic achievement and, 71(t), 72
  competition and, 141–142(n1)
  See also Families
Parental preferences, home-schooling and, 110
Parents, education of, and home-schooling, 100, 101(t), 102
PCEs. *See* Postcompulsory entitlements
Pedagogical approaches, education management organizations and, 172–173
Peer effect
  supply curve and, 151
  voucher students and, 160
Pell Grants, 192–193
Pennsylvania, 99

Personnel and organization, education management organizations and, 173–174

Pierce v. Society of Sisters, 6, 163

Places, expansion of, supply responsiveness and, 147

Political tolerance, 52, 53(t), 58(n16)

Postcompulsory education, 179–180, 194
finance and, 180
sponsorship of, 180
See also Postsecondary education

Postcompulsory entitlements (PCEs), 19
comprehensiveness and, 184
costs of, 186–187
definition of, 180–181
design of, 188
efficiency of, 183, 186–187
eligibility and, 181, 184
endogenous growth theory and, 189
equity and, 182, 183, 185, 187, 188, 190–191, 194(n1), 194(n2), 195(n3)
feasibility of, 192–193
finance and, 184, 188–189
flexibility in offering supply and, 185
flexibility in timing and, 184–185
freedom of choice and, 183, 185–186
funding of, 189–190
government subsidies and, 182, 188–189
income-contingent loans and, 191, 195(n4)
properties of, 182–183
public information system and, 182
regulation of, 191
size of, 182, 190–191
social benefits of, 188–189
social cohesion and, 183
special education needs and, 185
sponsorship of, 181
support services and, 192
vouchers and, 183

Postsecondary education, 194
vouchers and, 180–183
See also Postcompulsory education

Private-independent schools
civic education and, 52, 53(t), 58(n16)
SATs, socioeconomic status and, 111–112, 111(t)
SATs and, 101(t), 102
school choice, community and, 88(t), 89, 90
school choice, students and, 85, 87(t), 89, 90
school choice and, 80
schools choice, household, mothers and, 84–85, 86(t), 90
test scores and, 106, 107(t), 108
See also Private schools

Private-religious schools
civic education and, 52, 53(t), 58(n16)
SATs, socioeconomic status and, 111–112, 111(t)
SATs and, 101(t), 102
school choice, community and, 88(t), 89, 90
school choice, students and, 85, 87(t), 89, 90
school choice and, 80
schools choice, household, mothers and, 84–85, 86(t), 90
test scores and, 106, 107(t), 108
versus public schools, effectiveness of, 46, 57(n9)
See also Private schools; Religious schools

Private schools, 3, 4(t), 5
academic achievement and, 46–47
advantages to, 150
civic education and, 52, 53(t), 58(n16)
elasticity of supply of, 151, 151(t)
enrollment in, 21, 126–128
enrollment in, and competition, 126(t), 135, 143(n6)
enrollment in, and public schools, quality of, 123
finance and, 161
funding of, 1, 2, 3, 9
governance of, 6–7
growth of, 147–148, 148(t), 149, 159
national data on, 147–148
outcomes of, 12–13

Private schools *(continued)*
  production of, 11
  school supply and, 145–146, 146–151
  sponsorship of, 6
  supply responsiveness and, 146–147,
    149, 151–152, 157–158, 157(t), 160,
    162(n5)
  technology of private schooling,
    supply curve and, 150
  tuition and, 177
  versus public schools, and student-
    teacher ratio, 134–135, 143(n15)
  See also For-profit private schools;
    Private-independent schools;
    Private-religious schools
Privatization
  debate over, 2–3
  dimensions of, 3, 4(t), 5–14
  ideological appeal of, 55–57
Product, uniform educational, and
    education management
    organizations, 170–171
Production, 3, 4(t), 10–12
  competition and, 119
  markets and, 30–31
Productive efficiency
  markets and, 43
  vouchers and, 35, 38
Productivity, home-schooling and, 103
Publication bias, 121, 129–130
Public Choice, 120
Public information system,
    postcompulsory entitlements and,
    182
Public School Choice, 53
Public schools, 4(t), 5
  academic achievement and, 46–47
  civic education and, 52, 53(t)
  differences among, 22
  education management organizations
    and, 8, 11, 174
  funding of, 1–2, 9–10
  governance of, 7–8
  home-schooling versus, 102–112
  outcomes of, 13
  production of, 11–12

  quality of, and private schools,
    enrollment in, 123
  SATs, socioeconomic status and, 111–
    112, 111(t)
  SATs and, 101(t), 102
  school choice, community and, 88(t),
    89, 90
  school choice, students and, 85, 87(t),
    89, 90
  school choice and, 80, 82
  schools choice, household, mothers
    and, 84–85, 86(t), 90
  sponsorship of, 6
  test scores and, 106, 107(t), 108
  versus private-religious schools,
    effectiveness of, 46, 57(n9)
  versus private schools, and student-
    teacher ratio, 134–135, 143(n15)

Reagan administration, 165
Recurrent education, 179, 194
Regulation, 66
  of education management
    organizations, 166, 167
  of home-schooling, 95, 112–114,
    115(n1), 115–116(n7)
  of markets, 31
  of Milwaukee Parental Choice
    Program, 153
  of postcompulsory entitlements, 191
  of vouchers, 36–37
Religion
  home-schooling and, 94, 100, 101(t),
    109–110, 114
  school choice and, 90
Religious schools
  church and state entanglement and,
    146
  civic education and, 52, 53(t), 58(n16)
  civic order and, 146
  growth in, 147–148, 148(t), 149, 159
  number of, in Milwaukee Parental
    Choice Program, 153–154, 154(t),
    156(t), 157(t), 160
  school choice and, 80
  social tolerance and, 146, 161(n2)

supply responsiveness and, 146
See also Catholic schools; Private-
religious schools
Retraining institutes, 179

Satisfaction, parental and student,
school choice and, 161(n1)
SATs
characteristics of takers of, 101(t), 102
competition and, 128
home-schooling and, 99–100
school type and, 106, 107(t), 108
socioeconomic status and, 111–112,
111(t)
See also Achievement tests; Test scores
School choice, 17–18, 22
Catholic schools and, 80
caveats and, 42–43
community and, 88(t), 89, 90
competition and, 120, 121
determinants of, 84–89
economics of, 80–83
families and, 61, 79
home-schooling, private schools,
public schools and, 80–83, 82, 85,
87(t), 88(t), 89, 90
household, mothers and, 84–85, 86(t),
90
income and, 82
intradistrict, 142(n4)
markets and, 31, 32, 33–34
motivation and, 81–83
parental and student satisfaction and,
161(n1)
program design of, and supply curve,
150–151
religion and, 90
religious schools and, 80
students and, 85, 87(t), 89, 90
See also Competition; Freedom of
choice
School maintenance, education
management organizations and,
174
School managers, efficiency of, 45–46
School organizations

public and private characteristics of, 3,
4(t), 5–14
types of, 3, 4(t), 5
School owners, efficiency of, 45–46
Schools
contracts and, 66–67
families and, balance between, 62, 63,
66–68
families' preoccupation with, 64–66
regulation of, 66
social purpose of, 34
School Standards and Framework Act of
1998, 77(n1)
School supply, 145–146
academic achievement and, 147
civic attitudes and, 147
elasticity of, 148–149, 150, 151, 151(t)
importance of, 146–152
Scotland, 58(n13)
Secular schools
number of, in Milwaukee Parental
Choice Program, 153–154, 154(t),
156(t), 157(t), 158–159, 160
supply responsiveness and, 146
Segregation, 2
Sensitivity analysis, 121, 129–130, 136–
137, 142–143(n10)
SES. *See* Socioeconomic status
Social acceptance, home-schooling and, 114
Social benefits, postcompulsory
entitlements and, 188–189
Social cohesion
home-schooling and, 108–110,
115(n6)
markets and, 51–52, 58(n14), 58(t)
postcompulsory entitlements and, 183
vouchers and, 36, 39
Social tolerance, religious schools and,
146, 161(n2)
Socioeconomic partitioning, 58(n13)
Socioeconomic status (SES)
academic achievement and, 69–70,
70(t), 71–72(t), 72
families and, 68–70, 70–71(t), 72
SATs, school type and, 111–112,
111(t)

Special education
  education management organizations
    and, 176
  in Milwaukee Parental Choice
    Program, 161
  postcompulsory entitlements and, 185
Sponsorship, 3, 4(t), 6, 22
  postcompulsory education and, 180
  postcompulsory entitlements and, 181
Standardized testing, home-schooling
    and, 103
Standards, home-schooling and, 110
Standards movement, 65
Students
  distribution of, by religious
    orientation, in Milwaukee Parental
    Choice Program, 154–157, 155(t),
    156(t), 160
  school choice and, 85, 87(t), 89, 90
  vouchers, peer effect and, 160
Student-teacher ratio, public versus
    private schools and, 134–135,
    143(n15)
Supplemental Educational Services, 53
Supply and demand, competition and,
    121, 122, 123, 142(n6)
Supply curve
  design of school choice program and,
    150–151
  factors influencing, 149–151
  identification of, 148–149
  peer effects and, 151
  technology of private schooling and,
    150
Supply responsiveness, 146–147, 149
  expansion of places and, 147
  in Milwaukee Parental Choice
    Program, 152–161
  research on, 151–152, 159–160
  tuition and, 152, 162(n6)
Support services
  home-schooling and, 113
  Milwaukee Parental Choice Program
    and, 153
  postcompulsory entitlements and, 192
  vouchers and, 37

Teacher quality, competition and, 126,
    134–135, 143(n14)
Teacher salaries, competition and, 134–
    135, 143(n14)
Teachers' unions, markets and, 32, 56–57
Technology
  home-schooling and, 104
  of private schooling, and supply
    curve, 150
Tennessee Class Size experiment, 65,
    143(n18)
Test scores
  accountability, home-schooling and,
    113
  competition and, 44–45, 45(t), 126–
    128, 139, 142(n8)
  home-schooling and, 99–100, 105–
    106, 107(t), 108, 113
  private-independent schools and, 106,
    107(t), 108
  private-religious schools and, 106,
    107(t), 108
  public schools and, 106, 107(t), 108
  See also Achievement tests; SATs
Tests of Achievement Proficiency, 105
Texas, 5, 95, 124, 126, 127
Timing, postcompulsory entitlements
    and, 184–185
Title I, 9
Training courses, 179
TTC. *See* Tuition tax credit
Tuition
  private schools and, 177
  supply responsiveness and, 152,
    162(n6)
Tuition tax credit (TTC), 1, 2, 22, 26–27,
    41; equity and, 50

United Kingdom, 58(n13)
Universal Pre-School Programs, 67
Universities, 179
University of Phoenix, 175
Unsafe Schools Choice Options, 53
U.S. National Institute of Education, 181
U.S. Office of Economic Opportunity, 24

U.S. Supreme Court, 6, 7, 11, 25, 163
Utah, 99

Vermont, 24, 128
Veterans Education and Benefits
    Expansion Act of 2001, 195(n6). *See
    also* GI Bill
Virginia, 115(n2)
Virtual charter schools, 8
Voice, 32
Voucher programs, 23–26
    evaluation of, 47–49, 48(t), 49(t)
    See also individual programs
Vouchers, 1, 2, 19, 22
    design and, 36–37
    equity and, 35, 38–39, 50, 58(n12)
    extensive and expensive evaluations
        of, 55
    finance and, 36
    freedom of choice and, 35, 38
    Friedman plan and, 40

incompatibilities, trade-offs and, 39–
    41
Jencks plan and, 40
market experience and, 54
postcompulsory entitlements and, 183
postsecondary education and, 180–
    183
productive efficiency of, 35, 38
public discussion of, 24
regulation of, 36–37
social cohesion and, 36, 39
support services and, 37

Wages, competition and, 125(t), 136
Washington state, 99, 127
Ways with Words (Heath), 73
West, E. G., 57(n8)
West Virginia, 99
Wisconsin, 24

Zelman v. Simmons-Harris, 25

About the Authors

Clive R. Belfield, Associate Director of the National Center for the Study of Privatization in Education at the Teachers College, Columbia University, is the author most recently of *Education Privatization: Causes, Consequences, and Planning Implications* (2004). **Henry M. Levin,** Director of the National Center for the Study of Privatization in Education, is coauthor with Belfield of *The Economics of Higher Education* (2003).